D0881131

Towards the Understanding of
Karl Marx

Towards the Understanding of
Karl Marx

A Revolutionary Interpretation

by

Sidney Hook

Expanded Edition
Ernest B. Hook, editor

**With contributions by Paul Berman and Lewis S. Feuer and
Historical Introduction by Christopher Phelps**

 Prometheus Books

59 John Glenn Drive
Amherst, New York 14228-2197

Published 2002 by Prometheus Books

Inquiries should be addressed to
Prometheus Books, 59 John Glenn Drive, Amherst, New York 14228–2197
VOICE: 716–691–0133, ext. 207; FAX: 716–564–2711
WWW.PROMETHEUSBOOKS.COM

06 05 04 03 02   5 4 3 2 1

Library of Congress Cataloging-in-Publication Data

Hook, Sidney, 1902–1989.
    Towards the understanding of Karl Marx : a revolutionary interpretation / Sidney Hook ; edited, with an introduction by Ernest B. Hook ; historical introduction by Christopher Phelps and contributions by Lewis S. Feuer and Paul Berman.—Expanded ed.
        p. cm.
    Includes bibliographical references and index.
    ISBN 1–57392–882–8 (alk. paper)
    1. Karl Marx, 1818–1883. 2. Historical materialism. I. Hook, Ernest B., 1936– II. Title.

HX39.5 .H628 2002
335.4—dc21

                                                    2002070508

Printed in Canada on acid-free paper

The dedication of the 1933 edition read:

"To, C.K.H.
IN FRIENDSHIP"

C.K.H. was Carrie Katz Hook (1898–1988),
Sidney Hook's wife from whom
he was intermittently estranged.
They divorced in 1935.

This expanded edition is dedicated to
remembrance of the public libraries of
New York City, its public schools, and the
City College of New York of the first three decades
of the twentieth century.
Whatever their deficiencies they provided the
resources which enabled a child of the proletariat
from a barren intellectual background to find his path
to eventual fulfillment in the world of ideas.

CONTENTS*

---

*Page numbers listed here and elsewhere in the book in brackets denote those of the expanded edition and appear in brackets on the top of each page. Page numbers not in brackets are those of the original edition and appear at the bottom of each page of the reprinted text.

THE MUTABLE UNMUTED SIDNEY HOOK
(1902–1989)

TOWARDS THE UNDERSTANDING OF KARL MARX
AND TOWARDS THE UNDERSTANDING
OF SIDNEY HOOK

BY ERNEST B. HOOK

I

My father had many lovable qualities. Particularly lovable was his ability to admit that he had been mistaken about some past view. He did not see this as an admission of intellectual weakness. He thought admitting openly and honestly that he had been wrong was the natural position of a reasonable person when, in the light of observation and experience, he concludes he had erred. Another part of wisdom, he believed, was continually reexamining one's position.

From many observations I infer he regarded these attitudes as the application to one's personal, professional, and political life of the logical aspects of the "scientific method"—as conveyed to him initially by the razor-sharp brilliance of his first mentor, the logician and philosopher of science Morris Raphael Cohen at the City College of

New York—and the deeper insights and implications for the scientific method of pragmatism—as conveyed to him later by the greater and gentler wisdom of his second mentor, John Dewey, at Columbia University.

These traits stayed with him as long as I knew him, to his very last days.[1] So he had no difficulty in admitting in later life that he had been wrong about many things in the book republished here. He wrote, for instance, in 1983, fifty years after the publication of *Towards the Understanding of Karl Marx*: "history which according to Marx is the acid test of historical predictions showed that I was

---

1. He once wrote to a journalist with whom he disagreed, "even when I find myself . . . in disagreement with you again, I shall on the basis of what I have just read, re-examine my own position more carefully. I have been wrong about many things but I am not too old, even approaching 84, to learn." (Letter to Stephen Chapman, 28 March 1986, as quoted in *Letters of Sidney Hook: Democracy, Communism, and the Cold War*, ed. Edward S. Shapiro [Armonk, N.Y.: M. E. Sharpe, 1995], p. 373.) I heard him at age eighty-five, about a year before his death, arguing vigorously in the hallway of the Hoover Institution at Stanford University with M. S. Bernstam, a Russian émigré demographer. "Michael," he said, "I was wrong to oppose the Helsinki agreements. I thought they gave too much away. I didn't realize how much impact the human rights clauses would have upon internal events in the Soviet Union." "You were right to oppose them, Sidney," Bernstam retorted. "We would have done those things even without the Helsinki agreements." "No," he persisted, "I was wrong!" "Sidney, you were right!" "I was wrong!" They did not have a chance to delve more deeply into matters before I foolishly interrupted to lead him off to some family event. Only in retrospect did I marvel at the interchange. But there had to be good reasons for any change. As he approached death, he was asked what he would say if confronted in the afterlife by the Almighty, wrathful about his nonbelief (since age twelve). He would say simply, he said: "Forgive me, Lord, but you did not give me enough evidence."

wrong [in this volume]—together with Marx—about capitalism, and even more so about the Soviet Union."[2]

Were he to rewrite it today he would alter a good deal in what he wrote in 1932, notably those sections which, despite lack of explicit reference to the USSR, implied that the Soviet Union had a hopeful future, praised Leninist approaches, or left the impression that the term "Leninist democracy" (like a Stalinist "People's democracy") could be anything but an oxymoron.[3]

Yet many—not all—statements in *TUKM* which now initially seem doctrinaire or foolishly optimistic on closer inspection appear carefully qualified. Unlike other Marxist expressions circulating in 1933, his formulation clearly conceded it might be mistaken and altered in the light of future developments. For instance he noted if, contrary to his exposition, "ever a time comes when in a class [e.g., a bourgeois] democracy the group which controls the state uses it in the interests of the class which its [the state's] economic institutions oppress, or if ever in a true democracy [i.e., one in which in accord with communist theory economic class divisions are abolished] a situation arises in which a minority resorts to force to overthrow the decision of a majority—*the Marxian theory will have to be revised*" (emphasis added).[4] One may readily find similar

2. Letter to Jeff Beneke, 8 November 1983, Sidney Hook Papers, The Archives, Hoover Institution on War, Revolution and Peace, Stanford University, California, Box 41, #3.

3. See for instance pages 287–90, and 304–13 of this volume (1933 pagination).

4. P. 311 of this volume.

examples—more or less explicit.[5] And, of course, revise Marxian theory he did in his later writings on the pertinent points, after the welfare state in the West established the first cited condition necessary to require such revision.[6]

---

5. After claiming that "one of the most striking consequences of the still incomplete Russian revolution . . . [is] . . . the progressive elimination of national, cultural and racial hostilities among its heterogeneous peoples" [!] he notes explicitly that he is not saying that "after the socialist revolution has been completed there will no longer be social oppositions." He simply asserts "*as an hypothesis to be tested in practice* [emphasis added] that social oppositions will not be accompanied by economic oppression" (p. 247). (Next to this in the margin of one of his own copies, now in my possession, he wrote "hypothesis false.") And his suggestion (p. 248) that "the *truth* of Marx's theory of the class struggle can be established only in the experience of social revolution, i.e. *after* class society has been overthrown" (emphases added) implies of course prior to that time its truth is not established, but must remain conjectural, and implicitly subject to modification. In answer to the query (p. 289) "Why cannot the revolution be made peacefully? Why may not the ruling class voluntarily surrender its power rather than risk defeat or the destruction of the whole of society in civil war?" he retorted, "When has this ever been the case?" implying of course should that *occur*, one would have to reconsider matters, as indeed he did with the historical developments after World War II.

6. He has written extensively about the relationship of subsequent historical developments to the alteration of his views. See for instance: "Spectral Marxism," pp. 54–71, in Sidney Hook, *Marxism and Beyond* (Totowa, N.J.: Rowman and Littlefield, 1983), and also: "From 'Scientific Socialism' to Mythology," pp. 1–63, in Sidney Hook, *Revolution, Reform, and Social Justice: Studies in the Theory and Practice of Marxism* (New York: New York University Press, 1975).

It was not just the emergence of the welfare state that led to alteration of his views. He realized subsequently that the historical consequences of Lenin's actions could not be explained by Marx's (or Lenin's) historical materialism, e.g., Sidney Hook, *The Hero in History: A Study in Limitation and Possibility* (New York: John Day, 1943), esp. chap. 10, "The

Until, in preparing this chapter, I read the archival files, I thought he came to repudiate and abandon almost all of the views he expressed in this volume, although never his admiration, perhaps critical sympathy is a better term, for Marx and his work. Certainly I always sensed he feared some overenthusiastic new readers might be inspired inappropriately to foolish views or actions. He alluded in the 1950s and later to what he felt had been the pernicious influence in the 1930s upon its readers, many of them friends or students, who remained wedded to its doctrines long after he had abandoned them in the light of historical developments.[7]

Russian Revolution: A Test Case," pp. 184–228. See also Lewis S. Feuer, "From Ideology to Philosophy: Sidney Hook's Writings on Marxism," pp. 35–53, in *Sidney Hook and the Contemporary World: Essays on the Pragmatic Intelligence*, ed. Paul Kurtz (New York: John Day, 1968), reprinted in this volume.

7. Thus I was surprised he wrote in his autobiography (*Out of Step*, p. 178) that *Towards the Understanding of Karl Marx* had little impact on intellectual life either in or outside the academy in the United States. Perhaps he was excluding the relatively small number of individuals caught up with or interested in Marxist doctrines. Subjective evidence from subsequent testimonials suggests the volume increased those numbers or (for I find it difficult to establish this point quantitatively) at least reinforced the fervor and dedication of those already committed to an independent Marxism in the United States. Certainly the book received many reviews and, with the exception of the Communist press, mostly a favorable or at least a sympathetically critical reception. Perhaps he had the impression that he had already converted those susceptible intellectuals with his numerous written and verbal expositions of his view of Marxism in the early 1930s prior to the book's publication. I don't think his view of the book's lack of impact resulted from either false modesty or "denial" in the psychoanalytic sense. For he wrote in the same section of his autobiography, that he had been given to understand the volume had great influence in England, and had drawn many Oxford and Cambridge students

He occasionally quoted to me the admiring comments of others on the book, yet left me with the impression that he regarded himself as having been very foolish and that he now repudiated its message. I sensed mixed feelings, wonder, yet regret, at his own ability to have had impressed yet misled many gifted individuals.

Yet he always seemed proud of the work. And indeed, in preparing this introduction I discovered a letter that he wrote in 1976, forty-three years after first publication, that indicated I might have misjudged his own later views of it. This was a reply to an inquiring publisher who, in a letter seeking to reprint *TUKM*, informed him that one philosopher had recommended the work as the best introduction ever written to Marx's thought, but added tactlessly that another said Hook probably wanted to forget he ever wrote it.[8]

In some atypical surprisingly immodest remarks—

---

into the Communist movement! (The only documentation of its actual effect in England of which I am aware, separate from the few reviews it received there, is a letter to him by Bertrand Russell, cited in his autobiography, *Out of Step*, p. 178). He wrote this autobiography fifty years after the events, and clearly without consulting the extensive files, clippings of comments and reviews of it, as well as his own correspondence which are now organized at the Hoover Institution Archives. Comments by others who came to maturity in the mid and late 1930s in the United States indicate that the volume did have considerable influence. Irving Kristol, for instance, a student in the late 1930s, has written that in his Trotskyite phase he must have read it at least six times. (Irving Kristol, "Life with Sidney: A Memoir," p. 27 in *Sidney Hook: Philosopher of Democracy and Humanism*, ed. Paul Kurtz (Amherst, N.Y.: Prometheus Books, 1983).

8. Letter from William H. Y. Hackett (Hackett Publishing Company, Inc.), 17 October 1976, to Sidney Hook, Sidney Hook Papers, The Archives, Hoover Institution on War, Revolution and Peace, Stanford University, California, Box 41, #3.

written I infer in the heat of righteous indignation—he replied: "It is not only the best introduction ever written about Marx's thought but the best exposition. Far from wanting to forget I wrote it, I am proud to have written it. Events since 1932—when I finished the [manuscript]—in the U.S., the U.S.S.R. and mainland China have refuted the theory of historical materialism as well as Marx's economic predictions. [But the] trouble with almost all *other* [emphasis added] interpretations of Marx is that they make his assertions irrefutable by any empirical evidence and hence present Marx as anything but a scientific thinker. . . . I have had many requests to reprint it but have been too busy to write a new long introduction made necessary by historical developments."[9]

His views, he wrote later, began to alter even before the book was published.[10] Stalin's imposition in the early 1930s upon German Communists of the theory that the German Socialists were "social fascists" prevented a united front against the Nazis and enabled Hitler to come to power in January 1933 while the book was in press. He

---

9. Sidney Hook to William H. Y. Hackett, 15 December 1976, Sidney Hook Papers, The Archives, Hoover Institution on War, Revolution and Peace, Stanford University, California, Box 41, #3.

10. A letter from Richard J. Walsh (John Day Company) to Sidney Hook, 1 August 1932, indicates that the volume had been submitted for publication probably in July 1932. Walsh agreed to bring it out the following March but thought it would be somewhat difficult for the general audience. He suggested that expansion may help to make it, as he termed it, somewhat popular. It is not clear how much alteration was made subsequently. Walsh wrote that they wanted the final manuscript not later than November first (1932). Sidney Hook Papers, The Archives, Hoover Institution on War, Revolution and Peace, Stanford University, California, Box 41, #3.

informed another inquiring publisher in 1983 that when he wrote the work in the fall of 1932 he was actively supporting the Communist ticket of Foster and Ford for president "in the expectation that the communists would abandon their criminally stupid theory of Social-Fascism according to which the Social Democrats were the twins of Fascists—and unite with the Social Democrats to fight Hitler if he came to power. . . . *This expectation explains my silence about the anti-humanist, anti-Marxist features of the Soviet Union* [emphasis added]. . . . It was only on January 30, 1933 when instead of combating Hitler, Stalin reaffirmed the theory of social-fascism that I realized that the retention of the theory was designed to make Hitler's accession to power possible in the hope that Hitler would go to war against the West, and the USSR would pick up the pieces. The German Communists on orders from the Kremlin proclaimed about that time 'Nach Hitler, kommen Wir.' "[11] (In essence, "First Hitler, then us," or "After Hitler, our turn.")

Perhaps he did change his views about the USSR as abruptly as this passage might imply. But I suspect his political position about the Soviet Union as well as his perspective about this book changed more gradually and somewhat differently than this passage, written hurriedly a half-century later, seems to imply. His autobiography, as well as all his comments to me over the years, suggests that the Moscow trials in the mid-1930s were as important

---

11. Sidney Hook to Jeff Beneke (Shoe String Press), 8 November 1983, Sidney Hook Papers, The Archives, Hoover Institution on War, Revolution and Peace, Stanford University, California, Box 41, #3.

if not more so than Hitler's rise to power in leading him to modify his views of the promise of the Soviet state.[12]

Yet for all the book's silence about the antihumanist and anti-Marxist practices of the Soviet Union, even ten years after the first Moscow trials, as late as 1945, he allowed a Portuguese translation of *Towards the Understanding of Karl Marx* without apparent modification. And at the end of 1947 he authorized an Italian translation (which never appeared) although expressing the wish that the publisher would include "a brief Introduction, which I am prepared to give them without charge" (8 December 1947). Nothing had come of this by the end of 1949, and when approached by an agent again about the project, his views had hardened. He replied in early January 1950 that he would only allow an Italian translation if it included an introduction clearly intended to be revisionary. And a week later he wrote that he was not planning to reprint the work in English. This appears to have put an end to the discussion of

---

12. Re the Moscow trials, see especially pp. 218–47 of *Out of Step*. He notes explicitly they were "a decisive turning point in my intellectual and political development" (p. 218). Of even greater pertinence, "The upshot of the Moscow trials affected my epistemology too. I had been prepared to recognize that understanding of the past was in part a function of our need to cope with the present and the future, that rewriting history was in a sense a method of making it. But the realization that such a view easily led to the denial of objective historical truth, to the cynical view that not only is history written by survivors but that historical truth is created by survivors—which made untenable any distinction between historical fiction and truth—led me to rethink some aspects of objective relativism. Because nothing was absolutely true and no one could know the whole truth about anything, it did *not* follow that it was impossible to establish any historical truth beyond a reasonable doubt. Were this to be denied the foundations of law and society would have to be denied" (pp. 218–19).

any translation as well. I strongly suspect the emergence of Stalin's Soviet Union as the clear chief threat to the world after the defeat of Hitler and his allies finally led to his aversion in 1949–50 to letting the volume reappear unaltered.[13]

Yet even as late as 1983 he wrote to another publisher that he would agree to its republication with a new introduction, albeit one of one hundred pages.[14] I can find no evidence that he ever began work on one. But a listing of typographical errors and marginal comments in one of his copies supplemented by photocopies in the Hoover Institution Archives of notations in another copy suggest at least he contemplated such.[15]

13. Franz J. Horch to Sidney Hook, 18 November 1947; Sidney Hook to Franz J. Horch, 19 November 1947; Sidney Hook to Franz J. Horch, 8 December 1947; Franz J. Horch to Sidney Hook, 31 January 1949; Max Pfeffer to Sidney Hook, 29 December 1949; Sidney Hook to Max Pfeffer, 5 January 1950, and 12 January 1950. Sidney Hook Papers, The Archives, Hoover Institution on War, Revolution and Peace, Stanford University, California, Box 41, #3.

14. Sidney Hook to Jeff Beneke (Shoe String Press), 8 November 1983. Sidney Hook Papers, The Archives, Hoover Institution on War, Revolution and Peace, Stanford University, California, Box 41, #3.

15. The photocopies are in Box 41 of the Sidney Hook Papers, The Archives, Hoover Institution on War, Revolution and Peace, Stanford University, California. One of the volumes from which these were copied has disappeared; the other is in my possession. It is not clear when these notations were made.

II

Sidney Hook described his political evolution fully in his autobiography.[16] But I must emphasize here two related very consistent aspects of his views from the late 1930s onward. Despite his opposition to capitalism and the capitalist states in the 1930s and 1940s, he strongly supported the war against the Axis of the Nazis and militaristic Japan.[17] Present-day readers may be unaware that for this view Trotskyites and other Marxist militants denounced him (as some still do!) as an apostate Marxist.[18] His view

---

16. Sidney Hook, *Out of Step: An Unquiet Life in the Twentieth Century* (New York: Harper & Row, 1987).

17. He told me he had, without my mother's knowledge, made inquiries about enlisting shortly after the United States entered World War II, when he would have been thirty-eight or thirty-nine. But the recruiting officer did not seem interested in someone of his age and family situation. And his eyesight would have kept him out in any case. (I suspect, from some other remarks he made in a different context, of having harbored as a child unrequited or thwarted hopes of becoming a great general.)

18. Thus Alan Wald (*The New York Intellectuals: The Rise and Decline of the Anti-Stalinist Left* [Chapel Hill: University of North Carolina Press, 1987]) implies those who abandoned Leninist-Trotskyite positions were hypocritical opportunists selling out for position, power, or money! Sidney Hook's changes in views about Marxism he claims (p. 293) were due to "social pressures"—source unspecified—and, he implies, the consequence of a personal experience of "post-war prosperity"! But Hook's changes in views began long before the end of World War II, and despite not because of any "social pressures" from those close to him. Indeed, the suggestion that "social pressures" ever had any effect upon the views of Sidney Hook is farcical. (Hook's favorite quotation, cited frequently throughout his entire life, was, "Follow your own course and let people talk," which, in fact, originated with Marx (not Dante as Marx thought erroneously). (Anonymous, *Lectura Dantis,*

was that imperfect as capitalist democracy might be, at least if it survived there would be a chance to improve conditions. If Hitler and his allies won, there was little chance to do so, given the dark ages to follow.

After the defeat of Hitler, despite his admiration for Marx he viewed the "Marxist" states of Stalin and his allies as the greatest menace to the continued existence or future possible achievements of democracy and freedom throughout the world. He fought vigorously with tongue and pen the dedicated agents, simpleminded dupes, foolish "independent" revolutionists, and uninformed do-gooders whose activities served directly or indirectly, consciously or unconsciously, the Stalinist cause. And on the same grounds that he allied himself with the forces of capitalist democracy against Hitler, he supported policies, positions, and election of many anti-Marxists with whom he disagreed on social and economic matters as well as ideology, in the fight against Communism even while disagreeing on other issues.[19]

4:111, 1989.) See also "Sidney Hook on Alan Wald," *Contentions* (publication of the Committee for the Free World [March 1988]: 7–8) for a surprisingly restrained rejoinder to Wald. For attacks on Hook during World War II for his stand supporting the war, see among others David Merian [a pseudonym of Meyer Schapiro], "Socialism and the Failure of Nerve—The Controversy Continued," *Partisan Review* 10 (September–October 1943): 473–76; and the rejoinder to this: Sidney Hook, "Faith, Hope and Dialectic: Merian in Wonderland," *Partisan Review* 10 (September–October 1943): 476–81. These were the aftermath of a lengthy exchange: Sidney Hook, "The New Failure of Nerve: Part 1," *Partisan Review* 10 (January–February 1943): 2–23; Sidney Hook, "Part Two: The Failure of the Left," *Partisan Review* 10 (March–April 1943): 165–77; David Merian, "The Nerve of Sidney Hook," *Partisan Review* 10 (May–June 1943): 248–57; and Sidney Hook, "Politics of Wonderland," *Partisan Review* 10 (May–June 1943): 258–62.

He strongly defended Ronald Reagan's characterization of the Soviet Union as an "evil empire" and was critically sympathetic to those responsible democratic political elements on the right (or the left) which opposed the Soviet menace and their sympathizers. For taking such an approach some labeled him a "cold warrior" and others a "neoconservative." Some sections of the academy anathematized him and unfairly caricatured his views. He rejected the label "neo-conservative."[20] He always classified himself as either a democratic socialist or a social democrat. I never heard him comment on being called a "cold warrior." But if it was meant pejoratively, I am sure he would have said, "Yes, but whatever you may mean by the term, I am a cold warrior who believes that waging a tough cold war is the best approach to achieving survival *and* freedom, to preventing *both* a hot war and supine capitulation to an international totalitarian movement."[21]

Nevertheless, through all the years of his opposition to self-styled Marxist regimes and Marxist movements throughout the world, of his denunciations of the machi-

---

19. For some of his final political views, see "Reaffirmations," pp. 596–606, in *Out of Step*. See also, e.g., Sidney Hook, "A Critique of Conservatism," in his *Marxism and Beyond* (Totowa, N.J.: Rowman and Littlefield, 1983), pp. 208–18, and Sidney Hook, "Bread, Freedom, and Free Enterprise," in his *Political Power and Personal Freedom* (New York: Criterion, 1959), pp. 83–94.

20. See pp. 11, 305, 306, 312, in Shapiro, *Letters of Sidney Hook*.

21. He wrote, "I am proud of being a 'cold war liberal.' " (Letter to William Phillips, 14 March 1984, in ibid., pp. 343–44. See also "In Defence of the Cold War: *Neither Red nor Dead*," in Sidney Hook, *Marxism and Beyond* [Totowa, N.J.: Rowman and Littlefield, 1983], pp. 187–96.)

nations of Stalinists and their fellow-travelers and successors in the Kremlin and elsewhere, of his blasts at the hypocrisy and intellectual confusion of Trotskyites and anti-anti-communists, he never abandoned his regard for Marx as an intellectual thinker. Even into the 1950s not only did he regard himself as a "Marxist" but he happily referred to himself as such.[22] He stopped doing so, he stated, because he felt that circumstances had evolved to the point where he had an apparently unique view of Marxism. He would jauntily note even Marx himself lived to say, "I am not a Marxist," in umbrage at the line taken at the time by the bulk of his later disciples.

I believe several factors contributed to his identification with Marx as an inspiring fighter for human freedom. His own early intellectual life had been vastly influenced by Marx's writings. He was happy initially to embrace an unequivocal revolutionary position he described as Marxism. But he read into Marx's work what many others did not see there. He saw threads of rationalism, reason, a sense of democracy, decency and fair play, and most importantly an endorsement of the scientific approach *and thus by implication the capability to admit and rectify error*. Thus as even the mature Marx was, Sidney Hook believed, capable of admitting error, of learning from experience, and thus revising and changing his position, as he was, so true Marxism must logically have within it the seeds of such a self-correcting policy not just with regard to tactics and the need for revolution, but even, heretical though it was, to *aspects of its ideology*. Those Marxist movements that are intransigent, that deny this capability of correcting ideological and other error are then not Marx's true

heirs.[23] And should somehow Karl Marx return to earth
matured and seasoned by the experience of the twentieth
century, *he* would concede his earlier errors just as
Sidney Hook had conceded *his*.

Nevertheless, I always suspected him, despite his
dogged rationalism, of inconsistently being a bit too
willing to bend a point for those thinkers he admired or
individuals he loved.[24] I think Sidney Hook's reluctance in
his later years to abandon his identification with Marx was
likely based on sentiment and sympathy with a person
whose writings were influential in his early life and into
whose "ambiguous legacy," as he tellingly termed it, he
read perhaps a bit too much of his own sense of human
dignity, fair play, striving for freedom, and even the
humane pragmatism of John Dewey.[25] Indeed, some
would maintain that even in his "revolutionary" days,
Sidney Hook had done the latter![26]

---

23. See, e.g., Sidney Hook, "Karl Marx versus the Communist Movement," in his *Marxism and Beyond* (Totowa, N.J.: Rowman and Littlefield, 1983), pp. 3–22.

24. Including among other examples, Marx in the first category and
family members in the second. For some elaboration, see Ernest B. Hook,
"Eulogy to Sidney Hook," *Free Inquiry* (fall 1989): 41–43, or "Tribute,"
in *A Service of Remembrance: Sidney Hook*, Hoover Institution, Stanford
University, California, 1989, pp. 9–16.

25. See, e.g., Sidney Hook, "Evaluation of Marx's Contributions," in
Marx and the Marxists: The Ambiguous Legacy (New York: Van Nostrand Reinhold, 1955), pp. 35–48, esp. pp. 47–48.

26. He had been a Marxist first, and remained one while studying with
John Dewey. But Sidney Hook's doctoral thesis (which comprised his
first book, *The Metaphysics of Pragmatism* [Chicago: Open Court, 1927;
reprint, Amherst, N.Y.: Prometheus Books, 1996]) had nothing to say
about Marxism.". . . What Marx Might Have Said Had He Been a Pupil

All this naturally gives rise to the question, how much of his interpretation, in either this volume or elsewhere in his 1930s exposition of "Marxism," is Marx and how much is Sidney Hook? He told me that someone remarked to him at the time his volume first appeared: "This is your own stuff, why don't you develop it as your own? Why attribute it to Marx?" Indeed, why not? I inferred it never occurred to him at the time that he was doing something not analytical and derivative, but original and synthetic.

Is this volume then simply, as he wrote in 1983, an introduction to and exposition of the real thoughts of Marx? Or is it, whatever its title, and despite the many hypotheses and claims that history has shown to be false, rather an independent, effective, forceful, humanist, lucid, genuinely new revolutionary synthesis of promise honed from Marx's and other European ideologies, and from the American pragmatism of John Dewey? I for one, despite what he said, take this view, a view which gives the work a greater originality than Sidney Hook himself thought it had. But I recognize my personal bias may interfere with rational evaluation.

---

of John Dewey" appeared in the subtitle of Max Eastman's review of *TUKM* in the *New York Herald Tribune Books,* 13 April 1933, p. 6. In partial defense, Hook noted many years later in his autobiography that among others, even Bertrand Russell had seen a philosophical kinship of the thought of Dewey and Marx, a kinship he, Hook, traced to their Hegelian origins, their acceptance of Darwinism as a basis for a world-view, their opposition to atomism, and "their common emphasis of democracy." *Out of Step,* p. 139.

III

Despite all this, I have had deep reservations about allowing *Towards the Understanding of Karl Marx* to be republished. Its reappearance violates his only specific injunction to me about his professional afterlife (although, when I last discussed it with him, about a year before he died, he appeared less concerned about the matter than before). More than ten years have passed since his death in 1989, but allowing it to be reprinted still feels like an act of betrayal. Why, then, have I finally allowed an imploring publisher to reissue it?

First, it is of value as a historical document. Its lucid prose explains better than any other document of the times why the thought of Sidney Hook had such great appeal to American Marxists in the 1930s and 1940s who were not blindly sectarian. Second, its reappearance with a better index and with extensive commentary about the historical background of the volume and its reception provides information not readily available to many scholars of the period.[27] Third, its reappearance allows me to correct the

---

27. I sent to the author of the historical introduction of this volume for background material, photocopies of all the reviews and comments upon *TUKM* that I could find in the Hoover Archives. Some were not mentioned by Barbara Levine in her *Sidney Hook: A Checklist of Writings* (Carbondale and Edwardsville: Southern Illinois University Press, 1989), p. 6, including one in Yiddish. I suspect the archives' holdings were those originally collected by the publisher and that there are many other reviews of *TUKM* not in the archives or mentioned by Levine. At the time I commissioned a historical introduction, I had been unaware of the work of Richard Downing Horn (Ph.D. diss., Princeton University, 1997): *The Perils of Pragmatism: Sidney Hook's Journey through Philosophy and Politics, 1902–1956* (Ann Arbor, Mich.: UMI Dissertation

[26]

record in an appropriate place on Sidney Hook's own final
views of the work, to which I have alluded above, and
which some contemporary self-styled scholars of the work
of Sidney Hook still do not appreciate. Fourth, it enables
me to provide in the same volume an explanation for the
reader who may not have read *Out of Step*, Sidney Hook's
autobiography, not only from where Sidney Hook came in
writing *TUKM*, but an indication of his subsequent trajectory, the rationale for that trajectory, and how through all
of that, the basic integrity of his approaches—willingness
to admit error, a humane and scientific pragmatism, and
hopes for human freedom and full achievement of human
abilities—remained unchanged. Fifth, as I noted, he himself in his later years was not adverse to reissuing the
volume, only to reissuing it without the lengthy new introduction he believed it required. While he never thought it
worth the effort to write such, he did of course subsequently write a good deal of other things about Marx and
the Marxists which indicate his later views. So in this
reissue I can in particular refer the reader otherwise unfa-
miliar with them to these works, for instance, his
insightful, pithy comments on Marx, Lenin, Trotsky, and
others that appeared in his annotated sourcebook, *Marx
and the Marxists: The Ambiguous Legacy* (New York: Van
Nostrand Reinhold, 1955), which are too little known.
Sixth, reissue provides a rationale for republication of
Lewis Feuer's essay on Sidney Hook, which, supplemented with comments here, may serve as an accessible,
integrated, and brief surrogate for the introduction to
Towards the Understanding of Karl Marx that *he* would

Services), microform no. 9727034, in particular vol. 1 (1902–1928), and
vol. 2 (1929–1939), to which I also direct the reader.

have written. Seventh, republication may at least indirectly lead to appreciation of the remaining vast corpus of
the work and wisdom of Sidney Hook in areas other than
political philosophy and social affairs. While I recognize
as well as anyone my own bias, I think the work of the
later Sidney Hook in those other spheres is, unjustly, not
sufficiently known. Those who have disagreed with his
uncompromising public political positions—which
includes a large segment of the academy and journalists
reporting upon the academy, especially those among the
"politically correct"—have tended to ignore or dismiss the
significance even of the nonpolitical work by Sidney
Hook. Appreciation of his work in the philosophy of education, the philosophy of history, the ethics embedded
within pragmatism, the nature of pragmatism itself, and
even on philosophical issues concerning the end of life has
tended to be subdued by political currents.[28] Eighth, no

---

28. I am not suggesting that his work has been *un*appreciated. Rather,
there has been an emotional reaction, almost a conditioned reflex among
many, not all, who are aware of his political work, some only by reputation, to resist evaluating *any* of his post-1930s writings on their merits.
Some of his outstanding later nonpolitical contributions include *The Hero
in History: A Study in Limitation and Possibility* (New York: John Day,
1943); *Education for Modern Man: A New Perspective*, 2d ed. (New York:
Alfred Knopf, 1966), especially the chapter "The Good Teacher"; the
essay *"The Quest for Being"* (originally published in 1953) in the volume
of the same name (1961; reprint, Amherst, N.Y.: Prometheus Books,
1991) and also in the same volume, "The New Failure of Nerve" (1943)
and "Religion and the Intellectuals" (1950); "Science and Mythology in
Psychoanalysis" in the volume he edited in 1959: *Psychoanalysis[,] Scientific Method and Philosophy* (New York: New York University Press);
"Pragmatism and the Tragic Sense of Life" (1960) in his volume of the
same name (New York: Basic Books, 1974). See the Appendix, esp. pp.
[466]–[476] of this volume for a list of works by and about him.

longer is it likely that the reissue of *TUKM* will have upon any readers the same galvanizing effect it had among many in the years of the Great Depression. Revelations in the 1990s in the wake of the demise of one of the most notorious incarnations of self-styled Marxism—the Soviet Union and its satellite governments—have undermined the naive enthusiasm about Marxism that existed among many intellectuals since the 1930s.[29]

If despite all of this, Dad should confront me in our afterlife, and ask why I ignored his explicit injunction not to reprint the volume, I have a defense prepared. I will attempt to hoist him with his own petard. "I *thought*," I will say, "that of all people, *you* would have preferred not a legacy of blind obedience but rather one of sympathetic independent judgment." His retort might be: "Yes, but I would have hoped for an *intelligent* judgment too!" I know out of parental affection he would not say that, should he think it. But if I telepathically detect the thought, I will again expound points one to eight above, and attempt to explain why he should, once again, change his mind. But perhaps time will prove him to have had the greater wisdom on this calculated risk.

---

29. Among other things, these released documents have established the truth of every claim that Sidney Hook made in his later life about the Soviet Union, its open and clandestine activities, the Communist Party in the United States and elsewhere as a conspiratorial organization, and the presumption that Communist Party members were likely, albeit not necessarily inevitably, agents of the Soviet Union in the classroom and elsewhere throughout American cultural life. The reader who at this late date still doubts this should examine, for instance, the issues of the past ten years of the *Newsletter of the American Historians of Communism*.

IV

Those who knew Sidney Hook well were aware of his deep-grained sense of fair play. As long as I knew him, his razor-sharp polemical skills never diminished expressions of demands for equal hearing of his principled opponents—that is, those he believed were not conscious hypocrites, deliberately dishonest. Indeed, with some wonderment I often heard him engage with great sympathy in discussion with well-intentioned individuals with whom he disagreed markedly. (I suspect he saw, in those among them who were young and enthusiastic, a bit of his earlier self.) I cannot resist sharing a specific example that pertains to this volume.

I was astonished to find in the Hoover Institution Archives a letter of 23 May 1934 to an editor at Polemic Press imploring him to issue speedily, as a separate publication, a lengthy critique of *Towards the Understanding of Karl Marx* by one Paul Mattick! Even though he disagreed with Mattick, regarding the tract as hyperorthodox and mystical, he urged the publisher to "Rush it to the printer as soon as you can because the dear chap has received something like a raw deal from the M.M." [*Modern Monthly*]![30] There is something warm about that wish to

---

30. The letter reads in part: "Dear Solon: After re-reading Comrade Mattick's criticism of my book, I am more than ever convinced that POLEMIC PUBLISHERS ought to publish it. I think it is only just to Mattick to print his essay as a separate brochure. My recommendation of his essay as a timely contribution to Marxist discussion in no way affects my evaluation of the validity of his arguments. I do not believe that Mattick establishes anything which he does not beg at the very outset. . . . When I get around to writing my reply ANTI CRITIQUE [never written]

help a principled even if sadly mistaken opponent who has
received a raw deal publish a criticism of his own book!
That characteristic I observed as long as I knew him.

I shall pay my respects both to [Max] Eastman and Mattick. I did not
intend to bother with Eastman but reading Mattick convinced me that
Eastman's position must be more systematically criticized. The reason is
that Mattick's position makes Eastman's point of view both possible, and
to many, quite plausible. You see Mattick's line is probably the best of all
the orthodox ones with its acceptance of the myths of inevitability, spontaneity, organicism, and its identification of principles with things . . . in
short, outright mysticism. The best though it may be, it can easily be shot
full of holes. My task is to [show] that if this is Marxism, then not a
single one of Eastman's stale criticisms can be answered, and then to
indicate that Eastman['s] criticisms can easily be met from the point of
view of my interpretation and [that] Eastman's own 'creative engineering
Marxism' reveals an ignorance of both the nature of science and philosophy. . . . Please do not hold Mattick's manuscript up but rush it to the
printer as soon as you can because the dear chap has received something
like a raw deal from the M.M. [Presumably, the *Modern Monthly*]
apropos of his article which is better than most of the editors of the
Monthly are in a position to appreciate and which is certainly more
important for the development of Marxist ideas in America than all the
bunk about artists in Bohemia, etc. Give me a ring as soon as you get this
so that I know what's what." (Capitalization and underlining as in the
original.) Letter to "Solon," 23 May 1934 (probably S. L. Solon,
although he was himself then an editor at the *Modern Monthly*). Sidney
Hook Papers, The Archives, Hoover Institution on War, Revolution, and
Peace, Stanford University, California, Box 41. The comments on Max
Eastman reflect the recently ended six-year published exchange
(1928–33) with him (mostly in the *Modern Quarterly* and then *Modern
Monthly*). Despite the comment in this letter, I can find no evidence that
Hook wrote a reply to Mattick or anything further until many years later
re Eastman's views then of Marxism. Hook's key paper in the exchange
with Eastman was in *Modern Quarterly* 4 (May–August 1928): 388–94.
For specific citations to all the thrusts and parries, see page 2 of Barbara
Levine, *Sidney Hook: A Checklist of Writings* (Carbondale and
Edwardsville: Southern Illinois University Press, 1989). Hook discusses
Eastman and the exchange in pages 137–39 of his *Out of Step*.

Another trait was his sense of humor, including, not least, the ability to laugh at or tell a joke at his own expense.[31] The introduction to his interview with the deceased Karl Marx that he conducted in 1955 and which is reprinted in this volume, captures only incompletely his sense of humor.[32] He would have roared with laughter at the writer Paul Berman's subsequent sly dig at the extraordinary fact that the more mature Karl Marx now explicitly agreed on all matters with Sidney Hook! And he would have laughed even more had he been able to read Berman's posthumous interview with *him*. Presumably inspired by Hook's ability to communicate with revolutionary spirits of the past, Berman himself conducted an interview with the deceased Sidney Hook, which seems an appropriate piece with which to conclude this volume.

Berman has caught his tone so well, I can practically hear the interchange. And, he tells us, deceased (Marxist-Leninist and/or Stalinist) communists will find themselves in hell condemned to debate Sidney Hook. I suspect, however, Sidney Hook will be first engaged in some higher philosophical discourse elsewhere. But if Berman is correct, then at the same time on the same podium Sidney Hook must surely be in heaven, or at least enjoying himself wherever he is as if he *were* in heaven, however warm the flames around him!

---

31. These characteristics are captured marvelously in Adrienne Koch, "Personal Reflections on Sidney Hook," in *Sidney Hook and the Contemporary World: Essays on the Pragmatic Intelligence*, ed. Paul Kurtz (New York: John Day, 1968), pp. 28–31.

32. That appeared originally as Sidney Hook, "Marx in Limbo: An Imaginary Conversation," *New Leader* 38 (2 May 1955): 14–17, reprinted in "Karl Marx in Limbo," in Sidney Hook, *Political Power and Personal Freedom* (New York: Criterion Books, 1959), pp. 389–96.

Lest all these comments still not be enough to deter any misinterpretation or misapplication of the contents of the volume itself, I note one historical fact. That same young Sidney Hook was the progenitor of the older Sidney Hook who, however proud he may have been of his earlier achievements, in the light of historical developments and personal observation and experience eventually rejected his earlier views about the paths to full achievement of both human freedom and human potentialities.

So reader, reflect: if it happened to the young Sidney Hook, it can happen to you! If you regard yourself as honest, conscientious, and reasonable, then think seriously about the implications. The young author of this seductive revolutionary volume—reprinted here for the benefit of intellectual scholarship, not naive activism—later conceded his errors and cheerfully admitted he had learned from experience and was simply mistaken about many matters. He did *not*, incidentally, abandon his belief that in some circumstances social and political revolution *is* warranted. But he came to believe that, despite the demagoguery of zealots, the goals of a revolution may usually be achieved by other means and that a violent revolution, especially one led by a narrow, sectarian, doctrinaire faction, will lead with high probability to the very abuses, if not worse, that it sought to overthrow.

Read seriously then and reflect upon his later writings. For I hope that it does not require your experience of the deeds of another Stalin, of the too-belated recognition of the consequences of a Lenin, a Mao, or a Pol Pot to lead you to his later insight: that you can learn from the tragedies of history which others have experienced without undergoing something similar yourself.

For otherwise, you, too, like the Leninist and Stalinist communists of the past, will wind up in hell, condemned to debate Sidney Hook.

ACKNOWLEDGMENTS

I am grateful for the encouragement of the many surviving friends of Sidney Hook to whom I spoke concerning the wisdom of my decision to republish this volume for scholarly purposes. (At many stages, because of some vexations, I was prepared simply, to drop it.) I am indebted to the Archives of the Hoover Institution on War, Revolution and Peace, located at Stanford University, and in particular, to Dale Reed, for preserving and organizing the papers of Sidney Hook. His skillful oversight in arrangement and indexing of these files enabled me to follow the traces of this volume readily. I extend my gratitude to Mary A. Read of Prometheus Books who, with graciousness and tact, oversaw a number of mind-numbing details that arose in publishing an expanded edition of this type, many of them unanticipated at the time the venture was planned. Ranjit Sandhu undertook the extensive and complex new index, which integrates the new material and the double pagination of the republished volume I requested. All scholars using the volume will be in his debt. Many "typographical" errors in the original (1933) edition of *Towards the Understanding of Karl Marx* have been detected in preparing the expanded edition and its index. Current, and probably 1930s, rules of punctuation and grammar would require their alteration. Nevertheless, as the errors detected do not appear to impair the intended meaning, they have been left in situ.

HISTORICAL INTRODUCTION

CHRISTOPHER PHELPS

Towards the Understanding of Karl Marx was praised by reviewers in 1933, created its author's reputation as an adroit and learned interpreter of Marx, and subsequently achieved the status of a classic in the commentary on Marx and Marxism. But soon after its release, the book fell out of print for almost seventy years. At last, with this new edition, readers of every persuasion, whether curious about the New York intellectuals, American philosophy, political theory, or Marx and Marxism, may read *Towards the Understanding of Karl Marx* and judge for themselves its significance and meaning.

The book's reissue has special value in light of the contemporary renaissance of pragmatism. John Dewey's philosophy of experimental naturalism implicitly informed young Sidney Hook's understanding of historical materialism in *Towards the Understanding of Karl Marx*. In the past two decades, in fields ranging from legal studies to literary theory, pragmatism has undergone a rebirth. As in Dewey's time, pragmatism today is a minority point of view within philosophy, but its cultural influence extends throughout the humanities. Those hoping to grasp its social and political implications will find few more useful pragmatist-informed political interpretations than *Towards the Understanding of Karl Marx.*

THE POLITICS OF PHILOSOPHY

The argument of *Towards the Understanding of Karl Marx* requires acquaintance with the spectrum of socialist debate in the first half of the twentieth century. As its subtitle declares, the book advances a "revolutionary" interpretation of Marx. By that Hook did not mean that his view was new or unprecedented. Rather, he concurred with those who had argued that Marx's essential purpose was his revolutionary opposition to capitalism and class society. This interpretation stood in contrast to that expounded by the thinkers of German Social Democracy in the decades prior to the First World War. Because it boasted the largest membership of any socialist party in the world and therefore dominated the Second International (1889–1914), because its leaders were in several cases protégés of Marx and Engels, and because its theorists spoke of "orthodox" fidelity to Marx, Germany's Social Democratic Party had both considerable prestige and a special claim on Marxist theory, conditioning not only European but American understandings of Marxism. The central purpose of *Towards the Understanding of Karl Marx* was to set this record straight by contesting the interpretation of Marx made by German Social Democrats such as Karl Kautsky, Edward Bernstein, and Rudolf Hilferding, whose views Hook, in the opening lines of his book, declared "the abandonment of the revolutionary standpoint which was central to Marx's life and thought."[1]

Towards the Understanding of Karl Marx, therefore, should be understood as an important theoretical contribution to one of the fundamental debates in twentieth-century politics, that between revolutionary socialism and social democracy. This contest, though it may seem arcane at the opening of the twenty-first century, has had repercussions of enormous historical significance. The political difference between the two currents is not, as is commonly misunderstood, that between reform and revolution or between democracy and dictatorship. Rather it is a difference over the *method* of pursuing social reforms, the *types* of reforms to be pursued, the *kind* of democracy envisioned, and the *strategy* for obtaining democracy. Social democracy found classical expression in the trade union bureaucracies, labor parties, and welfare states of Western Europe. It has tended to favor parliamentary and legislative activity within the parameters of the existing government and society. Revolutionary socialism, which historically generated many sizeable mass movements desirous of a new society, including the Russian Revolution of October 1917, has criticized such reformism as a misguided and self-defeating compromise with class society. It has advocated only those changes which it believed would strengthen the position of the working class, sought

---

1. See this edition of Sidney Hook, *Towards the Understanding of Karl Marx* (which follows the 1933 pagination), ix.

through revolutionary action to dismantle what it viewed as the repressive apparatus of the state and to abolish the rule of capital, and aspired to replace class domination with democratic socialism from below.[2]

Though bound up closely with this political divide, the *philosophical* dispute between revolutionary socialism and social democracy has distinctive features. Both types of socialism claim a birthright in Marx, but their account of the philosophical implications and contours of Marxism is incompatible. Revolutionary socialism—in Hook's youth still known as "communism," a word not yet associated unequivocally with the new class states dominated by Communist Party bureaucracies—was represented in *Towards the Understanding of Karl Marx* by two figures who opposed the Second International's capitulation to the First World War and reformism: Polish-German activist Rosa Luxemburg and the Russian Bolshevik leader V. I. Lenin. Although the major theorists of the SPD considered themselves orthodox Marxists, they had, Hook argued, actually created a mechanical, fatalistic ideology, with a deterministic emphasis upon an ostensible "science" of social development, a positivism contrary to Marx's actual worldview, which emphasized practical action. Although Marx had sometimes spoken of revolution as "inevitable," that did not mean, Hook maintained, that Marx saw it as automatic or fated, a certainty of History. Marx knew, he suggested, that revolution would require human action informed by theory—*praxis*. That Lenin and Luxemburg

---

2. For further elaboration of this distinction, see Rosa Luxemburg's pamphlet *Reform or Revolution* (New York: Pathfinder, 1970), first published in 1899, revised in 1908, whose influence upon Hook is clear in *Towards the Understanding of Karl Marx*.

understood this crucial point, the need for a conscious revolutionary subject prepared to act decisively, made them more faithful to Marx, in Hook's estimation, than the "orthodox" minds of German Social Democracy.

Hook's reconstruction of the theory of *praxis* was a product of the mutual influence upon him of pragmatism, which maintained that the veracity of ideas is best tested by evaluating their consequences in practical experience, and of the continental Marxism of Georg Lukács and Karl Korsch, who had entered into opposition against the economic determinism and fatalism of Second International reformism and whose debt Hook expressly acknowledged in his preface. Later in life, beginning around 1939, Hook would develop affinities for the very kind of gradualist politics that he objected to in *Towards the Understanding of Karl Marx*, but his understanding in 1933 of the most significant debates within socialist theory accounts for why his "revolutionary interpretation" of Marx began not with Marx himself but with the layers of controversy surrounding Marx, set in historical context.

CRITICAL RECEPTION IN 1933

With unemployment and bank failures at an all-time high, with capitalism appearing to many observers, even outside the socialist left, to be in ruins, a new book by an American scholar about the author of *Capital,* appearing on the fiftieth anniversary of Marx's death, generated tremendous interest. A surprising number of daily newspapers reviewed *Towards the Understanding of Karl Marx,* generally according it high praise for filling a gap in the limited English-language literature on Marx. Several reviewers concluded that any American university professor who risked writing sympathetically about Marx must surely have an independent mind. The *New York Evening Post* called Hook "a courageous pioneer," and the *Philadelphia Public Ledger* proclaimed him "not only one of the very few bona fide academicians in America who knows anything about Marx, but . . . one of a still smaller company who dares write about the founder of socialism." As might be expected, not every newspaper admired Hook's stance. To the *Louisville Courier Journal*, "A difficulty arises in the fact that Professor Hook himself makes no pretense of detachment, which is honest and which is consistent with his evident view that partisanship is necessary to a real grasp of Marxism, but the fact is bound to arouse combativeness now and then in the unbeliever."[3]

In journals of opinion, superlatives abounded. Harold Laski, writing in the *New Republic,* called *Towards the Understanding of Karl Marx* "the most stimulating introduction so far written in English. . . . It marks an epoch in the study of its subject." In the *World Tomorrow*, Reinhold Niebuhr hailed Hook as "the ablest interpreter of Marxian philosophy in our nation." Although Ross J. S. Hoffman in

3. N. G., "Marxian," *New York Evening Post* (30 March 1933); S. C., "Hook Celebrates Marx Anniversary," *Philadelphia Public Ledger* (13 May 1933); Russell Briney, "Marxian Theory and Practice," *Louisville Courier Journal* (9 April 1933). For other newspaper reviews, see A. B. E., "Karl Marx," *Boston Transcript* (12 April 1933); "An Interpretation of Marx Undertaken by a Writer," *Pittsburgh Press* (14 May 1933); Karl Scholz, "Marx Interpreted for the Moderns by Sidney Hook," *Philadelphia Record* (26 March 1933); F. M., "An Intelligent Treatise on Marx," *Providence Journal* (2 April 1933); and F. B. B., "Karl Marx," *Springfield Union* (2 June 1933).

Commonweal warned of passages that "offer difficulty to minds unused to the recondite language of professors of philosophy," Herschell Bricker of the *North American Review* called *Towards the Understanding of Karl Marx* "a simple, clear interpretation not only of the Marxian teachings, but also of the whole history of the Marxian movement, in short, a book to supply any intelligent reader with enough information about Marx to discuss The Revolution." Edmund Wilson, himself at work on the history of socialist thought that would become *To the Finland Station*, vouchsafed, "If anybody wants a lucid guide to what Marx and Engels really thought as distinguished from what the various Marxist parties think they ought to have thought, Sidney Hook is the man for him to read."[4]

Scholarly reviewers were no less fulsome in their praise. Selig Perlman, writing in the *American Political Science Review*, called *Towards the Understanding of Karl Marx* "the best presentation of the social philosophy of Karl Marx in the English language." Academic compliments, however, came seasoned with a general opposition to Marxism. In the *Journal of Philosophy,* George H. Sabine held that Marx's philosophical concept of the dialectic, which Hook elaborated and defended, was "not a logical method, but an art of propagating moral and reli-

4. Harold J. Laski, "Introduction to Marx," *New Republic* (28 June 1933): 186–87; Reinhold Niebuhr, "The Ablest Interpreter of Marx," *World Tomorrow* 16 (August 1933): 476; Ross J. S. Hoffman, "The Prophet of Communism," *Commonweal* 18 (18 August 1933): 390–91; Herschell Bricker, "The Literary Landscape," *North American Review* 236 (July 1933): 96; Edmund Wilson, "Taking the Marxist Dialectic Apart," *New Republic* (4 August 1937): 366–68. See also Lewis Carliner, *Progressive Education* 10 (October 1933): 354–55; untitled review, *Current History* 38 (August 1933): vi.

gious convictions." In the *American Economic Review*, Joseph J. Senturia found Hook's position on the labor theory of value a "brilliant but sterile exercise in logic in defense of an obsolete theory." Perlman, similarly, wished Hook would turn his attention away from elucidating "the real Marx" toward "another subject, perhaps more important in the present juncture, namely, the puzzling deviation of the conduct of Western societies from that laid down by the Marxian prognosis," meaning, presumably, the failure of the working classes in the advanced capitalist countries to seize power.[5]

In the United Kingdom, where the book was issued by the leftist publisher Victor Gollancz, the *Economist* objected that Hook was guilty of "barely specious apologies for Marx's theoretical structure," when Marx was in actuality "a great reformer and propagandist genius who never cared very much for disinterested scientific analysis." But the *Times Literary Supplement* held that Hook "writes well and clearly—or as clearly as is possible on such a subject," and the reviewer for the *South Wales Argus* wrote, "Whether we are Communists or not, it is well to see exactly what Marx really taught. For this purpose the student will find nothing in English so full and adequate as this volume." Hook's own impression was that England was the country where the book had its greatest influence, especially at Oxford and Cambridge, where it

---

5. Selig Perlman, *American Political Science Review* 27 (August 1933): 657–58; George H. Sabine, *Journal of Philosophy* 30 (9 November 1933): 634–37; Joseph J. Senturia, *American Economic Review* 23 (December 1933): 687–89. See also George E. G. Catlin, *Philosophical Review* 44 (January 1935): 73–75.

"converted many readers—or strongly confirmed them in their leanings—to a revolutionary outlook."[6]

COMMUNIST AND SOCIAL DEMOCRATIC CRITICISM

Acclaim in daily newspapers, journals of opinion, and the universities throws into sharp relief a major irony of the book's reception: writers on the left, rather than opponents of Marxism, delivered the fiercest criticism of *Towards the Understanding of Karl Marx*. The two most well-established and sizeable tendencies in the world socialist movement in the interwar decades were Communism and social democracy, and neither found *Towards the Understanding of Karl Marx* much to its liking.

A remote observer might have expected that the American Communist Party—the main pole of attraction for revolutionary socialists after its founding in 1919—would herald a favorable book on Marx, especially from an intellectual so close to its cause as Sidney Hook. Hook had endorsed the Party's electoral ticket in 1932, and had helped draft the pamphlet of its artistic and intellectual

6. "Marx and Lenin," *Economist* (9 September 1933); untitled review, *Times Literary Supplement* (30 August 1934): 591; J. O., "The Ideas of Karl Marx Explained," *South Wales Argus* (2 August 1933); Sidney Hook, *Out of Step* (New York: Harper and Row, 1987), p. 178. One of the few surviving bits of the book's publishing data is that Gollancz printed 2,000 copies in May 1933 and an additional 1,000 copies in February 1934 (Christine Woodland, Active Archivist, University of Warwick Library, letter to author, 7 August 1997). If the tabulation of the American publisher, John Day, was comparable, then the original edition sold about 6,000 copies, a respectable number given the economic crisis.

supporters, *Culture and the Crisis* (1932). Many of his
personal friends, including his first wife, belonged to the
Communist Party. But Hook's relationship with the Communist Party was increasingly contradictory, as a result of
developments in the Soviet Union. In the course of the
1920s, the Soviet government, which Hook had believed
was founded in democratic workers' councils, became
increasingly authoritarian as the power of its bureaucratic
officialdom, led by Joseph Stalin, expanded.[7] In the late

---

7. In a 1934 article for the American Workers Party's *Labor Action*,
Hook praised workers' councils as "the organs of working-class democracy." A related article by Hook, for the Carnegie Endowment's periodical
International Conciliation, suggested this ideal state of affairs: "The political basis of the workers' State is the occupational activity of its citizens.
The Workers' Councils are the democratically administered instrumentalities for organizing and controlling production, administering justice, and
conducting the national defense. As the expression of the workers, it is the
ultimate source of all authority responsible to no one but itself, and the
best judge of its own interests." Did the Soviet Union live up to the ideal?
No, but the problem lay not in initial aspiration but in later corruption: "In
one of his writings on the work of the Soviets, Lenin wrote that 'the Soviet
State is a million times more democratic than the most democratic bourgeois republic.' If we approach the problem of democracy not from the
formal point of view of the registration of consent but of the actual power
to control the conditions and direction of social life, Lenin's characterization will undoubtedly be found to be, in the main, still correct although
less so than in his own times. (Since 1924 there have been progressive
restrictions on workers' democratic control and a growing intolerance of
the expression of dissident communist opinion. And this despite the fact
Russia is far more stable today than she was in Lenin's times!)" If anything is remarkable about this 1934 article, indeed, it is Hook's description of the Soviet Union as a "crippled workers' democracy," which
despite the term "crippled" concedes the existence of a modicum of
democracy. Perhaps the article was written much earlier than its formal
date of publication, because by 1934 Hook was generally given to deny
categorically that any democracy whatsoever existed in Stalin's Soviet

1920s and early 1930s, the Soviet state was urging upon its global supporters a "Third Period" rhetoric that justified fierce denunciations of any potential "misleaders" of the working class, especially social democrats. In this context, which encouraged the reduction of theory to sectarian dogma, the American Communist leadership concluded that Hook's interpretation of Marxism was incompatible with its own. Just a few months before the 1933 publication of *Towards the Understanding of Karl Marx,* parts of which had already appeared in periodical format, the Party launched a full-scale ideological purge of him. The attack involved a distortion of Hook's ideas, imputing to him the very politics of social democracy his book had challenged. An article by V. J. Jerome in the *Communist*, the Party's official organ, claimed, "Nowhere—not in Marx, not in Engels, not in Lenin, nowhere except in German revisionism can Hook find the true Marxism! Better spoken: Not in Marx, nor in Engels, nor in Lenin, but in German revisionism, in Bernstein, in Kautsky, in Hilferding, can Hook mirror *his own* Marxism."[8]

Union; in fact, he would soon reject the term "workers' state" as a description of the Soviet Union, given the powerlessness of Soviet workers. This, however, Hook found to be a violation, not fulfillment, of the original Leninist project, which remained a valuable model: "If we remain true to the Marxist and Leninistic conception of the workers' state as a workers' democracy and agitate in these terms, much greater headway in reorienting the working masses toward revolutionary action can be made." Sidney Hook, "Marxism and Democracy," *Labor Action* (1 May 1934): 5; "The Democratic and Dictatorial Aspects of Communism," *International Conciliation* (December 1934): 452–564.

8. V. J. Jerome, "Unmasking an American Revisionist of Marxism," *Communist* (January 1933): 55–56. Just prior to publication of the book, Hook was summoned to a meeting with top Party officials on the legendary ninth floor of Communist Party headquarters on East Thirteenth

In actuality, *Towards the Understanding of Karl Marx* persistently took to task the views of Bernstein, Kautsky, and Hilferding, and favored Marx, Engels, and Lenin. Hook retorted that Jerome "violates every principle of Leninist accuracy by taking sentences and phrases from the context of my writings, thereby giving the reader an impression of my views which is the *precise opposite* of what I actually wrote." He characterized Marxism as "the theory and practice of social revolution," and explained his belief that German Social Democracy had turned Marxism into a science of social development and thereby succumbed to the lull of reformist practice, whereas Lenin had "restored Marxism to its original spirit and developed its doctrines in an analysis of the problems of revolutionary theory and practice in the era of finance capitalism." But the Party's top leader, Earl Browder, upheld Jerome's association of Hook with Bernstein, calling both "revisionists," and declaring with finality that Hook had "an understanding of Marxism in conflict with that of the Communist Party and the Communist International."9

Street, where he was asked to defend his philosophical positions in a lengthy session. See Hook, *Out of Step*, pp. 158–65.

9. Hook's reply is found in Earl Browder, "The Revisionism of Sidney Hook," *Communist* (1933): 134, 145, 286. There were several ancillary phases of Stalinist criticism. One issued from William Cunningham and Paul Evans, teachers at a small left-wing college in Mena, Arkansas. Cunningham, an Oklahoman CP activist and novelist, would in the 1940s go to work for the Soviet news agency TASS in New York. He and Evans maintained in the school's bulletin that Marx, contrary to Hook's interpretation, *did* intend a science of economics. In a reply disparaging attempts to make Marxism an economic science rather than a method of action and to settle political disagreements by rote citation, Hook wrote, "The failure to do justice to this activistic and revolutionary aspect of Marxism, is at the source of the social democratic deviations

The Communist position that Hook was an admirer of social democracy hit "a new high for argument by misquotation and downright distortion (and that at a time when there is no dearth of talent in that direction)," as one radical critic of both Hook and official Communism put it.[10] Excoriation of *Towards the Understanding of Karl Marx* as soft on social democracy, despite the book's con-

---

and distortions of Marxism." The Communist Party of Great Britain launched related attacks on Hook, chiefly in its publication *Labour Monthly.* By "twists and maneuvers," claimed the *Labour Monthly* reviewer, Hook seemed to oppose the Second International but in reality opposed the Marxism of Lenin and the Third International: "It is not surprising that that other great bourgeois student of Marxism, Professor Laski, should have found this book so worthy of his august praise." The Hungarian Stalinist philosopher L. Rudas, writing in a subsequent issue of *Labour Monthly,* claimed that since Hook was not a member of the Communist Party he could not possibly be a Marxist: "Being outside the Communist Party he of course knows that he can be neither a communist nor a dialectical materialist nor a Marxist." By contrast, the British Communist autodidact T. A. Jackson, in his 1936 book *Dialectics*, noted with fairness that Hook was a critic rather than an accomplice of German social democracy. But Jackson mockingly urged sympathy for Hook because "he has had an academic training inflicted upon him," and was cool toward Hook's conclusions. See William Cunningham, "Misunderstanding Marxian Economics," *Commonwealth College Fortnightly*, 15 February 1934, 2–3; "Sidney Hook Replies," *Commonwealth College Fortnightly*, 15 June 1934, 2–3; Paul Evans, "On Sydney [*sic*] Hook's Reply," *Commonwealth College Fortnightly*, 15 July 1934, 2; P. A. S., "Towards the Understanding of Marx," *Labour Monthly* (December 1934); L. Rudas, "The Meaning of Sidney Hook," *Labour Monthly* (March 1935): 313, 319, 320; T. A. Jackson, *Dialectics* (New York: International, 1936), p. 123. For Hook's reply to Rudas, see Hook, "Philosophical Burlesque: On Some Stalinist Antics in Philosophy," *Modern Monthly* 9 (May 1935): 163–72.

10. Jim Cork, "The Marxism of Sidney Hook," *Workers Age* 2 (1 October 1933): 4.

sistent criticism of social democratic method and conduct, represented a simple attempt to discredit Hook in the eyes of those who were unlikely to read the book on their own given such devastating reviews from the highest authorities in the Communist movement. In 1933, the charge of social democracy was anathema to the Communist ranks. The Communist leadership's broadside probably derived from the perception—basically accurate—that Hook was by temperament unsusceptible to Party control, that he was unlikely to abide Soviet doctrinal pronouncements, and that he was developing profound doubts about the state and class structure of the Soviet Union, even if none of those doubts were yet explicit in *Towards the Understanding of Karl Marx*.[11]

Social democrats, for their part, found little comfort in Hook's interpretation—certainly none of the sympathy for their heroes that Communist polemics suggested lay at the heart of the book. Consequently, the social democratic response to *Towards the Understanding of Karl Marx* was equally sharp. However, the critics of *Towards the Understanding of Karl Marx* from a social democratic position were far less numerous, perhaps because social democratic intellectuals in the United States, in contrast to their European counterparts (who for the most part did not drop their rhetorical attachment to Marxism until after the Second World War), were then, as now, more concerned to outline a centrist strategy for socialism than to explore Marxism as theory or doctrine.

Two notable social democratic reviewers of the book

---

11. For a more extensive discussion of Hook's break with Communism, see Christopher Phelps, *Young Sidney Hook: Marxist and Pragmatist* (Ithaca, N.Y.: Cornell University Press, 1997), pp. 74–78, 84–89.

were David Berenberg and Morris Cohen. Berenberg, writing in the *City College Alumnus* (Hook had graduated from City College in 1923), found *Towards the Understanding of Karl Marx* "always vivid and at times brilliant" but was disturbed that Hook "cannot mention Kautsky, Hilferding, or Plekhanov without an implicit sneer." In this sense, Berenberg comprehended Hook's revolutionary criticism of social democracy with far greater accuracy than Jerome or Browder. But he too resorted to ad hominem attack when he attempted to counter Hook's criticism of the British Labour Party and the American Federation of Labor for failing to organize unskilled workers by charging Hook with "parlor communism." Hook, Berenberg held, is "a man cloistered and remote from the scene of the struggle, whose sole information comes from the writings of impatient revolutionaries, whose nerves are agreeably stimulated by this very impatience and violence of temper."[12]

Far more painful to Hook in personal terms was a polemic against *Towards the Understanding of Karl Marx* by his undergraduate mentor, philosopher Morris Cohen, published in the social democratic youth journal *Student Outlook*. Cohen was a left-liberal, not a Marxist. He was also a devastatingly logical teacher of philosophy whose challenges sometimes extended to the point of cruelty. These characteristics were evident in his review of *Towards the Understanding of Karl Marx*. Cohen claimed that his former student had presumed a need for violent revolution, overemphasized the revolutionary instincts

---

12. David Berenberg, untitled review of *Towards the Understanding of Karl Marx*, *City College Alumnus* 29, no. 5 (1933): 71–72.

and capacities of the working class, ignored intermediate classes (such as farmers and small shopkeepers), and, in general, indulged in wishful thinking: "Why should society submit to a bloody revolution from which it might never recover if the same result can possibly be brought about by less sanguinary though slower methods?" Hook, Cohen charged, was "hypnotized by the sacred cows of revolutionary phraseology."[13]

Moderate socialists, finding their politics under criticism from the left, have often charged their critics with a utopian lack of realism, cautioned that restrained tactics are the most prudent for advancing socialist interests, and equated revolution with indiscriminate violence. But *Towards the Understanding of Karl Marx* was actually far subtler, especially on the topic of violence and class struggle, than Cohen and Berenberg's criticism implied. In regard to force, Hook started from the premise that cant about morality was often manipulated by the ruling class in bourgeois societies:

---

13. Morris R. Cohen, "Notes on Prof. Hook's Understanding of Karl Marx," *Student Outlook* 3 (November–December 1934): 31–34. Cohen's polemic was not merely against a former student but a former *disciple* who had defected from his point of view to the pragmatism of John Dewey in the mid-1920s. This personal and philosophical history, as much as political difference, probably accounts for the severity of the upbraiding. In a personal letter, a pained Hook called the review "grossly unfair": "I regard your 'notes' as both unjust and discourteous, not to speak of their mischievous effect. I still cherish, however, the memory of my intellectual indebtedness to you. Even though doctrinally and temperamentally we are far apart, I have learned many lessons well from you. Among them has been to put truth first." Hook to Cohen, 12 January 1935 (Sidney Hook Papers, The Archives, Hoover Institution on War, Revolution and Peace, Stanford University, California, Box 41, #6; reprinted by permission); see Phelps, *Young Sidney Hook*, pp. 23–24, 28–30, 100–104, and Hook, *Out of Step*, pp. 42–44, 53–68, for more on the Hook-Cohen relationship.

Having already made its revolution by force, it now taught that the use of force was in principle a crime against civilization. And this in the face of the facts that the bourgeois state and law functioned by the use of force; and that the struggle between capital and labor, upon which bourgeois civilization rested, took the form of open civil war whenever workers were driven to defend themselves as a result of intolerable oppression.

Nonviolent resistance could in some cases achieve certain revolutionary ends, Hook observed, but in other instances—including the periods prior to the First World War and before the rise of fascism, together responsible for millions of deaths—"excessive legalism and pacifism" had rendered socialist movements impotent. Hook believed that Marx, Engels, and Lenin had been too optimistic about the possibility of a peaceful transition to socialism in the United States, and he concluded that the weight of probability was with the exercise of coercion. But Hook never held force *requisite;* indeed he pointed out that Marx made no fetish of force.[14]

The critical difference between Hook and his social democratic opponents was less about the appropriateness of violence than about class and state. As Hook wrote, it was "Marx's theory of the state which distinguishes the true Marxist from the false":

For it is the theory of the state which is ultimately linked up with immediate political practice. The attempt made by 'liberal' Marxists throughout the world—even when they call themselves orthodox—to separate the existing eco-

---

14. Hook, *Towards the Understanding*, pp. 282, 285–86.

nomic order from the existing state, as well as their belief
that the existing state can be used as an instrument by
which the economic system can be "gradually revolutionized" into state capitalism or state socialism, must be
regarded as a fundamental distortion of Marxism.

Whereas social democrats believed that elections, education, and legislation within a strategy of gradualism were
the appropriate means of social change, for Hook history
demonstrated that elites were capable of rendering all of
those means inadequate if their power to rule were threat-
ened. Socialists were remiss to restrict themselves to legal
and electoral tactics alone, which would all but guarantee
their ultimate failure.[15]

Hook was among those who by the early 1930s concluded that both Communism and social democracy had
sacrificed whatever claim they once held to authentic
Marxism. The political conciliations and accommodations
of social democracy and the increasing dogmatism and
authoritarianism of the Communist movement, combined
with the failure of both to halt the advance of fascism in
Europe, stimulated the emergence of a small, diverse third
camp of socialism in the late 1920s and early 1930s.
Almost lost to memory in recent discussions of socialism's
fate is this alternative tradition of socialism from below, to
which Hook contributed many clarifications, especially
regarding "workers' democracy"—an anticipated transitional society along the way to socialism, resistant to both
bureaucratic and capitalist rule. The composition of the
independent Marxist left was often forged out of necessity
as much as choice. Hook, for example, had tried during the

15. Ibid., pp. 291–97, 270–71.

time he was writing *Towards the Understanding of Karl Marx* to preserve a relationship with the Communist movement, but, probably because of his privately expressed reservations about its top-down structure and policy errors, the Party hierarchy sanctioned a deluge of abuse for *Towards the Understanding of Karl Marx*. Among Marxists who were neither Communists nor social democrats—a spectrum comprised of multiple competing small groups as well as unaffiliated individuals—Hook's ideas were never received uncritically. They did, however, receive a more thorough and comprehending criticism than they had received at the hands of the Stalinist and social democratic left.

PAUL MATTICK: SCIENCE, INEVITABILITY, AND SPONTANEITY

By far the most exhaustive assessment of *Towards the Understanding of Karl Marx* was Paul Mattick's pamphlet *The Inevitability of Communism: A Critique of Sidney Hook's Interpretation of Marx* (1935). A German revolutionary who migrated to the United States in 1926 and became an industrial worker in Michigan and Illinois, Mattick was one of a small circle of "council communists," including the Dutch leftists Anton Pannekoek and Herman Gorter. At once idiosyncratic and orthodox, his pamphlet displayed both profound intellectual engagement and a pronounced sectarian streak.[16]

16. Paul Mattick, *The Inevitability of Communism: A Critique of Sidney Hook's Interpretation of Marx* (New York: Polemic, 1935). On

The problem gnawing at Marxism, Mattick argued, was not dogmatism but lack of principles. Mattick thought Hook mistaken to set Marxism apart from science proper (which Hook took to rise above particular class loyalties), "since *all* scientific methods, regardless of the material with which they deal, are in part subjectively conditioned." In this, Mattick anticipated some contemporary sensibilities in the philosophy and history of science. Yet his intention was not to deny universalist possibilities or rational ambitions. He meant rather to underscore that "there is no distinction to be made between science and Marxism," and that under German Social Democracy, "Marxism *was not* converted into a science but, first practically and then also theoretically, completely *abandoned*." Another orthodox tenet defended by Mattick against Hook was that of the inevitability of communism: "An analysis of capitalist society, which implies looking into its own inner laws of development, permits no other conclusion, on a scientific basis and with the acceptance of the theory of value, than that communism is inevitable."[17]

Mattick's life and thought, see Paul Mattick Jr., "Mattick, Paul," in *Biographical Dictionary of Neo-Marxism*, ed. Robert A. Gorman (London: Mansell Publishing Limited, 1985), pp. 286–89; and *Root & Branch*, whole no. 10 (1982), a special issue of that libertarian socialist journal on "The Marxism of Paul Mattick."

17. Mattick, *The Inevitability of Communism*, pp. 7, 9, 44. The issue of the relationship of science to Marxism was of general interest on the left in the 1930s. Many Communist critics of the book, for example, raised it. It was also important for the movement aligned with Leon Trotsky, the dissident Russian revolutionary who was in exile from Stalin's Soviet Union. The Trotskyist movement was, in the 1930s, the core tendency in the revolutionary anti-Stalinist socialist camp. Both Trotsky and his followers were concerned to demonstrate that Marxism was not merely a method of revolutionary action but *also* a science of

This love for orthodoxy, science, and inevitability, not to mention Mattick's confidence that accumulation would lead without question to a collapse, giving rise to a new society, was distinguished from the similar stance of many Communists by Mattick's simultaneous enthusiasm for spontaneity and libertarianism. Unlike Hook, who in the 1930s upheld Bolshevism despite his growing personal discomfort with subsequent events in the Soviet Union, Mattick opposed Bolshevism completely. To him Bolshevism and social democracy were equally reformist, both the Second and Third Internationals had distorted Marxism, the Bolsheviks were merely "*radical* social democrats," and neglect of spontaneous working-class revolutionary upheaval accounted for "the mechanism of Kautsky and Lenin." Mattick opposed socialist parties of *any* variety. All real revolutionary movements, he argued, were spontaneous—"the *revolution is not a party matter but the affair of the class*"—and to the class, rather than the party, revolutionaries should look: "Today the party is nothing more than a hindrance to the unfolding of real class consciousness. Wherever *real class consciousness* has been expressed, in the last thirty years, it has assumed

social development, that such a conception of Marxism need not take on a reformist political cast, and that Marxism's fallibility and inability to make predictions only made it *typical* of science. Although Trotsky and Hook had personal and published exchanges at about this time (see Phelps, *Young Sidney Hook*, pp. 91–96), Trotsky never directly reviewed *Towards the Understanding of Karl Marx*. For a Trotskyist reply to *Towards the Understanding of Karl Marx*, see Ruben Gotesky, "Marxism: Science or Method?" *New International* 1 (December 1934): 147–51; 2 (March 1935): 71–73; 2 (May 1935): 106–109; see also the favorable review by Felix Morrow, a friend of Hook's who was a Trotskyist, in *Saturday Review of Literature* 9 (22 April 1933): 550.

the form of committees of action and workers councils."
Political parties, Mattick held, automatically substitute
themselves for the mass movement: they had only blunted
the edge of spontaneously formed councils, and they grew
in size and influence as class consciousness receded. Revolution as a party matter, he pronounced, "belongs to a
period which is already surpassed—the period of
reformism, for which Marxism had frozen into an ideology and whose position Hook, in spite of all his criticism, after all now approves."[18]

Mattick's conflation of organization with reformism led
him, like the Communists, to characterize Hook as a
reformist and to charge that Hook "in his zeal has abandoned Marxism itself." One could have asked for few
more apt corroborations of Hook's suspicion that claims to
orthodoxy are essentially religious in impulse. Such denunciation undercut Mattick's more favorable comments,
such as his assertion that *Towards the Understanding of
Karl Marx*, "in comparison with the hitherto embryonic
Marxism in the United States . . . is without doubt to be
regarded as an advance."[19]

But violence of dissent can obscure proximity of perspective, and so it was with Hook and Mattick. For while
Towards the Understanding of Karl Marx conveyed a
mostly favorable disposition toward Lenin and his emphasis on party organization, Hook's values were democratic. Hook, like Mattick, favored workers' councils, or
soviets, as the revolutionary basis for the reconstruction of
society from below. He distinguished Marx's vision of
revolution from the conspiratorial putsch. And in his dis-

18. Mattick, *The Inevitability of Communism*, pp. 31, 34.
19. Ibid., pp. 34, 40.

cussion of the "dictatorship of the proletariat," Hook held that the phrase did not condone despotism; rather, it specified an intermediate formation following the revolutionary triumph but preceding the attainment of communism, that is, a workers' state that would require the forcible suppression of counterrevolutionary terrorism but would prepare the way for socialist democracy. Representative institutions of the producers would govern, with administrators kept to working-class wages, elected delegates subject to recall at any time, and no standing army separate from the armed population (measures drawn from Lenin's *State and Revolution*).[20]

---

20. Later Hook would come to believe that "to be a Leninist was tantamount to surrendering any kind of belief in democratic socialism" (*Out of Step*, p. 516), but in the 1920s and 1930s he did not find the two incompatible. In a series of reviews on Russia for the *Saturday Review*, for example, he suggested that "the true hero of the Russian revolution," rather than any one individual, was "the Bolshevik party, of which Lenin was an integral part, and which prepared itself for action only by the interstitial processes of self-criticism." He praised the "character of the Bolshevik party as a whole, which, despite the waverings of some of its leaders, mustered sufficient intelligence, flexibility, and will to action to insure a practically bloodless triumph." And, he wrote, "It is remarkable, and yet the documentation on the point is compelling, that during the whole period of storm and stress in 1917 and 1918 the principles of centralized democracy within the Bolshevik party were faithfully adhered to. Minority opinion within the organization has never been given such latitude in expression since. This very freedom to take issue with the party leadership proved to be really a source of strength, for in addition to the greater flexibility in approach, critical awareness, and anticipation of difficulties confronting proposed policies which resulted from party democracy, there were fewer defections and less bitterness and waste of energy, than would have been the case if latter-day methods of treating intraparty opposition had then prevailed." Only after 1923, with the rise of Stalin, did Hook believe the revolution went awry: "Lenin's death and

Yet unlike Mattick, who identified a new form of exploitative class rule in the Soviet Union, Hook in *Towards the Understanding of Karl Marx* begged the question of disturbing tendencies in post-1917 Russian history. Consider, for example, Hook's rejoinder to Robert Michels's thesis that all of modern social organization tends toward bureaucracy:

> In a socialist society in which political leadership is an administrative function, and, therefore, carries with it no economic power, in which the processes of education strive to direct the psychic tendencies to self-assertion into "moral and social equivalents" of oligarchical ambition, in which the monopoly of education for one class has been abolished, and the division of labor between manual and mental worker is progressively eliminated—the danger that Michels' "law of oligarchy" will express itself in traditional form, becomes quite remote. In addition, the organization of the communes or soviets demands that all producers in the course of their work be drawn into the "social planning activities" of society. Of necessity they become politically conscious. And where political consciousness is widespread and the means of production held in common, bureaucracy cannot flourish.[21]

---

the abandonment of the principles of international revolution for the theory of socialism in one country mark the proper dividing line between the two epochs of Russian development." Hook, "Russia in Solution," *Saturday Review* (8 April 1933): 521–22; "Interpreting Soviet Russia," *Saturday Review* (16 February 1935): 494–95; and "What Happened in Russia," *Saturday Review* (1 June 1935): 10–11. At the same time, Hook criticized Lenin's epistemology as flawed; see Hook, "The Philosophy of Dialectical Materialism," parts 1 and 2, *Journal of Philosophy* 25 (1 and 15 March 1928); and Phelps, *Young Sidney Hook*, pp. 115–17.

21. Hook, *Towards the Understanding*, pp. 312–13.

But already by the time Hook wrote, the Soviet experience had contradicted this scenario entirely. Mattick's characterization of the USSR as "state capitalist," while arguable, was at least an explicit attempt to come to terms with the realities of exploitation, bureaucracy, and state in the Soviet Union. The relative deficiency of *Towards the Understanding of Karl Marx* in this respect was a result of Hook's attempt in 1932–1933 to preserve a friendly relationship with a Communist movement that espoused a set of values and politics increasingly at odds with his own understandings of Marxism and Leninism. In the next few years, Hook would develop a much more penetrating assessment of Soviet society and would spell out in great detail the types of structural measures and subjective standards necessary to enhance the likelihood of democratic consequences issuing from revolutionary efforts.[22]

---

22. In his autobiography, Hook recounted, "In *Towards the Understanding of Karl Marx*, I did not compromise on any theoretical point in which I thought Marx, Engels, or Lenin were wrong, confident in my naïveté that these criticisms would be taken in the context of my new persuasive restatement of the social philosophy of Marxism as a whole. I did refrain from criticizing certain unhealthy developments in the Soviet Union, realizing already that I could get no hearing for my views among those I was trying to influence if I were to identify myself with any of the warring political factions" (*Out of Step*, p. 177). Once apart from the Communist milieu, Hook did in fact identify himself with one such faction, the American Workers Party. For Hook's sharply focused political assessment of Stalinism in that period, see Sidney Hook, ed., *The Meaning of Marx* (New York: Farrar & Rinehart, 1934).

MARXISM AND PRAGMATISM

A crucial philosophical issue that Mattick's pamphlet failed to address was the relationship of Marxism to pragmatism. As a favorite student of John Dewey at Columbia University in the 1920s, Hook had been influenced by the experimental method of pragmatism, the major American-born contribution to twentieth-century philosophy. Among the basic tenets of pragmatism (sometimes called, with potentially misleading consequences, "instrumentalism") are the propositions that ideas are the cumulative result of human experience and that doubts about whether any particular idea is warranted are best resolved by putting it to the test of practice. This method pervaded the interpretation of Marxism advanced by Hook in *Towards the Understanding of Karl Marx.*

Many commentators—admirers and critics alike—have extrapolated far more from *Towards the Understanding of Karl Marx* about Hook's views on the relationship of pragmatism and Marxism than the text explicitly warrants. Dewey's name, for example, never appears in the book. Nonetheless, an obvious pragmatist sensibility permeated certain passages in *Towards the Understanding of Karl Marx*, such as its assertion that "there is nothing *a priori* in Marx's philosophy; it is naturalistic, historical, and empirical." And some of its sentences might have been written by Dewey: "If practice and successful action are criteria of intelligibility, then critical intelligence may be defined as an awareness of the technique, procedures and instruments involved in all directed activity"; "any problem which cannot be solved by some actual or possible practice may be dismissed as no genuine problem at all." Yet Hook's declared focus, it must be underscored, was the interpretation of *Marxism,* not pragmatism.[23]

The implicit coincidence of Marxism and pragmatism in Hook's thought was either treated superficially or ignored by most writers. Communist critics pounced upon his pragmatist leanings as a bourgeois deviation. Scholarly commentators were too taken by the novelty of a serious American Marxist to pay much heed to Hook's pragmatism. An exception was Hook's erstwhile mentor, Cohen, who charged that Hook's attempt "to unite pragmatism and the belief in moral free will with economic determinism and with too simple dogma as to the class struggle, leads to insuperable difficulties." Another was literary critic Llewellyn Jones, who took an opposite tack: "Mr. Hook has already been accused of re-writing Marx's theories in terms of Deweyan instrumentalism. He has abundant justification, however, not only in Marx's own words but in Lenin's, for stressing the instrumental character of Marxian thought. For Marx not only specifically denied that his determinism meant fatalism and that his economics were objective, but wherever he uses the word revolutionary we can read instrumental: indeed it is obvious that the two words are almost synonymous." Where Cohen's tone was peremptory, Jones's enthusiasm went far beyond what Hook himself was prepared to argue.[24]

A more sophisticated criticism of Hook's pragmatist understanding of Marxism came from independent socialist journalist Benjamin Stolberg in the *Nation*. While

---

23. Hook, *Towards the Understanding of Karl Marx*, pp. 5–6, 184, 76.

24. Cohen, "Notes on Prof. Hook's Understanding of Karl Marx," 31; Llewellyn Jones, "Sidney Hook on Karl Marx," *New Humanist* 6 (July–August 1933): 39.

he found *Towards the Understanding of Karl Marx* an "index of the intellectual awakening in our higher social learning," Stolberg found fault with Hook's "gentle obsession": "that Marx was a revolutionary pragmatist, in the technical sense of the term." Hook had, Stolberg wrote, attributed to Marx "the theory of knowledge as well as the social psychology of pragmatism." While the book was "the most significant contribution which has yet to appear in America," Hook was mistaken to impute Deweyan characteristics to Marx: "Marxian 'instrumentalism' has none of the worship of empiricism of the pragmatists. It is calculated to advance revolutionary tactics within a strictly a priori social logic. It learns from means only when they are inclined to serve its ends, while pragmatism is the idolatry of endless means. Pragmatism, indeed, is the most sophisticated expression of the planlessness of modern capitalism."[25]

A related criticism came from Greenwich Village radical Max Eastman, who, though of an earlier generation, had also been a student of Dewey's, had also turned to revolutionary socialism, and had for five years been involved in a running polemic with Hook in small journals of the independent left. Eastman found *Towards the Understanding of Karl Marx* "a delightfully intelligent daydream of what Marx might have thought and said had he been a pupil of John Dewey." He admitted that both Marx and Dewey, as a product of their common Hegelian training, had arrived at a philosophical position combining knowledge with programs of action. Yet there the similarity ended:

25. Benjamin Stolberg, "The Americanization of Karl Marx," *Nation* 136 (12 April 1933): 414–15.

Perhaps the most obvious difference is that according to the Marxian scheme the philosopher has to feel that his program-of-action will be fulfilled. The Deweyite, on the other contrary, regards this "quest of certainty" as one of the survivals of a barbarous faith. For this reason Sidney Hook, with his gallant determination to make Karl Marx a thorough Deweyite, is compelled to wish away and wipe out of Marxism altogether the very central pillar of its temple, the belief in "historic determinism." He does this by mere arbitrary dictum—by telling you "what Marx means when he speaks of the historic inevitability of communism." And what Marx means, of course, turns out to be, not that communism is inevitable but that it is possible, an alternative worth striving for and which we may help to "make true" by believing in it. It was Marx's uncomprehending followers, Hook has told us elsewhere—men like Kautsky, Bernstein, Plekhanov, Lenin—who translated his thoroughgoing instrumentalism into the "mythical language of the inevitability" of communism. But Marx's *language*—as you see above—was just as mythical as theirs. If Marx said *inevitable* when he meant *possible,* perhaps they suffered from the very same feebleness of mind! There is no end to this kind of "interpretation."[26]

26. Max Eastman, "An Interpretation of Marx: Sidney Hook's Daydream of What Marx Might Have Said Had He Been a Pupil of John Dewey," *New York Herald Tribune Books*, 13 April 1933, p. 6. In his autobiography, Hook mistakenly ascribed this subtitle to an imagined review by Eastman of his 1936 book, *From Hegel to Marx*, and then commented, with unknowing wit, "it would have been more appropriate had it been directed at my earlier work, *Towards the Understanding of Karl Marx*," Hook, *Out of Step*, p. 139. Eastman's review was part of an exchange between the two men over seven years, which is retraced in Phelps, *Young Sidney Hook*, pp. 38–44, 96–100.

Eastman, in contrast to Mattick, was not critical of Hook for abandoning the postulation of communism's inevitability; he did, however, fault Hook for denying the concept's origins in Marx.

Plausible answers to each of these challenges were already present, in outline form, within *Towards the Understanding of Karl Marx*. Stolberg's identification of pragmatism with "capitalist planlessness"—mirrored in Trotskyist identifications of pragmatism with petty-bourgeois philistinism and, later, in New Left identifications of pragmatism with technocratic or corporate liberalism— gave due consideration neither to Dewey's criticisms of capitalism (which hardly give cause to think pragmatism a natural counterpart to capitalism) nor to the grounds on which Hook had argued in *Towards the Understanding of Karl Marx* for a consistent experimentalism: "Any social theory—the test of whose truth would involve a change in the existing property-relations or balance of class forces— will be denounced as a dangerous untruth by the class in power. That is why no true social development is possible in class society." Neither Stolberg's nor Eastman's criticisms of Hook's pragmatism, moreover, addressed Hook's distaste in *Towards the Understanding of Karl Marx* for the "vicious variety of Jamesian pragmatism" manifest in Bergson's influence upon Sorel—namely, the subjectivist idea that, "Any thinking is valid which gets you where you want to go." Here was an explicit repudiation of vulgar instrumentalism, of pragmatism taken to mean "whatever works for me." While Eastman was correct that Marx had written of communism as inevitable, Hook was also correct that for Marx this did not make revolution any the less dependent upon subjective human choices, *practice,* which in "itself becomes an historical factor in making the revolutionary ideal come true." Nor did Eastman come to terms with Hook's overarching thesis that the unity of Marx's thought lay in his method, and that any particular conclusion reached (say, the inevitability of communism) was "tentative and contingent" and "may be impugned without necessarily calling the method into question, especially when new results are won by a fresh application of the method."[27]

Thus, the social and political implications of pragmatism, sure to generate considerable intellectual interest today as pragmatism experiences new ferment in the humanities, were not conclusively addressed in the immediate aftermath of initial publication of *Towards the Understanding of Karl Marx*. Perhaps a more successful Marx-Dewey dialogue can now take place. Given the renewed interest in pragmatism among American intellectuals, Hook's philosophical position may generate appreciation rather than the skepticism that it originally faced, and given the moral and political collapse of bureaucratic Communism since the Eastern European revolutions of 1989, the book's implicitly democratic interpretation of Marxism is likely to meet with greater sympathy, too. Whether *Towards the Understanding of Karl Marx* is taken as a faithful elucidation of the core of the Marxist tradition, as a brilliant example of revolutionary socialist thinking in the interwar years, as a distinctively American and pragmatist emanation, or as all three at once, it is without doubt a superb exercise in intellectual clarification, an important contribution to social thought, and a

27. Hook, *Towards the Understanding of Karl Marx*, pp. 105, 51–52, 114, 5.

summons to action. Its meanings are likely to reverberate with many readers still, despite the gulf between the present and the occasion of its genesis.

Towards the Understanding of
Karl Marx
Sidney Hook

ABOUT THE AUTHOR

SIDNEY HOOK was born in New York City. He received his B.S. from College of the City of New York in 1923; his M.A. from Columbia in 1926, and his Ph.D. from Columbia in 1927. He has studied in Berlin, Munich, and done research at the Marx-Engels Institute in Moscow. Mr. Hook has twice been awarded a Guggenheim Fellowship.

He is the author of *The Metaphysics of Pragmatism,* and a co-author of *Essays in Honor of John Dewey.* He has contributed to the *Encyclopaedia of the Social Sciences* and to many magazines including *Journal of Philosophy, International Journal of Ethics, The Monist, Mind, Archiv feur Philosophie, The New Republic, The Modern Quarterly* and *The Philosophical Review.*

Mr. Hook is assistant Professor of Philosophy at Washington Square College, New York University, New York City, and lecturer at the new school for social research, New York City.

PREFACE

THIS BOOK, written to commemorate the fiftieth anniversary of the death of Karl Marx, offers an interpretation of the activity and thought of one of the outstanding thinkers of the nineteenth century. It is written in the hope that it may clarify some of the fundamental problems and issues of Marx's philosophy around which controversy has raged for decades. To those who are already acquainted with the writings of Marx and his followers, it is hoped that this book will suggest a fresh point of view. To those who are not acquainted with Marx, it is offered as a guide to further study.

The occasion for which this book has been written and the unhomogeneous nature of the reading public to which it is addressed have determined the content and method of its presentation, and have compelled the author to forego a systematic historical exposition and a detailed critical analysis of the themes treated. These will be given in subsequent studies. But it is hoped that Marx's leading ideas have been here presented with suffi-

[*70*]

cient clarity to produce a lively appreciation of their meaning and impact in the world to-day. If in addition the reader is led to independent reflection upon the material submitted and the point of view from which it has been interpreted in the following pages, the objectives of the author will have been attained.

Experience has shown that no book on Marx can expect to be received with anywhere near the same detachment as a book on the Ammassalik Eskimo or a treatise on the internal constitution of the stars. Marx's ideas are so much a part of what people fear or welcome to-day, his doctrines so intimately connected with the living faith and hate of different classes and so often invoked by groups with conflicting political allegiances that the very sight of his name arouses a mind-set on the part of the reader of which he is largely unconscious. Every critical student of Marx—as of any disputed text or epoch—must, however, make the effort to distinguish between the meaning disclosed by analysis and his own evaluation of that meaning. Such an effort in Marx's case is singularly difficult, for even when we become aware of our prejudices we do not thereby transcend them; but it is an effort which must be made if we would do justice to both Marx and ourselves.

In order to facilitate this process of discrimination, the author believes it may be helpful to state explicitly certain methodological cautions that are generally taken for granted in subjects less heatedly controversial. He also hopes that by making his own position clear at the outset, much misunderstanding will be avoided.

This book is not written by an "orthodox" Marxist. Indeed the author regards orthodox Marxism, in the form in which it flourished from 1895 to 1917, as an emasculation of Marx's thought. He holds that Marx himself was not an orthodox Marxist. Orthodoxy is not only fatal to honest thinking; it involves the abandonment of the revolutionary standpoint which was central to Marx's life and thought. This has been amply demonstrated by the historic experience of the German Social Democracy, the leaders of whose center and right wing regarded themselves as orthodox Marxists *par excellence,* and who were quick with the epithet of heretic against all who sought to interpret Marxism as a philosophy of action.

The very use of the term "orthodoxy" is an anomaly in any revolutionary movement. Its derivation is notoriously religious. Its meaning was fashioned in the controversies between Roman and Byzantine Christianity. Its associations more naturally suggest a church and the vested privileges of a church than an organization of enlightened and disciplined men and women fighting for the emancipation of society. Wherever there are people who insist upon calling themselves orthodox, there will be found dogma; and wherever dogma, substitution of a blind faith or a general formula for concrete analysis and specific action.

One cannot be orthodox at any price and a lover of the truth at the same time. This was clearly demonstrated by the tenacity with which "orthodox" Marxists, who in practice had long abandoned Marx and Engels, clung to the latter's anthropology in the face of the most conclusive findings of modern anthropologists. If the acceptance of Morgan's outmoded anthropology is necessary to orthodox Marxism, the author must be damned as an heretic on this point as well. Morgan was a great pioneer anthropologist. But no one to-day can accept his universal schema of social development for the family and other institutions, without intellectual stultification.

This book is not an attempt to revise Marx or to bring him up to date. Such a procedure is impermissible in what presumes to be a critical, expository account of Marx's own theories. The fact that the neglected aspects of Marx's thought, to which this book calls attention, have impressive contemporary implications, explains, perhaps, why this study was undertaken, but it does not constitute an introduction of a foreign point of view into the doctrines discussed.

No author can guard himself from the will to misunderstand. But he can diminish the dangers of distortion by inviting the reader to follow the argument in its own terms and to judge it in the context of the views opposed. The emphasis upon the rôle of activity in Marxism, as contrasted with the mechanical and fatalistic conceptions of the social process which prevail in orthodox circles, lays the author open to the charge of smuggling in philosophical idealism. But Marx's *dialectical* materialism has always appeared to be idealistic to those who, having reduced all reality to matter in motion, find themselves incapable of explaining the interaction between things and thought except on the assumption that the mind produces what it acts upon. This last assumption is frankly idealistic but it is not involved in dialectical materialism.

Due to the limitations of space, a great deal of material bearing upon the central issues of the discussion has been omitted. Some important philosophical problems have not even been mentioned. It should be borne in mind, however, that what is left unsaid on these matters as well as on others—relevant or irrelevant—is not thereby denied, unless it is logically incompatible with the implications of what *is* said. No form of criticism is more unconscionable than that which proceeds on the assumption that an author intends to exhaust his subject-matter and then urges against the position taken that it implicitly denies views, which, in virtue of necessary selection, it has no opportunity to treat. This caution is added, not to prevent the reader from raising difficulties, but rather to insure that the difficulties which are raised bear relevantly upon the issues discussed. The author is quite aware that the position sketched in this book is not free from difficulties. He even states some of them. A position which has no difficulties is too easy to be true, or if true, too trivial to be of practical import in this world. On the other hand, because all positions have difficulties is no reason for refusing to take one. On some subjects—especially the subjects treated in this book—no one can escape taking a position. For every position towards the question of social change—including the dead point of indifferentism—has social consequences. The intelligent thing to do—so it seems to the author—is to take a position, recognize the difficulties and participate coöperatively, with all those who share the position, in their solution.

The author wishes to state his indebtedness to two contemporary writers: Georg Lukács, whose *Geschichte und Klassenbewusstsein* stresses the significance of the dialectic element in Marx's thought and links Marx up —unfortunately much too closely—with the stream of German classical philosophy; and to Karl Korsch whose *Marxismus und Philosophie* confirms the author's own hypothesis of the practical-historical axis of Marx's thought, but which underestimates the difficulties involved in treating the formal aspect of Marx's thought from this point of view. The text and footnotes carry acknowledgments to non-contemporary writers.

Some of the material in the early chapters was originally printed as an article in the *Symposium* of July, 1931; thanks are due to the editors for permission to reprint it here. The *Symposium* article together with an earlier article on "Dialectical Materialism" in the *Journal of Philosophy* for 1928 contained material whose phrasing has given rise to serious misinterpretation. This has been corrected in the body of the book.

SIDNEY HOOK

New York,
January 1, 1933.

PART I

THE QUEST FOR MARX

"Rétablir la vérité historique n'est pas seulement une question de conscience; c'est aussi une question d'un intérêt pratique immédiat."

—SOREL.

1

INTRODUCTION

THE world to-day stands in the shadow of the doctrines of a man dead barely fifty years. The social philosophy of Karl Marx, comparatively unknown and ignored in his own lifetime, exercises a stronger influence upon the present age than the social theories of any of our contemporaries. History is being made in its name. A new philosophy of life, avowedly Marxist in inspiration, is slowly emerging to challenge the dominant attitudes and values of Western and Oriental cultures.

And yet, as soon as one devotes oneself to the study of Marxian doctrine, one discovers that there exists no canonic formulation of its position. Marx's literary activity, extending over a period of forty years, is for the most part extremely controversial. None of his writings contains a definitive and finished expression of doctrine. He himself lived to say, *"Je ne suis pas un marxiste."* Various conflicting interpretations of his philosophy have split the ranks of his professed followers as well as those of his critics. There has been a greater eager-

3

[78]

ness to discuss the truth of his doctrines than to establish their meaning.

The situation is no different to-day than it was when Marx was first discovered by "bourgeois" thinkers. The academic German professors, after the conspiracy of silence against Marx had been broken in the nineties, charged that Marx's conclusions were vitiated by the presence of irrelevant moral considerations. Later, neo-Kantians as well as religious socialists made the contrary charge that Marx's conclusions were vitiated by the absence of such judgments. Some said that Marx was overemphasizing the importance of revolutionary will; others, that he was paralyzing human effort in a monstrous economic fatalism. Both were agreed that his thought was a contradictory mess of analyses, prediction, faith, and passion. Each critic had his counter-critic; and every attempt at synthesis brought forth another campaign of polemics. Add to these academic lucubrations not only the denunciatory defence of the "orthodox" Marxists, but the shrill outcries of preachers, publicists and minor literati, who rushed to refute Marx without stopping even to read him, and the atmosphere of the discussion is set. To some it appeared to be an intellectual circus; to others, another illustration of the class war.

Of itself, however, this diversity of interpretation is not an unusual thing in the history of thought. There has been hardly a single thinker of historical importance who has not paid a price for having disciples; who has not been many things to many men. There is no can-

4

onic life of Christ as there is no canonic interpretation
of Plato. But in Marx's case, the natural diversity of
interpretation was reinforced by the introduction of an
explicit political axis into the discussion. In addition, a
peculiar way of arriving at those interpretations complicated matters. The unity of his thought was sought
solely in his conclusions and not in his method of arriving at them. The systematic results were examined and
not the systematic method. It was uncritically assumed
that unity and simplicity were synonymous; so that in
the face of complex findings, often apparently contradictory, it was concluded that his thought lacked unity.
Simplicity, however, is an attribute of content; unity,
of organization. If Marx's thought possesses unity, it is
to be found not in his specific conclusions but in his
method of analysis directed by the revolutionary purposes and needs of the international working class. The
method, to be sure, is to be checked in the light of his
conclusions; but the latter are derivative, not central.
They are tentative and contingent. They may be impugned without necessarily calling the method into
question, especially when the new results are won by a
fresh application of the method. Just as it is possible to
dissociate the Hegelian method from the Hegelian
system (as Marx and Engels repeatedly insist), so it
is possible to dissociate the Marxian method from any
specific set of conclusions, or any particular political
tactic advocated in its name. This is another way of
saying that there is nothing *a priori* in Marx's philoso-

5

phy; it is naturalistic, historical and empirical throughout.

To distinguish between Marx's method and his results is *not* to separate the two any more than to distinguish between the essence of scientific method and the scientific findings of any particular day—which are sure to be faulty and incomplete—is to deny any organic connection between them. Ultimately the validity of scientific method depends upon its power to predict, and wherever possible, to control the succession of natural phenomena. It is this progressive power of prediction and control which justifies us in retaining scientific method even when we have discarded or modified the physics of Ptolemy, Copernicus and Newton. Similarly the validity of Marx's method depends upon whether it enables us to realize the class purposes in whose behalf it was formulated.

But here the similarity between "science" and "Marxism" ends. This does not mean that Marxism is not a "scientific" method, that is, adequate and efficient to secure its goals. The distinction sought flows from the recognition that the natural sciences and the "social sciences" are concerned with two irreducibly different subject-matters. This difference in subject-matter compels the further recognition that values—class values—are essentially involved in every attempt to develop a methodology and program of social action. The distinction therefore means that in so far as Marxism is a method of thought and action designed to achieve a class goal, it is something more than science, or less; for science, as such, although it may be used in behalf of class purposes, has no class character. The truth or falsity of its propositions have nothing to do with the class struggle even when the class struggle is the objective reference of its propositions. It is not denied that the direction scientific research has taken has often been determined, to a not inconsiderable extent, by the economic, political and "moral" interests of the classes which have endowed laboratories and subsidized scientists. But since this applies to the false theories which have arisen as well as the true, the difference between the true and false cannot be explained by class or social considerations. To affirm the contrary is to confuse categories.

In Marx's theories, on the other hand, a class bias and a class goal are presupposed. His doctrines do not merely describe the phenomena of class society and class struggle. They are offered as instruments in waging that struggle, as guides to a mode of action which he believed would forever eliminate class struggles from social life. As instruments they can function effectively only in so far as they approximate objective truths; but as objective truths, they cannot be effective instruments without reference to subjective class purposes. Marx's philosophy is a dialectical synthesis of these objective and subjective moments. By subjective is meant not unreal or uncaused—for obviously class purposes are conditioned by the socio-economic environment—but a mode of response which is directed by *conscious* will or desire. The *range* of possible class goals which can be willed at any moment in history is determined by objec-

7

tive social factors, but neither the willing nor the *specific* choice at any definite moment of time can be explained without introducing other factors. These latter we call subjective in relation to the first set; but in relation, say, to what a particular member of a class wills, they are objective. To overlook this distinction and to speak of Marxism as an "objective science," is, therefore, to emasculate its class character. The disastrous consequences of such a procedure both in logic and historic fact will be examined in subsequent chapters.

2

ON HISTORICAL UNDERSTANDING

$\mathbb{T}$HE system of thought associated with Karl Marx, and which is loosely designated as Marxian, differs from all other social theories and methodologies in that it is the fighting philosophy of the greatest mass movement that has swept Europe since the rise of Christianity.[1] It cannot be neatly cut from its highly charged historical context and examined exclusively in the light of its verbal consistencies. For it is not an armchair philosophy of retrospection, but a philosophy of social action; more specifically, *a theory of social revolution.* Developed in the course of a lifetime of social action on the battlefield of the class struggle, it bears evidence of the occasions which provoked it and the purposes which directed it. Marx began his adult life as a revolutionist, fought like one and was exiled in consequence of being one. And although he died of

---

[1] Marx himself says in *The Communist Manifesto* that the communist theories "only express in general terms the circumstances of an actually existing class struggle, of an historical movement going on under our own eyes." They are not based upon ideas or principles set up or discovered by some *"Weltverbesserer."*

9

the effects of eating dust for so many years in the British Museum, during those years he never lost touch with the daily struggle of the working classes throughout the world. He had participated in the fighting of 1848, but his own best weapons were the weapons of dialectical criticism.

Not only were Marx's doctrines developed in the course of the social struggles and experiences of his own lifetime; after his death they were taken up by others in the continuation of that struggle. A whole movement sprang into existence with Marxian slogans and arguments. More accurately, the existing working-class movement in Germany became in name, if not in fact, Marxian. This movement had a life greater than any member within it and a task to perform unique in the history of social revolt, *viz.,* consciously to develop a philosophy which would aid it in winning its battles. This task demanded not a set of petrified dogmas but a revolutionary flexibility in theory and practice. There soon developed a literature, tradition and mode of analysis directly inspired by the writings and personality of Marx. The dangers of doctrinal orthodoxy in the early years, before the German Social Democracy had won a free field for action, were not great. Marx was alive to guide it. Its problems were his problems. And after his death, Engels acted as its official mentor. But before many years had passed, the movement was confronted by new specific tasks and problems. They flowed naturally from the altered conditions—social, technical, national, and psychological—which the expansion of industrial capitalism brought with it in the last quarter of the nineteenth century. Active response to changed conditions was immediate, for no movement can live without flexible readjustment to a shifting milieu. Things were done first to meet the demands of the moment and justified later. The interpretation of the causes and consequences of such action was formulated in Marxian terms. No program of action was so foreign that it could not be brought under Marxian formulas; no declaration of policy or principles so recondite that it could not be supported by some text.

What happened was merely this. Confronted by new conditions which generated new tasks and new conceptions of those tasks, followers of Marx decided upon the reasonable thing to do and defended it as the orthodox Marxian method of doing it. But what determines the policies which men, confronted by a common problem, regard as "reasonable"? When it is not a question of the logical fitness of means to ends, the "reasonable" policy is derived ultimately from something they *wish* to do. That is to say, their purposes and values are logically, if not psychologically, prior to their immediate program of action. It was natural, then, that with the development of different aims and purposes there should arise different interpretations of Marx. In almost every European country successive generations brought forth new attitudes and perspectives. Some few men like Bernstein in Germany, Sorel in France and Struve in Russia developed within the span of their own lifetime conflicting conceptions of the nature of Marxism. Nor must it be imagined that all of these interpretations were unusually artificial or far fetched. The very individuals who combated them in the name of orthodoxy, fell back upon a conception of Marx which was itself a selected portraiture, one which possessed many of the defects of the views opposed and few of their virtues. The defects were a failure to consider all the available texts and contexts, to evaluate their relative weight, to distinguish between the method employed and the tentative character of the results won by the use of that method, and most important of all, an inability to grasp the central importance of Marx's class bias. The virtues were an openly avowed flexible policy to the passing events of the day, an attempt to steer a straight course in the new currents of science and philosophy, and a refusal to regard fundamental theoretical issues as finally closed.

These conflicting doctrinal interpretations of Marxism were not mere variations on one intellectual theme. *There were different patterns of social response projected by different groups in a struggle to dominate the socio-economic scene.* They were ways of making history, innocently paraded as methods of reading it. They told more about the orientation of these groups to the living issues which agitated them than they did about Marx.

Significantly enough, the history of Marxian interpretation offers a curious confirmation of the Marxian criticism of all cultural ideology: different social classes react differently to the same social object. These differences express themselves first, in disparate emphases of interpretation, then, in conflicting evaluation, and ultimately, in opposite modes of social action. Their class point of view becomes an objectified part of what they are trying to understand. But if this be so, one asks in irritated bewilderment, what is the common subject-matter of all these interpretations? What is the objective historical reference of these varying interpretations, and is objective truth about such reference possible?

Before we despair of attaining objective truth about social questions, which are of necessity viewed differently by different social classes, let us pause for a moment to point out that this situation has its logical analogue in the predicament historians find themselves whenever they seek to offer a definitive explanation of an historical event. It is a methodological commonplace to-day that the history of man is not something that can be automatically read off from a chronological record. It involves interpretation, selection, and construction. Its criteria of what is probable and relevant are ultimately drawn from the present.[2] The consequences of this commonplace, however, are startling. For as we go from one period to another, interpretations of the past are altered. The meaning of the past seems to be a moving shadow of the wider experiences and purposes of the present. Not only is this true of events which do not carry their meaning upon their face; it is just as true of the thought of men who have

[2] Cf. the writer's "A Pragmatic Critique of the Historico-Genetic Method" in *Essays in Honor of John Dewey*, New York, 1929.

left a corpus of writings behind them. No better illustration of this can be found than the history of Platonic interpretation. How many philosophical portraits of Plato have circulated in the world mart! And how unmistakably do these portraits display the lineaments of their painters! Plato as a Moses-speaking Attic, as a Christian Father, as a mystic Pythagorean, as a dramatist of the life of reason; the first Aristotelian, the precursor of Kant, of Hegel, of Cantor and the modern theory of continuity; "the father of all orthodoxy and the source of all heresy"—these are only some of the guises in which Plato has appeared in the history of thought. Here, as elsewhere, historical recovery is not the unveiling of ready-made fact in the stream of cultural tradition in the way in which excavation is the unearthing of definite material from the site of Troy. It is a selective emphasis whose verification is to be sought in some forms of contemporary or prospective activity.

But to return to Marx. If historical interpretation is contemporary orientation to living issues, why, it may be asked, was it necessary for the leaders of the working-class movement in Germany and other European countries to profess to be Marxian at all? Why did they not turn their backs upon the quest for the "real Marx" and devote themselves to fresh analysis of the problems at hand? Why did they insist upon calling themselves Marxist even when dissenters within the ranks called attention to their un-Marxian practice? In part the answer is to be found in the immense prestige which names and symbols carry in mass movements. New ideas introduce preliminary confusion even when they prove themselves to be instrumentally effective in realizing purposes. They are more likely to be accepted when they appear in the guise of old masks and slogans. Radicalism, too, is bound by the natural conservatism of habit. It learns soon enough that a movement without the means of adaptation to a changing environment is without the means of survival; but in the process of adaptation it clings all the more steadfastly to the symbols of its past. For the past is that of which it generally has most reason to be proud. The old faith once sincerely militant is still celebrated in a ritual; ideas and terms which once had definite practical import, become fetishes.

There were other reasons, aside from the "truth" of the doctrine, which contributed to keep alive the tradition of Marxism among socialists even when, as we shall see, their political parties were far from being Marxist in their practice. There was, first, the natural dislike to substitute one doctrine for another in the midst of the class struggle. "Never swap horses while crossing a stream" is a maxim that seems as plausible in politics as in war. Bernstein had good reason to recall it when meditating upon the fierce opposition which his attempt to revise Marx had called forth. The German Social Democratic Party almost voted his expulsion for what turned out later to be no more than terminological differences. In addition, there was the inflaming example of Marx's single-minded zeal and incorruptible revolutionary integrity. His hard-headed personal idealism, which was never stained by opportunistic compromise (in contrast with Lassalle), or warped by sentimental fanaticism (in contrast with Bakunin), provided a moral and political ideal which was all the more precious for being so difficult to attain. There was, too, the assurance of his intellectual genius to which even his enemies were compelled to make grudging admission. And who does not desire the glow of emotional security which comes from having a genius on one's side? There was, then, even on narrowly practical grounds good reason why those who sought to change the existing order—if only with a program of social reform—should still invoke the name of Marx long after they had given up trying to determine whether they were carrying on in his spirit. But the public avowal of Marxism necessitated taking over, defending and interpreting his doctrines. Later we shall discuss the fidelity of the interpretations offered. The most significant aspects of these interpretations—just because they affected the question of meaning—was the way in which they invariably expressed a present purpose and an immediately experienced class need.

At the turn of the century a virtual war broke out among socialists as to the real spirit and meaning of Marx's thought—a war as virulent to-day as ever before. The most influential of these contending positions must be stated and criticized before the import of the interpretation offered here can be grasped. The following chapters are not so much an historical excursion as an attempt to reveal the premises, purposes, and intellectual constructions of the four great movements which claimed to be carrying on in the spirit of Marx.

3

DER KAMPF UM MARX

$\mathbb{T}$HE struggle for the possession of Marx's spiritual bequest had already begun in Marx's own lifetime. Marx, himself, had called down a plague upon both the Marxists and anti-Marxists; but he watched with critical uneasiness the doctrinal deviations and false tactical moves of his adherents throughout the world and especially in Germany. As early as 1875, in a scathing criticism of the Gotha program adopted by his followers on the occasion of their union with the party of Lassalle, he complained that they were giving their socialism a nationalistic twist and that they had become infected with a servile faith in the bourgeois state.[1] No criticism was ever more prophetic. Before the next quarter of a century had elapsed these tendencies had become full blown and had flowered into a doctrinal interpretation of Marxism according to which it was no longer a philosophy of

---

[1] "Doch das ganze Programm, trotz alles demokratischen Geklingels, ist durch und durch vom Untertanenglauben der Lassellischen Sekte an den Staat verpestet." (Posthumously printed. *Neue Zeit*, Bd. IX, 1891, p. 574.)

social revolution, but a classless science of social development which countenanced open nationalistic and reformist practices.

If Marx's method of social analysis is valid, then the key to this doctrinal development is to be sought not in the ideas of a few individual leaders, but in the social and economic development of Germany. To this we must now turn.

The last quarter of the nineteenth century witnessed the emergence of Germany as an imperialist power of the first rank. With the conquest of foreign markets, opportunities for work increased—evidenced in the decline of emigration; prices on colonial raw material and consumption goods (rubber, tea, coffee, etc.) which were unprotected by tariffs, fell; and both the money and real wages of the highly organized skilled workers —but not of the unskilled workers in heavy industry or of the agricultural laborers—rose. The enormous profits of foreign trade and the superior technical organization of German industry enabled the state to maintain and extend the system of limited social insurance which had originally been adopted as safeguards against the revolutionary upsurge of the masses.[2] All this was not without its profound effects upon a working class efficiently schooled by state institutions in the traditions

[2] So effective was the system of state insurance that the president of the *Reichesversicherungsamtes* looking back upon its results was able to write, "The approval of the war credit by the Social Democratic Party represents the most beautiful success of German social reform." (P. Kaufmann, *Was dankt das kämpfende Deutschland seiner sozialen Fürsorge,* 1918, p. 11.)

of a nationalist culture. The skilled workers who felt that they stood to gain by the extension of the imperialism of the mother country were precisely those who were the most influential in the socialist trade unions; and the trade unions, then as now, had the socialist party in tow. The ideology of the trade unions, which centered around the day to day struggle for a higher standard of living, seeped into the political party. Although the party congresses still paid pious allegiance to the formula of revolution, the practices of the organization were exclusively devoted to a gradual social reform. The right-wing leaders stole a leaf from the scientific Marxists and urged that it was Utopian to oppose an imperialist expansion which followed with "iron necessity" from economic laws discovered by Marx himself; the only sensible policy was to put forward a colonial program which would relieve the pangs of economic penetration suffered by the natives. An enlightened, peaceful and civilized imperialism, accompanied by a liberal educational policy, would raise the cultural level of the indigenous population to a point from which it could appreciate the economic, social, scientific, and therefore, moral necessity of imperialist expansion.

With the growth of the party the domination of the trade unions in the interest of their immediate social politics increased. The trade unions were primarily interested in keeping their members at work. This was obviously bound up with the export of commodities. Exports demanded markets; markets a strong foreign policy. How, then, could the leaders of the trade unions reconcile their devotion to the immediate interests of the workers with a militant struggle against their own national imperialism? To be sure, they were aware that the lion's share of the profits of imperialist expansion fell not to themselves but to their employers. But then there were the concessions—the crumbs of bounty which fell from the table of superfluity. Certainly, cried Schippel and other reformist leaders, it was better to work than to hunger. To fight was out of the question. But fight they had to! On one sad day in 1914, in remembrance of the crumbs of concessions, they goose-stepped into battle to fight in a war brought on by imperialism.[3]

The orientation of the German Social Democracy towards practical immediate reform produced an important change in the social composition of the party. Numerous non-proletarian elements—petty bourgeois shopkeepers, professionals and intellectuals—began to stream into the organization. They did not stay in the rank and file, but, in virtue of their technical accomplishments and social connections, forged to the top of the party as functionaries, theoreticians and political representatives. Although the party membership still remained overwhelmingly proletarian, their strategic posts enabled them to wield an influence altogether disproportionate to their numbers. The growth of the trade

[3] For an interesting and well-documented analysis of the causes of the social patriotism of the German working class, cf. Zarchi, Mausa, *Die oekonomische Kausalität des Sozialpatriotismus*, Strasbourg, 1928.

unions, too, created an administrative apparatus whose standard of living was higher than that of the ordinary worker. The officials functioned so long in office that they lost contact with the actual raw experience of the industrial struggle and slowly acquired the narrow, self-centered ideology of the typical bureaucrat whose eternal archtype they always had before their eyes in the persons of the Prussian state officials. The persecution of the party and trade unions by their political opponents and the government often took the form of an economic and social boycott. This resulted in the rise of a not inconsiderable group of tradesmen and inn-keepers [4] who catered to the needs of the movement and consequently developed special interests not always compatible with the party line or the welfare of the membership. An amusing but very eloquent manifestation of the power of such groups was the existence of "The Association of Socialist Tavern-keepers" who at one time supplied more than seven per cent of the party representation in the Reichstag.[5]

As the years went by the party took on more and more the character of a benevolent organization with eschatological trimmings. The vested interests of the party bureaucracy in their posts were linked up with

[4] In Germany each political party has its own inns—*Lokale*—which serve as the centers of political and social life.

[5] Robert Michels' *Zur Soziologie des Parteiwesens in der modernen Demokratie,* Untersuchungen über die oligarchischen Tendenz des Gruppenlebens, revised, 2nd edition, Leipzig, 1925, contains a great deal of relevant material on this aspect of German Social Democracy, which does not justify, however, the theoretical conclusions he draws therefrom.

22

more material interests. By 1913 the German socialist party and trade unions owned in real property alone close to ninety million marks. This was, for them, substantial evidence that they were growing into socialism. When the decisive hour struck in 1914, they were in no mood to sacrifice all this.

Political events as well as the pressure of the socioeconomic environment contributed to enforcing the interpretation of Marxism as an "objective science" of social development with which only those blinded by illusion or self-interest could not agree. During the seventies the censor kept a wary eye open for militant class-conscious phrases and analyses. During the eighties, under Bismarck's exception laws the socialists played safe by choosing restrained and scientific language. (Engels' prediction of a European revolutionary disturbance for 1885 or thereabouts had failed to materialize.) During the nineties, after the exception laws had been abolished, the growth of the socialist vote to three millions provoked the feeling among the German leaders that they were a party of opposition rather than "the party of revolution." Their desire for social and intellectual respectability led them to stress the importance of systematic doctrine. Could a theory be dangerous which was grounded in real knowledge and expressed in heavy prose?

The practical and spiritual *embourgeoisement* of the German movement was not long in bearing theoretical fruit. The contradictions between Marx's revolutionary standpoint, of which there was still some lingering

23

memory, and the life activity of his "disciples," compelled the latter to seek some way of reconciling the
two which did not require too great a sacrifice of legality and security. Two ways suggested themselves to
square the practice of social reform with the theory of
Marxism. One of them was taken by the official party
under the intellectual leadership of those who called
themselves "orthodox" Marxists; the other by Bernstein
and others who were called "revisionist" Marxists.
Between these two a literary war broke out on an international scale.

4

THE ORTHODOX CANONIZATION

THE theoretical construc-
tions of orthodox Marxism were built out of phrases
and propositions drawn from Marx's own works. Indeed, Kautsky, Hilferding and others denied that their
orthodoxy constituted an interpretation. In their eyes
it was a faithful exposition of the doctrine. Nevertheless, there was a definite shift in the fundamental character of their expositions. Marxism was no longer regarded as essentially the theory and practice of social
revolution, but as a *science* of social development. The
official theoretical emphasis implied that it was not so
much a method of making history as of understanding
it after it had been made. It was offered as something
sachlich and free from value judgments, determining
action in the same way that a mountain slope determines the movement of a glacier. It was objective and
scientific in a strict sense. It carried the authority not
only of power but of knowledge. It tried to prove its
position by popularizing the deductions from the labor
theory of value in *Das Kapital* rather than by under-

25

scoring the revolutionary philosophy of the *Communist Manifesto* in which the labor theory of value in its distinctive Marxian form was not even mentioned.

The continued stabilization and expansion of capitalism, together with the programs of peaceful, evolutionary methods of social reform projected by the German Social Democrats, made the conception of socialism as an objective science of social development not only plausible but an effective talking point in winning converts from the parties of law and order. Gradually, reliance upon "processes at work in the order of things" became translated into the mythical language of the "inevitability" of the development of capitalism into socialism. Human need, evolution, and action, which Marx had taken as his starting points, now became theoretically—in strict logic but not in open avowal— a superfluous addendum to a self-contained system of social mechanics. Man was mortal; no less so the society in which he lived. And just as in one case human effort could only moderately influence the fatal day, so in the other. Cry out as the orthodox Marxists did against this interpretation of Marxism as a confusion of social *determinism* with social fatalism, it followed from their theories that the class struggle was a fact as objective as the force of gravitation, and that the social revolution was as ineluctable as an eclipse. Small wonder that this disguised natural necessity should have led to the characterization of "orthodox" Marxism as "astronomical" socialism!

And now an amazing thing happened. It was no

26

longer necessary, said the theoreticians, for a Marxist to be a socialist. Marxism was *wissenschaft;* socialism *weltanschauung.* Marxism was the science which proved that socialism as a state of society would come. All opposition and allegiance to socialism as an ideal were equally epiphenomenal. Socialism was coming! If you welcomed it, well and good—it might come a little sooner. If you did not, it would come anyway—perhaps a little later. In neither case would your attitude make a difference—or much of a difference. Into such a paralyzing doctrine did this pan-objectivistic interpretation of Marx eventuate.

Here is a citation from a key work of one such orthodox Marxist, which reveals the incidence of this position. Rudolph Hilferding prefaced his important treatise, *Das Finanzkapital,* as follows:

"The theory of Marxism as well as its practice is free from judgments of value. It is, therefore, false to conceive as is widely done, *intra et extra muros,* that Marxism and socialism are as such identical. For logically, regarded as a scientific system and apart from its historical effect, Marxism is only a theory of the laws of movement of society formulated in general terms by the Marxian conception of history; the Marxian economics applying in particular to the period of commodity-producing society. *But insight into the validity of Marxism which includes insight into the necessity of socialism is by no means a matter of value judgments and just as little an indication to practical procedure.* For it is one thing to recognize a necessity, and another thing to work for this necessity. It is quite possible for someone convinced of the final victory of socialism to fight against it." (p. x, 1910. Italics mine.)

This was a strange revolutionary theory indeed. It could explain the past and predict the future but had no function in the present. Experimentally there was nothing to distinguish it from a theodicy which, refusing to fathom the divine ways in any present event, read all of past history *ad hoc* and predicated nothing in the future but the Revolutionary Day of Judgment. And thus this brand of "orthodox" Marxism became to all who welcomed socialism a religion of consolation, and to those who opposed it, a doctrine of despair. It was the ideology not only of the German Social Democracy, but of the Second International which the German party dominated.[1]

Until 1895 the official theoreticians sought to justify

[1] The position of Kautsky and other leaders of the Center and Right was ambiguous and often contradictory. Not only did these contradictions crop up in theoretical writings but even in pamphlets devoted to questions of revolutionary politics. Kautsky, for example, could write in *Der Weg zur Macht:* "The socialist party is a revolutionary party but not a revolution-making party. We know that our goal can be attained only through revolution. We also know that it is just as little in our power to create this revolution as it is in the power of our opponents to prevent it. It is no part of our work to instigate a revolution or to prepare the way for it." (Eng. trans. by Simons, p. 50.) Later on Kautsky drifted more and more to the Right. In his criticism of the Gotha Program, Marx had written: "Between capitalist and communist society lies the period of revolutionary transformation of one into the other. Corresponding to this there is a political transition period in which the state can be nothing else than the *revolutionary dictatorship of the proletariat."* In 1922 Kautsky wrote: "Between the time of the pure bourgeois and the time of the pure proletarian democratically governed state lies a period of transformation of one into the other. Corresponding to this there is a political transition period in which the government as a rule will take the form of a *coalition government."* (*Der Proletarische Revolution und ihre Programm,* p. 196.)

themselves by appealing to Marx's closest collaborator
and literary executor, Frederick Engels. It was Engels
who during Marx's lifetime interpreted his central doctrines and after his death edited his manuscripts. But
this was no ordinary labor that Engels took upon himself. The exact intellectual relationship between the two
men has yet to be adequately tracked down. Certainly
there is no justification for the easy assumption made
by the self-styled "orthodox" that there is a *complete
identity* in the doctrines and standpoints of Marx and
Engels from the beginning of their friendship on. The
indisputable fact that they were minds of different order
would make that unlikely. Nor is there any more justification for holding with critics like Masaryk, Arturo
Labriola and Mondolfo that there was an essential difference between them. The truth seems to be that Engels
gave a characteristic emphasis to the doctrine of Marx
—an emphasis, however, which had far-reaching consequences upon the development of the doctrine in the
hands of the official party theoreticians. Already in his
Eugen Dühring's Umwälzung der Wissenschaft (one
section of which was written by Marx) we find a treatment of mooted problems of metaphysics, science and
ethical practice from the point of view of a monistic
system rather than of a unified method. But more important still, in bringing to completion and publishing
the second and third volumes of *Das Kapital* Engels
gave final currency to the notion that the economic
theories of Marx constituted a hypothetic-deductive system of the type exemplified by scientific theories *über-*

haupt, instead of being an illustration of a method of revolutionary criticism. In so doing Engels failed to develop the important sociological and practical implications of Marx's doctrine of the "fetishism of commodities." He devoted himself to the task of explaining how the law of the falling rate of profit could be squared both with the empirical fact that the rate of profit was the same irrespective of the organic composition of capital, and with the labor-power definition of exchange-value.

Nowhere, so far as I know, does Engels properly comment on Marx's own words in the preface to the second edition of the first volume, that political economy "can remain a science only so long as the class struggle is latent or manifests itself only in isolated or sporadic phenomena." It cannot be too strongly insisted upon that Marx did not conceive *Das Kapital* to be a deductive exposition of an objective natural system of political economy, but a critical analysis—sociological and historical—of a system which regarded itself as objective. Its sub-title is *Kritik der politischen Ökonomie.* Criticism demands a standpoint, a position. Marx's standpoint was the standpoint of the class-conscious proletariat of Western Europe. His position implied that a system of economics at basis always is a *class* economics. An implicit value judgment becomes one of the abscissae in terms of which its analytic equations are written.

Engels' interpretation of the economic doctrines of Marx as a closed deductive system was a matter of relative emphasis. It was controlled on crucial occasions by his revolutionary political instincts and corrected in his important letters on historical materialism. Engels, however, was living in London. And out of fancied political necessity the leadership was just as willing to revise him as to revise Marx. Indeed, Engels lived to see his very writings censored and distorted in order to make him appear to be supporting the party line. The revision of his introduction to Marx's *Klassenkämpfe im Frankreich,* the last publication of Engels, is a case in point. Even his protest at being made out to appear as a "peaceful worshipper of legality at any price" was coolly ignored.

In philosophy a corresponding shift occurred from Marx's naturalistic activism to a simplified materialism called dialectical but in reality mechanical. Here Engels' own formulations lent support to a theory of knowledge which constituted a definite shift in emphasis from Marx's own views as expressed both in the glosses on Feuerbach and *Die deutsche Ideologie.* In these writings Marx, true to his Hegelian tradition, pronounced crushing judgment on all mechanical materialisms which regarded man's sensation and thought as the passive automatic result of the impact of the environment upon the animal organism. He claimed that the chief defect of all previous materialism was its inability to explain *conscious* activity in general, and *cultural* selectivity in particular. The political passivism of Feuerbach's politics of love had one of its roots in his belief that sensations were literal images, knowledge-

31

bearing, carbon-copy reports of the objective world. For Marx, sensations were forms of practical, sensory activity (*praktische, menschlichsinnliche Tätigkeit*). They were not knowledge but the stimulus to knowledge which completed itself in action. They could not be anything else. Otherwise the social interaction without which the world cannot be transformed becomes impossible. If men cannot react upon and change their conditioning environment, social revolutions can no longer be regarded as a form of human activity but are reduced to incidents in some scheme of rational mechanics or energetics. But all social action and change is mediated by ideas in the minds of men. Ideas, therefore, cannot be passive images; they must be active instruments. In his *Ludwig Feuerbach und der Ausgang der klassischen Philosophie,* Engels, in an attempt to safeguard the materialistic foundations of *dialectical* materialism, did not sufficiently stress the place and importance of this active practical element in the Marxian theory of knowledge. He accepted the crude formula of Feuerbach according to which sensations are images and copies (*Abbilder* and *Spiegelbilder*) of the external world without explaining how it is possible for ideas, if they are *only* reflections, to help transform or revolutionize things. Instead of taking sensations as the material clues to knowledge, he identifies knowledge *with* sensations, and defines truth as the agreement between these sensations and the external world. How human beings can escape the magic circle of their sensations, how they can determine whether their sensations correspond with the external world, how, in fact, they can know that there is an external world, becomes, on this hypothesis, a mystery.

True, Engels attempted to solve this mystery by appealing to experiment and practice. But since experiment, as he saw it, results in sensations which are again taken to be cases of immediate knowledge, Engels was no nearer a non-sensationalistic criterion of truth and existence than the modern followers of Hume, against whom he used the "argument from experiment." In Marx the appeal to experiment and practice was legitimate, since as a close student of Hegel's *Phänomenologie des Geistes* he had already discarded the belief in the immediacy of knowledge. He considered the chief contribution of German classical philosophy, as opposed to metaphysical materialism, to be its emphasis on the *activity* of mind and corrected its idealistic distortion.

In 1892, in the preface to the English edition of *Socialism, Utopian and Scientific,* Engels went back to Marx; he there takes a definitely experimentalist view in which his earlier theory of sensations is virtually abandoned. But the orthodox German socialists based themselves, in their theory of knowledge, neither on Marx nor on Engels' final conclusions. They hardened into a systematic dogma the relative emphasis which Engels later abandoned. Their quotations are never from his last work. Instead of dialectical materialism, the materialism of the German socialists became sensationalist and mechanical, ignoring *praxis*.

And so the economics and philosophy of Social De-

33

mocracy became all of a piece with its politics. Only the revolutionary phrase remained as a foreign element in the new synthesis—an echo of the heroic days when Marx's ideas were principles of action.

5

THE REVISIONIST EXEGESIS

THE economic conditions of Europe at the turn of the century together with the peculiar "science" of Marxism conspired to make the Social Democracy a liberal reform group whose tactics bore no relation to their principles. And yet this did not prevent the intellectual leaders of the movement from mouthing the revolutionary phrases of Marx's early days. It was this dualism between the prosaic, class-collaborative activity of the organization on the one hand, and the lofty revolutionary tones of its holiday *Versammlungsredner* on the other, which gave Bernstein, the student of Engels and the teacher of Kautsky, his great opportunity. In his *Voraussetzungen des Sozialismus und die Aufgaben der Sozialdemokratie*— the *Das Kapital* of all subsequent revisionism—he declared to the mortification of his comrades that the Social Democracy ought "to find the courage to emancipate itself from a phraseology which in fact had long been outmoded and to be *willing to appear what in reality it already is to-day: a democratic, socialistic party*

35

of reform" [1] (p. 230, last edition). Bernstein did not disapprove of the practice of Social Democracy; he was intent, however, upon showing that the logical, theoretical counterpart of that practice was in flat contradiction with the theory which Marxists were professing. It was the effort to justify what the Social Democracy was actually *doing* which led Bernstein to utter that memorable sentence, "What is generally taken as the goal of socialism is nothing to me, the movement is everything." [2] In its colonial policy and agrarian program,

[1] "But is social democracy to-day anything beyond a party that strives after the socialist transformation of society by the means of democratic and economic reform? . . . Bebel . . . has entered the most vigorous protests against the idea that social democracy upholds a policy of force, and all the party organs have received these speeches with applause; nowhere has a protest against them been raised. Kautsky develops in his *Agrarian Question* the principles of the agrarian policy of social democracy which represent a system of thoroughly democratic reform straight through. The Communal Program adopted in Brandenburg is a democratic program of reform. In the Reichstag the party supports the extension of the powers and the compulsory establishment of courts of arbitration for trades disputes, which are organs for the furtherance of industrial peace. All the speeches of their representatives breathe reform. In the same Stuttgart where, according to Clara Zetkin, the 'Bernstein-ade' received the finishing stroke, shortly after the congress the social democrats entered into an alliance with the middle-class democracy for the municipal elections. Other towns in Wurtemberg followed their example. In the trade-union movement one union after another proceeds to establish unemployment funds, which practically means a surrender of the functions of a purely fighting trade union, and declares for municipal labor bureaus embracing equally employers and employees. In various large towns— Hamburg, Elberfeld—coöperative stores have been started by socialists and trade unions. Everywhere action for reform, action for social progress, action for democracy." (*Op. cit.*, pp. 231-232.)

[2] *Was man gemeinhin Endziel des Sozialismus nennt, ist mir nichts, die Bewegung alles.*

36

in its political collaboration with liberal parties and its trade-union activity, the true philosophy of the socialist movement was expressed. Why not make that philosophy explicit? To talk big was merely cant. And against this cant Bernstein opposed Kant. (*Kant wider cant.* The pun is Bernstein's.)

It is in Bernstein's neo-Kantianism and in the conditions which made for the revival of the ethical and political doctrines of Kant that the theoretical source of Marxian revisionism is to be found. With characteristic shortsightedness, the "orthodox" opposition restricted itself for the most part to a bitter criticism of Bernstein's economic deviations from Marx. Bernstein had challenged the accuracy of some of Marx's analyses which despite the fact that they did not treat of exact quantitative correlations or specific time coefficients, the "scientific" socialists regarded as literal predictions valid at any time: notably, disappearance of the middle class, the increasing severity of the business cycle and its corollary, the rate and quality of mass impoverishment. As a matter of fact, however, Bernstein's economic views were a form of immanent criticism. Allowing for the time factor, the development of finance capitalism and the rise of new industries, the "inconvenient" facts he cited could all be properly interpreted within the framework of the Marxian position. But it was Bernstein's ethical Kantianism which introduced the irreconcilable element in his discussion. For from it there followed as a matter of *principle* what the Social Democracy claimed to be doing as a mere matter of expediency.

37

The subdued Kantian tones of his original work became progressively stronger in subsequent publications
—of which his *Wie ist wissenschaftlicher Sozialismus
möglich?* (1901) is representative. Socialism as a science
has as its object the understanding of the socialist movement. It gives us knowledge of the causes and conditions of that movement. But it can never justify that
movement, for at its heart there are socialist claims,
demands, strivings. It is these ideal motives (*moralische
Interessen*) telling us what *ought* to be which gives
strength to the movement, not the knowledge of what
is. In fact, a conflict between scientific theory and ethical
practice is always possible. Not only may "what is" be
opposed to "what ought to be," but one "ought" may
be opposed to another "ought." To resolve these conflicts an objective ethical theory of the right and reasonable is necessary. Bernstein maintained that such an
objective theory must necessarily eschew naturalism and
embrace some form of the Kantian philosophy. That
was behind his oft-repeated reproach that the Social
Democracy was too naturalistic. With such an ethical
doctrine the socialist movement could now speak of
one's "ethical duties" to mankind, could now make explicit its "natural rights" doctrine already hidden in
such words as *Aus-beut-ung* (exploitation, *Beute,* originally meaning booty). The writings of F. A. Lange
and Hermann Cohen, together with those of other neo-
Kantians like Natorp, Staudinger and Vorländer, who
were developing socialism as an ethics and religion,
strengthened Bernstein in his views. When Bernstein

wrote, "The Social Democracy is in need of a Kant," it was not so much because of his interest in critical method as in ethical consciousness.

It is obvious that an objective classless morality furnished a beautiful premise for piecemeal social reform. The proletariat as the banner bearer of the ethics of the community could formulate demands and proposals which included its class opponents as part of the wider social whole. It could claim to be integrating not separatist; characterizing itself, as the occasion demanded, as the fulfillment of the prophets, of Christianity, of the French Enlightenment. Struggle was not for a class right but for a common right. The growth of ethical self-consciousness in the community is gradual. Consequently the methods of Social Democracy must be evolutionary. Class violence involves the negation of the fundamental rights of other classes as human beings. Consequently, Social Democracy must be peaceful. Phrasemongery about force and dictatorship of the proletariat was worthy of the followers of Blanqui and Bakunin, not of Marx. Class dictatorship means not social progress but a relapse into barbarism. Once more the *Volksstaat* of Lassalle (who had derived his conception of the state from Hegel—a conception excoriated by Marx in his *Critique of the Gotha Program*) reappeared as an undertone in the discussion, especially in Bernstein's defence of the worker's *Vaterland*.

Marx had written in the *Communist Manifesto:* "The proletariat has no fatherland," meaning that not the workers but the landlords and industrialists owned the country and that it was the task of the proletariat to expropriate them of it. Bernstein understood this to mean, however, that the worker had no nationality and that he was only a member of the international of have-nots. He protested that since the worker had become enfranchised as a citizen, this was no longer true. His duties as a citizen, his duties to the nation, were distinct from his duties as a member of a particular class. And so there began this blurring between the concept of class and country, class and public, class and people, which later on was to prove so fateful to the cause of the international working class. Economic classes were regarded as a species within the genus of the nation. Since the worker was a member of the nation before he was a member of an economic class, his duties as a citizen took precedence over his class interests. As a citizen, of course, he was free to agitate for the existence of a "people's state." And it was, indeed, with a heavy consciousness of their duties as citizens of the state that the German Social Democracy, which had come so close to expelling Bernstein and his followers from its ranks as heretics, voted the war-budget in 1914 for the defence of the potential *Volksstaat* in the actual *Vaterland*. This was not a capitulation to Bernstein but a logical fulfill-ment of the party's reformist past. When Wilhelm II proclaimed from the balcony of his palace in Berlin: "Ich kenne keine Partein mehr; ich kenne nur noch Deutsche," the Social Democrats, together with all other parties, applauded him to the echo. Before long the party and trade-union theoreticians were grinding out apologetics which Bernstein himself (who had been opposed in the fraction caucus to the approval of the war credits) courageously opposed. A representative passage which strikes the new note with utter frankness, follows:

"The masses know and feel that the fate of the nation and of its organized expression—the state—is also their fate. They feel themselves economically, politically and culturally bound to it through participation in the life of the community under the leadership of the state. Their economic welfare and future depends upon the state of the national economy which needs freedom of movement in order to develop. Trade unions can successfully negotiate conditions of work and wages only when trade and exchange are in full bloom. In this way the masses of workers are interested in the fate of the national economy and in the political validation of the state community. That is why they feel such an inner solidarity with the rest of the population in fighting off the dangers which threaten from without." (Winnig, A., "Der Krieg und die Arbeiterinternationale," in *Die Arbeiterschaft im neuen Deutschland,* p. 37. Edited by Thimme and Legien, 1915.)

The revisionists in their time were quite consistent—and honest. They were justified in reproaching the "orthodox" for acting in one way (always with the revisionists) and speaking in another (always against the revisionists). The hue and cry that went up against them in the party was an expression of intellectual confusion and troubled conscience as well. Auer, a member of the central committee, wrote to Bernstein confidentially: "Mein lieber Ede, so etwas tut man, aber sagt

41

man nicht." [3] In no important respect was Bernstein at odds with his party except in calling a dogma by its right name. It was Kautsky, himself, the man who led the theoretical onslaught against Bernstein, who confessed on the occasion of Bernstein's eightieth anniversary: "Since 1880 in political party affairs we have been Siamese twins. On occasions even Siamese twins quarrel with one another. And at times we did plenty. But even at those moments you could not speak of one without the other." [4] There can be no question but that Kautsky in essence is right. He and Bernstein were the Siamese twins of Marxian revisionism who differed only concerning the manner in which the practice of reformism could find adequate theoretical expression.

Bernstein, as an exponent of enlightened common sense, attributed the intellectual confusion of his fellow socialists to their pretended use of the dialectical method. In his own thinking he reverted to the sharp and exclusive dichotomies of the ideologues of the French Revolution for whom he always professed great admiration. Bernstein's conclusions can best be appraised in the light of his methodological starting-point, eighteenth century rationalism with its "terrorism of reason" mellowed by an acceptance of the theory of social evolution and a faith in human perfectability. So blunted was the appreciation of Marx's method on the part of his "orthodox" followers that the discussion with Bern-

[3] Quoted by K. Korsch, in *Kampf-Front*, Jan. 11, 1930.
[4] *Der Kampf*, 1930, p. 15.

stein raged around his specific conclusions, often around the wording of those conclusions, instead of his superficial rationalism.[5]

Bernstein's great merit lay in his intellectual honesty. He interpreted Marx and Engels as they appeared to him in their sober years—peace-loving, analytical, monocled scholars, devoted to the cause of social reform, with stirring memories of a revolutionary youth. The movement of which he was the literary head represented the strongest tendency in the alignment of socialist forces in Europe before 1918. It was Marxism as a liberal philosophy of social reform.

[5] In a conversation with me in the early summer of 1929, Bernstein (then seventy-nine) cheerfully admitted that he was, to use his own words, "a methodological reactionary." "I am still an eighteenth century rationalist," he said, "and not at all ashamed of it. I believe that in essentials their approach was both valid and fruitful." Towards the close of the conversation when I asked him whether he regarded this method to be the method of Marx, he lowered his voice and in confidential tones, as if afraid of being overheard, said, "The Bolsheviks are not unjustified in claiming Marx as their own. Do you know? Marx had a strong Bolshevik streak in him!"

6

THE SYNDICALIST HERESY

THE earliest critical reactions to the official Marxian orthodoxy manifested themselves in France. Here the traditions of Blanqui, Proudhon, and Bakunin still flourished. They were strengthened at the turn of the century by the existence of a socialist party whose left wing revealed the same divided soul between the revolutionary phrase and the reformist deed which possessed the German party, and a right wing which regularly fed ministers to a bourgeois coalition government. The republican form of government, the existence of a radical strata of the bourgeoisie which led the fight against clericalism, the hang-over of the democratic ideology of the French Revolution and the petty bourgeois socialism of 1848, obscured in the minds of many socialists the fundamental practical difference between a party of the proletariat and all other parties.

The trade unions, however, battling on the economic front, were compelled perforce to keep the main issue of the class struggle clear. They sought to free themselves from admixture with non-working class elements and to produce a pure proletarian socialist movement (*le socialisme ouvrier*). Syndicalism was the theory and practice of that movement. So fearful were they of the dangers of parliamentarianism that they restricted themselves to organizing direct economic action which arose in the spontaneous struggle of the class-conscious trade unions. All political activities were renounced. Power was to be won by the single weapon of the general strike. Anti-intellectualist in principle, as a protest both against the careerist leadership of the socialist party and the whole conception of political and theoretical guidance from without, they developed no systematic theory. They sought unity in the empirical practice of the defensive and offensive strike. Before long, however, they unofficially accepted the formulations of their position drawn up by a group of anti-intellectualist intellectuals of whom Sorel, Lagardelle and Pelloutier (who was also an important functionary) were the most outstanding. It was Sorel, an "old" Marxist, who attempted to lay the theoretical foundations of the movement.

If Bernstein was led to a revision of Marxism by an acceptance of the actual politics of socialist parties, Sorel undertook to revise Marx on the basis of a blank rejection of that politics. Even before Bernstein's criticisms had been noised abroad, Sorel had resolved to "revise Marxism with its own methods" (*renouveler le marxisme par des procédés marxistes*),[1] a task which suffered temporary interruption during the Dreyfus affair but

[1] *Matériaux d'une Théorie du Prolétariat*, p. 253.

45

to which Sorel again ardently devoted himself with the resurgence of political opportunism in France at the turn of the century.

The relation of Sorel and his followers to Marx has been sadly misunderstood. The current impression (circulated by the "orthodox" interpreters of Marx) that syndicalism was avowedly anti-Marxian in origin, intent and practice, is ungrounded. Its opposition was not so much to Marx but to what was being done in his name. Sorel for many years shared with Antonio Labriola the reputation of being the leading philosophic spirit among Marxists. Appalled, however, by the excesses of parliamentary ministerialism in France on the one hand and by the wave of trade-union reformism in Germany on the other, Sorel repudiated both the pacifist illusions of Jaurès and the sleepy, ambiguous formulae of Kautsky as equally foreign to the meaning of Marxism. Especially did he combat the fetishism of non-violence to which all the leaders of Western Social Democracy, with the exception of the Russians, were wedded. Marxism, he said, was the theory and practice of the class struggle. Since outside of the syndicalist movement the principle of the class struggle had been practically abandoned, only revolutionary syndicalism could be regarded as the true heir of Marxism. To be sure, there were minor criticisms of Marxian theory scattered throughout all of Sorel's writings; but wherever Sorel speaks of *la décomposition du marxisme* he explicitly refers to the reformist practices and the apologetic literature of official Marxism. Of Marx himself Sorel wrote in his

46

most important work: "No better proof perhaps can be given of Marx's genius than the remarkable agreement which is found to exist between his views and the doctrines which revolutionary syndicalism is to-day building up slowly and laboriously, keeping always strictly to strike tactics."[2] In his attack upon parliamentarians and state socialists on the right and the anarchist groups with their denial of the principle of authority on the left, Sorel could with justice claim some continuity with Marx; but his disregard of Marx's continued criticisms of the "no politics" cry of the Bakuninists and Proudhonians was so open that it bordered on quaintness. Since the latter were anarchists, Sorel claimed, what was true against them could not also be true for those who, like himself, condemned them.

Even more interesting in this connection is the note of cultural iconoclasm which Sorel sounds in his practical emphasis upon the class struggle, a note which was taken up by the international working-class movement only after the Russian Revolution. The economic and political conflicts between bourgeoisie and proletariat are at the same time cultural conflicts. Arrayed in mortal combat are two civilizations whose fundamental values cannot be arbitrated by an appeal to objective social duty. There is not even a significant common interest in the light of which these conflicting claims may be disinterestedly surveyed as partial interests. Duty, Sorel reminds those who have flown above the battle to get a larger view, has a meaning only "in a society in which

[2] *Reflections on Violence*, trans. by Hulme, p. 153.

all parts are intimately connected and responsible to one another."

Sorel was not content with underscoring the instrumental efficacy of revolutionary sentiment. He proceeded to develop a "logic" of sentiment on the Bergsonian model. It was this anti-intellectualistic current in Sorel which not only made *éclat* in the Catholic salons of the Third Republic but soon cost him the support of the syndicalist rank and file in whose presumable interests it had been elaborated. The classic expression of Sorel's irrationalism is to be found in his theory of the "myth." A myth for Sorel is any general notion, belief or fancy which drives men to great social action:

"Men who are participating in a great social movement always picture their coming action as a battle in which their cause is to triumph. . . . These constructions, a knowledge of which is so important for historians, I propose to call 'myths' . . . the syndicalist 'general strike' and Marx's 'catastrophic revolution' are such myths. (*Op. cit.,* p. 22.)

But how are such myths to be understood? By careful analysis? By distinguishing between what is description and what is prophecy? By disentangling the probable consequences of action from the desired consequences? Intuition forbid! A myth is not something which can survive analysis. It betrays a lack of intelligence even to try to analyze it. "It must be taken as a whole, as an historic force." Is not this equivalent to characterizing the myth of the general strike as Utopian? No, Utopian construction is the third member of the trinity of vicious abstractions whose other two members are socialist com-

promise and anarchist intransigeance. Utopias operate
with ideas which can be discussed and refuted; a *myth,
however, is an emotion which can only be enacted.*
It was upon this phantasy in a Bergsonian key that the
socialist movement was invited to stake its life.

By sheer intellectual violence Marx is transformed
from the theorist of social action into its poet; his
rational analyses are translated into romantic insights;
his attempt to explain the processes of production into
an indirect confirmation of the mysteries of creation.

"No effort of thought, no progress of knowledge, no
rational induction will ever dispel the mystery which en-
velops socialism; and it is because the philosophy of Marx
recognized fully this feature of socialism that it acquired
the right to serve as the starting point of socialist inquiry."
(*Op. cit.,* p. 164.)

This glorification of the violence incarnate in the
general strike was a clarifying influence in the foggy
atmosphere of parliamentary talk. It brought the "legalists at any price" to self-consciousness and forced them
openly to avow what they had already secretly confessed
to themselves; *viz.,* that they desired to constitute a new
administration, not to create a new state. But syndicalism itself provided no specific way by which the old
state could be destroyed except by professing to ignore
it. The general strike which it offered as a tactical pana-
cea was a highly abstract conception. The general strike
was regarded as a technical weapon which could be
used at will instead of a controlled politico-economic
reaction arising within a concrete historical situation.

It was taken as an isolated single economic act instead of a phase of a political revolutionary process. The syndicalists did not realize that a general strike could never of itself produce a revolutionary situation; that, on the contrary, its efficacy depended on whether it was itself produced *within* a revolutionary situation. Again the failure to think dialectically avenged itself upon them by driving them into a position which practically was no different from that of the orthodox Marxists whom they opposed. Their end was not linked up with their means.

Until 1914 the positive accomplishment of the syndicalist movement was to keep the French trade-union movement free from the views of parliamentary reformism. But like the I.W.W. in America, instead of building a revolutionary party, they proclaimed the slogan of "no party"; instead of relying upon their high fever of revolutionary sincerity to cure them of the infections of "dirty politics," they used as protection only the formula of "no politics"; instead of distinguishing between the legitimate organizational independence of trade unions from all political parties, and the inescapable acceptance of a political philosophy, they lumped both together, in the *Charte D'Amiens* of 1907, so that *organizational* independence in their minds meant *political* independence. But it really meant nothing of the kind. The economic struggle is always a political struggle. Even before the war it was clear that the state could not be snubbed out of existence because the syndicalist theory and program refused to recognize the necessity of fighting it on the political front. And during the war when the state smashed the syndicalist unions in America and corrupted the syndicalist movement in France, a classic demonstration was offered that the maxim, *to be is to be perceived,* was no more valid in politics than in philosophy.

Syndicalist philosophy had a twofold motivation. Politically it sought to convert a war of attrition for petty reform into a campaign of direct action for social revolution. It was a protest against the heterogeneous composition of the socialist parties, so many of whose leaders were *arrivistes,* indigent professionals, eloquent shopkeepers, and personalities from the fringe of hobohemia. Indicate that the "general strike" was a serious, perhaps a bloody business, and with one clean stroke you would sweep away all those intellectuals who had "embraced the profession of thinking for the proletariat." Theoretically, by denying that the future was predictable no matter how much scientific data might be at hand, it focused attention upon the necessity of risking something in *action.* The usual Bergsonian grounds were offered in denying that analysis could ever adequately render existence, especially in its dynamic aspect. Change could only be grasped in feeling; feeling could only be expressed in action. Thought followed action and derived its canons of validity from the successes registered. Any thinking is valid which gets you where you want to go. But since "where you want to go" is a feeling which defies description, the question "whether you have got to where you wanted to go" can only be decided *after* action, and then only by another feeling. The whole position runs out into a vicious variety of Jamesian pragmatism.[3]

The syndicalist movement was an embryonic revolutionary party. Because it did not recognize itself for what it was, it went to pieces and its revolutionary energy and zeal were dissipated. The most the syndicalists could do was to scare the state, not to conquer it. One critic aptly characterized them as "headless horsemen of the revolution riding furiously in all directions at once."

[3] Consistently embraced in Sorel's *De l'Utilité du Pragmatisme.*

7

LENIN: THE RETURN TO MARX AND FORWARD

VEN before Sorel had elaborated his syndicalist philosophy, a counter tendency to the official Social Democratic reformism had made itself felt from another quarter. In Germany this tendency was represented by Rosa Luxemburg, in Russia by Ulianov-Lenin. It was free from anti-intellectual demagogy and yet quite sensitive to every manifestation of revolutionary sentiment among the masses. Its interpretation of Marx differed as much from Sorel's as it did from Bernstein's. It reproached the syndicalists for overlooking the fact that every class struggle is a political struggle, for their refusal to make revolutionary use of parliamentary activity, and for their fetishism of violence. It criticized even more severely the supine parliamentarianism of the socialist parties, their naïve conception that every parliamentary debate was a class struggle, and their fetishism of non-violence.

As early as 1901 Lenin had taken the field against that variety of economism in Russia—ostensibly Marxian— which declared that the daily economic struggle must be left to produce simultaneously its own political activity and political leadership. As "tail-enders"[1] they held that to attribute to a political ideology any directive power upon mass movements was inconsistent with the theory of historical materialism. The political consciousness of a country can be no riper than its economic development. Arguing against this underestimation of revolutionary intelligence, Lenin writes:

"They fail to understand that an ideologist is worthy of that name only when he marches *ahead* of the spontaneous movement, points out the real road, and when he is able ahead of all others to solve all the theoretical, political, and tactical questions which the 'material elements' of the movement spontaneously encounter. . . . It is necessary to be critical of it [the movement], to point out its dangers and defects, and aspire to *elevate* spontaneity to consciousness. To say that ideologists cannot divert the movement created by the interaction of environment and elements from its path is to ignore the elementary truth that consciousness *participates* in this interaction and creation." ("A Conversation with Defenders of Economism," *Works,* Eng. trans. Vol. IV, p. 67.)

In a similar vein, but not so clearly by far, after the experiences of the Russian Revolution of 1905 Rosa Luxemburg wrote in her *Massenstreik, Partei und Gewerkschaften:*

". . . the task of the Social Democracy consists not only in the technical preparation and guidance of these strikes but, above all, in the political guidance of the entire movement.

[1] Tail-enders were those who believed that the political struggle is an automatic reflection of economic development, that a political party should follow, not lead, mass movement.

The Social Democracy is the most enlightened, the most class-conscious vanguard of the proletariat. It cannot and must not wait with folded hands fatalistically for the appearance of the 'revolutionary situation'—wait until that spontaneous people's movement may descend from heaven. On the contrary, in this case, as in all others, it must keep ahead of the development of things and seek to accelerate this development."

The consciousness to which Lenin and Luxemburg appealed was not mystic intuition but scientific knowledge. But scientific knowledge was not merely a disinterested report of objective tendencies in the economic world but a critical appreciation of the *possibilities* of political action liberated by such knowledge. The spontaneity which the syndicalists exalted at the cost of reflection was not enough. Unless a militant ideology or *theory* directed that spontaneous will, its energies would run out in sporadic and futile strike tactics. The proper direction of the labor movement implied the existence of a special class of professional revolutionists—a part of that movement and yet distinct in function—to make whatever spontaneity arose more effective. Marx was such a professional revolutionist. It was the height of absurdity on the part of those who sought to be orthodox to expect the course of economic development automatically to produce socialism. It could only produce by its own immanent movement the presuppositions of socialism. Power is bestowed neither by God nor the economic process. It must be taken. When Marx spoke of communism as being a result of a "social necessity," he was referring to the resultant of a whole social process, one of whose components was the development of objective economic conditions, the other, the assertion of a revolutionary class will. The task of a political party of professional revolutionists was to mediate these two interacting factors, to act as both vanguard and general staff of the revolutionary class struggle. The class struggle was not a simple, causal function of the tempo of economic development. That would mean fatalism. Economic forces and revolutionary organization, Lenin insisted, are not related to one another as mechanical cause and effect but are independent components of a *dialectical* whole—a dialectical whole being one which is continuously developing and whose parts are interacting with one another. To minimize the efficacy of the revolutionary idea which anticipates in present action the future direction of things on the basis of what they *were* and what we, as conscious willing beings, *are,* is to fall a victim to a bourgeois ideology.[2] Far from being Marxian it epitomizes all the policies of drift, compromise and caprice against which Marx waged war to the end.

Primitive economism has not reflected upon the real goal of the working-class movement. It has consequently confused means and ends. In so doing it has adopted the same passive attitude as the revisionists to the revolutionary class struggle. Theoretically the anarcho-syndicalist left and reformist-socialist right join hands. "That struggle is desirable which is possible, and the

[2] "What is to be Done?" *Works,* Vol. IV, p. 121.

struggle which is possible is the one going on now," wrote the *Rabochaya Mysl,* the organ of economism, in words which sounded quite similar to those of the "legal" Marxists, the Russian variant of revisionism.

It was Rosa Luxemburg who delivered the classic attack against revisionism from the standpoint of dialectical Marxism. The attack was at the same time an implied indictment of the official doctrinal orthodoxy. She began her famous pamphlet, *Reform oder Revolution,* by pointing out that there was a shadow of justification for Bernstein's refusal to take the professed goal of the socialist movement seriously. For after all how was that goal conceived by the "orthodox"? Generally as an economic collectivism of indeterminate organizational structure, with all sorts of features added by the private conceits of those who drew the picture. What organic connection, indeed, could exist between such Utopian constructions and the exigencies of the daily class struggle! No wonder that Bernstein confessed that the goal was nothing, the movement everything. The trouble was that both Bernstein and those who opposed him *shared the same mistaken premise* about the goal of the proletarian movement. That goal was not the organization of a socialist commonwealth (whose problems could only be intelligently met when they arose) but the *conquest of political power.* Like Lenin she held that only the presuppositions of socialism are automatically generated by the processes of capitalist production. The active seizure of power, however, which in a revolutionary crisis would put the working class at the helm

57

of state, depended primarily upon political intelligence, will and organization. The revolutionary dictatorship of the working class, ruling in the transition period from capitalism to socialism—only that could be the realistic goal of the movement. Here was an end which was organically related to the means used in the daily struggle. The ends must be recognized in the choice and character of the means employed. And there could no longer be any serious dispute about the means; they could not be of a kind that hindered the fulfillment of the end.[8]

The consequence of this shift of emphasis from a future state of society to a present struggle for power was impressive and far reaching. At one stroke it cut the roots from under those who believed in a *Kompensationspolitik*. There had been Social Democratic deputies who had been willing, as one reformist declared, "to vote appropriations for cannon in exchange for the people's electoral rights." And if the goal of the movement was socialism, regarded as an immanent phase of the economic development, there could be no objection to this exchange in principle. No matter how many cannon the Kaiser's army had, no matter how strong the existing state was, it could do nothing against the inevitable march of events. Why the same logic did not

[8] The organic unity of means and ends was a part of dialectical materialism. The proper analysis of the relation, distorted of course by an idealistic ontology, had already been made by Hegel (*Encyclopädie*, etc., Sec. 212; *Wissenschaft der Logik*, Lasson ed., Vol. II, p. 344), whom the Social Democratic theoreticians, with the exception of Plechanov, Lenin, and their circles, ignored.

militate against the demand for electoral reform was a mystery. But the suicidal character of such horse-trading tactics was not a mystery when, instead of the nebulous goal of socialism, there was substituted for it the conquest of political power and the dictatorship of the proletariat. If the state had to be captured, it was sheer insanity to begin by strengthening it.

The logic of the dilemma which Luxemburg and Lenin hurled at the official Social Democracy was clear. If practical reforms are the be-all and end-all of the movement, emphasis upon the goal conceived as the conquest of political power is bound to get in the way. When such emphasis is taken as something more than poetic myth, it becomes an irrelevant intrusion into the specific tasks in hand. One cannot significantly relate a struggle, say, for a two cent per hour increase in wages or a Saturday half-holiday with the conquest of political power. Bernstein was right in claiming that he had given theoretical expression to the reformist practices of German Social Democracy. If, on the other hand, the goal is the conquest of political power, reforms are to be regarded as the *by-products* of the class struggle. Immediate demands are not thereby stricken from the program—this was one of the errors of Daniel de Leon, the most orthodox of American Marxists— but are made the springboards of political agitation. No issue then could be too small if it served to intensify the class struggle. But every class struggle must be regarded as potentially a political struggle. It is directed not only towards improving the condition of the masses

59

—which is important enough—but towards wresting control of the state from the hands of the dominant class.

The work of Luxemburg and Lenin marked, so to speak, the beginning of the Marxian reformation.[4] The texts of Marx and Engels were to be read in the light of the original spirit behind them. In refusing to be "orthodox" at any price, Luxemburg and Lenin claimed to be more faithful to the ideas and methods of the men who originally inspired that orthodoxy than the formula-ridden pedants who anathematized them as heretics. The course of events has contributed to bringing these two Marxian interpretations into sharp opposition. One group was responsible for the German Republic; the other for the Russian Revolution. So wide did the rift grow that it became possible for the leaders of the first group to boast that they saved Western civilization from the chaos and barbarism advocated by the second; and for the leaders of the second to denounce the first as apostates to the cause of the working classes.

Historical accuracy demands, before we close this chapter, that we indicate some of the important differences which, for all their common opposition to Marxian orthodoxy, separated Lenin and Luxemburg. Lenin drew the proper logical conclusions from his rejection

[4] This figure of speech is merely a development of the metaphor which Engels himself used when he referred to Marx's *Capital* as the Bible of the international working class. Cf. one of his reviews of Marx's *Capital*, reprinted in *Marx-Engels Archiv*, Vol. II, p. 445; Engels' preface to the English translation, Vol. I, p. 30, Kerr edition.

of the theory of spontaneity in so far as they bore upon the question of organization. If the political party was to be the vanguard in the struggle for social revolution, it could not risk compromising its leadership by destroying its own organizational autonomy in relation to either the trade unions or the proletariat as a whole. Luxemburg demanded a form of organization which would more democratically reflect the masses outside of the party. This was a justified claim in so far as it was directed against the bureaucracy of the German party which not only lagged behind the radical sentiments of its members and working-class sympathizers but acted as a brake on their movement towards a more revolutionary position. It was unjustified, however, in so far as it was universalized to hold for all countries, especially Russia, where such a form of organization would involve the danger that the party might be taken in tow by unripe elements. Similarly, in her opposition to any alliance between the workers and the peasants in a revolutionary dictatorship, and in her slighting of the national question (*e.g.,* in her belief that in the era of monopoly imperialism national wars were no longer possible) there was revealed a too great reliance upon the theory of mechanical spontaneity. Perhaps her most significant difference from Lenin flowed from her analysis of imperialism. In her *Akkumlation des Kapitals* she contended that, with the exhaustion of the home market, capitalism must stride from one colonial country to another and that capitalism could only survive so long as such countries were available. As soon as the world would be partitioned among the imperialist powers and industrialized, the international revolution would of necessity break out, since capitalism cannot expand its productive forces and continue the process of accumulation indefinitely in any relatively isolated commodity-producing society, no matter how large.

Lenin denied that capitalism would ever collapse in any such mechanical fashion. Whoever believed that capitalism, no matter how severe its crisis, had no way out, was being victimized by the fatalistic pseudo-science of orthodox German Social Democracy. Without an international *organized* revolution, capitalism would never collapse unless it pulled the whole of civilization down with it in bloody war.

"Above all we must point out two widely spread errors. On the one hand bourgeois economists represent this crisis simply as a 'maladjustment,' as the elegant expression of the Englishman has it. On the other, revolutionists attempt to prove that there is absolutely no way out of the crisis. That is an error. There do not exist any positions from which there is absolutely no way out." (*Works,* German ed., Vol. 25, p. 420. An address delivered before the second congress of the Communist International, 1920.)

Peculiarly enough Lenin overlooks the incompatibility between his political activism and its underlying dynamic philosophy of interaction as expressed in *What's to be Done?,* and the mechanical correspondence theory of knowledge—defended so vehemently by him in his *Materialism and Empirio-Criticism.* Here he follows Engels word for word in his statement that "sensations are copies, photographs, images and mirror-reflections of things," [5] and that the mind is not active in knowing. He seems to believe that if one holds: (1) that mind enters as an active factor in knowing, conditioned by the nervous system and all of past history, then it follows that one must believe; (2) that mind creates *all* of existence including its own brain. This is the rankest idealism and idealism means religion and God. But the step from proposition (1) to (2) is the most glaring *non-sequitur* imaginable. As a matter of fact, in the interests of his conception of Marxism as the theory and practice of social revolution Lenin must admit that knowledge is an active affair, a process in which there is an *interaction* of matter, culture and mind, and that sensation is not knowledge but part of the materials with which knowledge works. This is the position that Marx took in his glosses on *Feuerbach* and in his *Deutsche Ideologie*. Whoever believes that sensations are literal copies of the external world, and that of themselves they give knowledge, cannot escape fatalism and mechanism. In Lenin's political and non-technical writings there is no trace of this dualistic Lockean epistemology; as we have seen above, his *What's to be Done?* contains a frank acceptance of the active rôle of class consciousness in the social process. It is in these practical writings in which Lenin concerns himself with the concrete problems of agitation, revolution and reconstruction, that his true philosophy is to be found.

[5] *Works,* Vol. XIII, Eng. trans., p. 195.

8

MARXISM AS METHOD

$\mathcal{W}$HAT shall we do in face of these conflicting interpretations of Marx? Add another? Who will decide among them? Why not shelve his theories, then, as a set of more or less ambiguous doctrines which exercised great influence over men because it permitted them to do what they wished to do in any case? Such a procedure, however, would fail to explain why the appeal was to Marx and not to St. Simon or Proudhon or Bakunin. There must have been aspects, at least, of Marx's doctrines which lent themselves to these different interpretations. The possibility we wish to entertain here is that the views considered above (which are by no means exhaustive) are, with the exception of Lenin's, one-sided emphases upon phases of Marx's thought and suffer from a common failure to appreciate the nature of Marx's dialectical method.

The significance of Marx's method as the clue to his doctrines is rendered all the more important by the vogue of critical interpretations whose chief point is that these doctrines are contradictory. And it is true that if they are considered in independence of the method they illustrate and the historical context in which they arose, they do appear contradictory. From these apparent contradictions has been born Sombart's *zwei Seelen* theory of Marx—as a thinker and as a hater; and the even more popular Dr. Jekyll and Mr. Hyde conception of Marx as a professional revolutionist and a fuzzy metaphysician. But the most elementary methodological caution has here been overlooked. The full import of a doctrine is not to be sought only in the formal analysis of isolated texts. It is to be derived from a consideration of these texts in relation to the positions and views they oppose. Just as the meaning of a proposition becomes clearer when we formulate its logical contradictory, so the import of a man's thought becomes more manifest when we know what the doctrines are which he is opposing. If the doctrines which he is opposing are themselves opposite, then we can expect that against one will be urged the accepted points of the other. If the critic has no clear idea of the positions which are being attacked, he runs the risk of converting the relative emphasis of different occasions into absolute contradictions. This is true of all the "critical annihilations" of Marx with which I am acquainted.

Marx came to critical self-consciousness by settling accounts with the varied intellectual traditions and attitudes of his day. He did not write textbooks and fill them with cold-storage truths. His writings were programs of action; his analyses a method of clearing the way for action. None of his works can therefore be understood without a comprehension of the opposing positions to which he makes explicit or implicit reference. Against the idealism of Bruno Bauer and his Young-Hegelian associates, Marx presents the argument for materialism. Against the passive materialism of Feuerbach, Marx defends the principles of activity and reciprocity which were central to Hegel's dialectic. Against the fatalism of both absolute idealism and "vulgar" (reductive) mechanism, Marx proclaims that human beings make their own history. As opposed to the revolutionists of the phrase, however, he adds that history is not made out of whole cloth but under definite, limiting conditions. It was as easy to characterize Marx as completely Hegelian in his method because he attacked the assumptions of atomic empiricism as to indict him as a "soulless" materialist for seeking a causal explanation of values. To the *wahre Sozialisten,* who sought to initiate a movement of social reform on the basis of absolute ethical principles like "social love" and justice, Marx declares that every realistic social movement must be a class movement. To simon-pure trade unionists struggling for a "fair day's wage for a fair day's work," he insists that every class struggle is a political struggle. Stirner's glorification of hard-boiled egoism with its perpetual declensions of "I, me and myself," he reveals as the social defence mechanism of a petty bourgeois soul desiring to save "its own." Against the classical school of economics, which had regarded its economic categories as valid for any historical system, he urges that economic categories are not Platonic Ideas but are as transitory as

the historical relationships which they express. Against
the historical school of economics, he vindicates the
necessity of analyzing the structure of political economy
independently of speculative fancies about its origin. As
opposed to the anarchist ideal of complete decentralization, he defends the principle of authority. To the Lassallean cult of the state, he counters with the idea of its
ultimate disappearance. He was as critical of petty bourgeois opportunism of the right as he was contemptuous
of the ultra-left sectarianism of men like Most and
Bakunin. The critics who made so much of Marx's contradictory positions never made an attempt to find a
point of view from which these alleged contradictions
turned out to be applications of the same principles and
purposes to different historical situations.

These historical situations as well as the wider social
horizons against which Marx's problems were formulated cannot be treated here. A complete treatment of
Marx's thought would have to include them together
with an account of the industrial transformations, the
political mass movements as well as the cultural developments of his age. Only then would we be applying
Marx's historical method to Marx's own work.[1] Even
so, the distinctive feature of Marx's thought would
hardly be in evidence, for Marx's age presumably was
the background of other thinkers from whom he vio-

---

[1] Interesting beginnings have been made in Mehring's biography,
Karl Marx, Geschichte seines Lebens, Berlin, 1919; in Gustav Mayer's
Frederich Engels I, Berlin, 1920; in the histories of the socialist move-
ment by Mehring and Beer; and in Riazanov's *Marx and Engels,*
Eng. trans., 1927.

lently differed. It is primarily that distinctive feature
which I wish to discuss.

Granted, then, that if Marx is to be completely understood, his background must be explained. What else
would we have to know about him? Obviously his purposes, his reaction to that environment and the logical
interest of his thought in theorizing about it. For only
in terms of these purposes can we understand his problems. The purpose of Marx's intellectual activity was
the revolutionary overthrow of the existing order. That
shines through all of his writings. Even his learned
economic treatises did not deceive the academic representatives of constituted authority in Europe—although
they did succeed in de-revolutionizing some of his
avowed followers. One can hear Marx's own voice in
the words which Engels pronounced upon him at High-
gate Cemetery in 1883: "Before all else, Marx was a
revolutionist." And it was as revolutionist that he approached his theoretical problems in sociology, economics, and philosophy. For him they were primarily the
theoretical problems of social revolution.[2] No presuppo-
sitionless treatment of the social sciences is possible. At

[2] That Marx's purpose was really one of the defining terms of his
problems and not an irrelevant psychological detail is evidenced by the
way in which he and Engels gauged the import of the social theories
of their opponents; first, by their probable influence on the formation
of revolutionary political organization; second, by their freedom from
the "muddled humanitarianism" which tended to wean these organizations away from militancy; e.g., for the possible disorganizing influence of Feuerbach, see *Briefwechsel zwischen Marx und Engels*,
Vol. I, Mehring's ed., pp. 7, 24, 45-48; and *Deutsche Ideologie*,
passim. For the dangerous influence of Grün and Proudhon, *ibid.*, I,
pp. 40-42.

their heart there lie certain irreducible values or *Stell-ungnahmen* which are, to be sure, historically conditioned by the social situation and the balance of class forces existing at any determinate period, but which cannot be logically *deduced* from it. Social science is class science; and what Marx means by science is not what is meant by the word to-day, but *criticism based on the observable tendencies of social development.*

The scientific approach to society involves the continuous application of ideals to the functioning of institutions and the continuous testing of those ideals by the social consequences of their application. Marx regarded those who restricted themselves to an objective description of social behavior, in which all notions of "what ought to be" are ruled out, as *apologists* of the existing order and of the ideals which social institutions embodied. And those who set up their "ought to be" as a categorical imperative, in independence of the limiting conditions of the given historical situation, he dismissed as Utopians. Marx was disinterested in the outcome of his inquiries only to the extent of drawing proper conclusions from his premises. He did not conceal his interests and bias but used them in order to reveal more effectively the interest of those who made a cult of impartiality. How it was possible for him to assert that his position was not impartial, and yet at the same time objective, is a problem which we shall consider below.

Marx's revolutionary motivation was no more uniquely his own than was his social background. Many of his contemporaries, both among the Utopians

(Owen) and reactionaries (Lorenz von Stein), felt the impact of what was essentially the same problem. And as for his purpose—the social revolution—it was the common goal of large numbers of German exiles, Blanquist Frenchmen, expatriate Poles and Russians. For some it was a religion in comparison with which Marx's faith seemed pale. It was the goal not only of a few individuals; it was the goal of a class. What, then, must we ask, is distinctive of Marx's thought, if it is neither his problems, his purposes, nor his conclusions? The answer suggested here is, that what is characteristic of Marx's thought is the *dialectical method* by which he undertook to solve these problems and attain his purposes.[3]

To distinguish between Marx's dialectical method and his conclusions is not to say that his conclusions are false; and to consider Marx's dialectical method is not to imply that it is an abstract instrument. On any specific occasion in which it is applied, Marx's specific purpose is part of it. Nonetheless it is possible to describe the general character of the method and indicate its larger philosophical and social implications.

[3] "The working out of the method which lies at the basis of Marx's criticism of political economy I regard as something hardly less important than the materialistic conception of history." (Engels in a review of Marx's *Introduction to a Critique of Political Economy*, reprinted in *Feuerbach*, Ducker ed., p. 118.) The method of abstraction, modified by historical description, which Marx uses in his economic analysis is only one specific application of the dialectical method.

PART II

THE PHILOSOPHY OF KARL MARX

"Marxismus ist ein revolutionäre Weltanschauung,
die stets nach neuen Erkenntnissen ringen muss, die
nichts so verabscheut wie das Erstarren in einmal
gültigen Formen, die am besten in geistigen Waf-
fengeklirr der Selbstkritik und im geschichtlichen
Blitz und Donner ihre lebendige Kraft bewährt."
—Rosa Luxemburg.

"'Our theory is not a dogma but a manual of
action,' said Marx and Engels."
—Lenin.

9

THE MARXIAN DIALECTIC

$\mathbb{A}$ WITTY Frenchman
once said that Marxism like Christianity has its bible,
its councils, its schisms, its orthodoxies and heresies, its
exegesis sacred and profane. And like Christianity it has
its mysteries of which the principal one is the dialectic.
This is not an infrequent judgment. There has hardly
been a critic of Marx who has not regarded the dialectical principle as either a piece of religious mysticism or
of deliberate mystification. In the writings of Marxists it
appears more often as a magic symbol than as a clearly
defined concept.

Yet the apparently mysterious character of the Marxian dialectic is due to nothing more than the Hegelian
terminology with which Marx, out of piety to Hegel's
memory, invested it, and to the refusal of Marx's critics
to translate its meaning from the technical idiom of
philosophy into the ever fresh experience of change,
growth and novelty. Thus it becomes clear that although
there is a significant continuity between the thought of
Hegel and Marx there are profound differences.

1. THE SCOPE OF DIALECTIC

Hegel was a man of vision who belied his own insights in order to assure the Prussian monarchy that its existence was part of the divine plan and, indeed, its final expression. Since the reasons he adduced were the most transparent rationalizations, both his system and his method fell into disrepute. Attempting to prove that all of existence was rational, therefore, necessary, and, therefore, good, he failed to make the existence of any *particular* thing intelligible. There was not much difference between his ruthless optimism which assured the rising German bourgeoisie that this was the best of all possible worlds and the sentimental pessimism of his arch-enemy, Schopenhauer, who held it was the worst. For neither system admitted that the world could significantly change one way or the other. For Hegel, change was merely appearance, for Schopenhauer, illusion.

Marx was an empiricist. If change was not real, nothing was real. Even if permanence and invariance were characters of existence, they could only be recognized in change and difference. The dialectic method of Marx is a way of dealing with what is both constant and variable in every situation. It is the logic of movement, power, growth and action.

The dialectic method is not opposed to scientific *method* but only to pseudo-scientific *philosophies* which overlook the specific context and tentative character of the results won in physical or biological investigation and seek to apply their findings to other realms without making the proper qualifications. It is not science but mistaken philosophies of science which use the "principle of the conservation of energy" or the doctrine of "the struggle for existence" to construct systems of social physics or social biology. The dialectic method is wider than scientific method if the latter is narrowly conceived to assert "only that exists which can be measured," for although it accepts the findings of science as an accurate report of the structure of the external world, it recognizes that there are other realms of experience, such as the arts and practical affairs, in which *qualities* and *activities* are the fundamental organizing concepts and not *quantities*. It distinguishes between types and levels of existence, investigates their interrelation, and synthesizes them in their order of temporal and structural dependence. In physics, the dialectic approach begins with the end-products of scientific analysis—its equations and abstractions—and instead of declaring as the metaphysical materialists do, "these alone are real," asks such questions as how these relational formulae are derived from concrete problems of practice, and how the invisible, inaudible, intangible world of mathematical physics is related to the many-colored world of familiar experience. In biology, it accepts the descriptions of the ways in which the structure of organs condition their present functions, but seeks for the evidence of past functions in present structure and attempts to discover how at any given time both the specific structure and the specific function of any organ are related to the *functioning* of the organism as a whole. Behind the facts and figures of social life, it sees the grim realities of the class struggle; in the struggle, possibilities of social development; in possibilities, plans of action. Marx used it to solve problems in political economy with which the unhistorical "classical school" wrestled in vain; Lenin, to correct the onesidedness of both Bukharin and Trotsky on the trade-union question.

The dialectic method is applicable to all levels of existence. On each level it reflects the novelties in the behavior of its subject-matter. When it deals with the structure of the atom, it does not introduce, as idealists do, will or purpose or feeling (Whitehead); when it deals with the rise and fall of civilizations, it does not interpret the historical process in terms of biological stimulus-and-response, as is the fashion with the "vulgar" behavioristic materialists (Watson).

Wherever the dialectic method is applied, it presupposes not the attitude of contemplation but of action. Freed from its idealistic *mésalliance,* it is genuinely experimental. It seeks objective knowledge of natural and social fact from the standpoint of the doer not the spectator. Indeed, the very meaning of what it is to possess objective knowledge of any ongoing process, involves the prediction of a future outcome, to achieve which, human activity enters as a necessary element. That is why Marx claimed that only in practice (*Praxis*) can problems be solved. Any problem which cannot be solved by some actual or possible practice may be dismissed as no genuine problem at all. The types and varieties of practice are determined by the existential context in which problems arise.

2. Some Contrasting Conceptions of Dialectic

A few words are necessary to distinguish the Marxian dialectic from older meanings of the term. Ancient dialectic—the "eristic" of the Sophists—as well as medieval dialectic, was not a method of demonstrating known truths or of discovering new truth. It was in the main a method of disputation whose primary aim was to trip up a speaker by showing that the implications of his statements were self-refuting. It seized upon ambiguities of terms, elliptical expressions, awkward grammatical constructions, to twist a meaning from words which was quite foreign to the intent of the one who uttered them. In this way dialectic was a method of proving anything, or more strictly, of *disproving* everything, since it showed that the speaker was contradicting himself and therefore talking nonsense. It was used in court room and public assembly and sometimes at philosophical exhibitions of low order. In common parlance this kind of dialectic is often used as a synonym for sophistry.

There was a more honorable sense of the term "dialectic" in ancient thought, illustrated by the writings of Plato. Dialectic is the process of thinking by which the dramatic conflict of ideas, as they arise in dialogue or monologue, is resolved by definition, differentiation and re-definition until one ultimate, luminously self-evident insight is reached in which the original conflict of ideas

77

is harmonized. For Plato, ideas are not mental events or physical things. They are meanings, essences, forms, and have no reference to existence. Dialectic, therefore, is the process by which the structure of logical systems is discovered.

In Hegel the dialectic method is not only a process by which logical ideas develop; it is a process by which all things in the world develop. For according to Hegel the very stuff of nature, society and the human mind is through and through logical. Plato's world is a frozen pattern of mathematical logic; Hegel's world is historical and organic. But in order to explain the rationale of historical development in physical nature and human culture, Hegel is compelled to endow his logical ideas or principles with efficient power. Just as in traditional theology thoughts in the mind of God created the world, so in Hegel's system the whole furniture of heaven and earth is the result of the development or unfolding of logical ideas. Marx abandoned the Hegelian dialectic because its logical processes were just as mysterious as the creation of Genesis. Despite the grinding of his elaborate intellectual machinery one could get no more out of Hegel's logic than was already in the world. The real task for the empirical philosopher, according to Marx, was not to show that the content of history was logical but that the content of logic was historical. This could be done only by taking logic in the widest possible sense so that it included all the processes by which knowledge was attained, and showing how the

problems and purposes of knowledge were always set
in some concrete historical context.

In contradistinction to Hegel, Marx's dialectic method
was applied primarily to human history and society.
Here he succeeded in doing what Hegel had failed to
do. Without denying the enormous complexity of the
factors involved, he offered a guiding thread into the
mazes of the social process. If followed, it leads not
only to a fruitful exploration of the past but to a course
of action which may free mankind from its major social
evils. The detailed application of Marx's dialectic
method is to be found in his economic theories, the
materialistic conception of history, and his philosophy
of state and society. In this chapter the dialectic method
will be expounded as it applies to the general questions
of culture, and an attempt will be made to derive and
state the formal characters of the method without for-
bidding terminology.

We may begin by contrasting Marx's philosophy of
culture with the most fashionable cultural theories of
Spengler, who in one sense is the greatest right-wing
disciple of Hegel, as Marx is the greatest among the
left-wing disciples. According to Spengler each culture
is an organic whole of institutions, habits, ideas and
myths; it is marked off in the same unmistakable way
from all other cultures as one individual is from another. Although each culture has its own life-cycle, the
formula of all cultural cycles is the same. It is a movement, to use Spengler's own terms, from culture to
civilization, from life to death. When a culture grows

old and cold, thought replaces feeling, mechanics life, law individuality. Each culture runs its own course in independence of all others; there is no significant diffusion of its cultural pattern. It is the morphology of these cultural patterns which interests Spengler most. Just as it is the whole nervous system which sees through the eye, the whole body which moves the arm, so it is the whole pattern of a culture which underlies its art, its religion, its mathematics, even its kitchen pots and pans.

When we inquire, however, what determines the character type or pattern of a specific culture, why the categories of finitude, quality, and natural order, are central to Greek culture while contemporary Europe and America are so much concerned with process, quantity and experience, why the "world-feeling" of medieval culture is so different from that of the Renaissance—Spengler, like Hegel, answers in terms of metaphysical abstractions. It is the *soul* or *spirit* of a people which expresses itself in its culture, and the spirit of a people in turn is an expression of spirit as a primary metaphysical reality. Indeed, Spengler even appeals to "the style of the soul" to account for the fact that different peoples have produced different types of mathematics. Spirit, soul, style, destiny—all these are one. They are the ultimate determining force of whatever exists. They cannot be explained; but they explain everything else:

"Style is not . . . the product of material, technique and function. It is the very opposite of this, something inaccessible to art-reason. It is a revelation of the metaphysical order, a mysterious must, a Destiny." (*Decline of the West,* I, Chap. VII.)

Here we have a conception of culture which is not empirical but essentially mystical (as are all objective idealisms); which at best accounts for the organization of a culture, not its development; which is fatalistic and denies to human beings genuine creative power; and which is distinguished for its cool disregard of the immense importance of cultural diffusion and social heredity in Western history.

The key weakness of Spengler's architectonic construction is to be found in his use of the terms "spirit" and "soul" to explain differences in culture. If spirit determines an existing culture, what determines spirit? And if spirit is self-determined, why cannot the culture-complex be self-determined? If spirit is the source of such different institutions as slavery, feudalism and capitalism, how account for the fact that they appear *when* they do, and in the *order* they do? Every culture shows a conflict between different groups which develop their own ideologies. How can the spirit of the age or people or nation account for these different expressions? Why did the reformation succeed in Northern Europe and fail everywhere else? Why did the "spirit of freedom" liberate Europeans from slavery and feudalism only to reimpose slavery upon the Negroes in America? It is clear that to invoke the soul of a culture as an explanation of a material culture is to invoke a mystery.

Marx's philosophy of culture already contains the ker-

nel of truth which Spengler wraps up in masses of
pseudo-erudition. Like all students of Hegel, Marx realized that every culture is a structurally interrelated
whole, and that any institutional activity, say religion or
law, can be understood only in relation to a whole complex of other social activities. But in two respects he
advances beyond his early master and those who have
either followed or plagiarized him since. He does not
claim that a culture is organic through and through and
that one principle can explain *all* its existing aspects,
from the latest frills in the culinary arts to the most
recent development of theoretical physics. He admits the
presence of relatively independent factors which do not
all possess the same weight, although they all arise out
of antecedent social processes and function in determinate ways in the *existing* social process. But more important, he seeks for the causes of cultural change
within the social process itself and not in the realm of
metaphysical abstraction. His method is realistic and
materialistic. He holds that any explanation of cultural
change must fulfil two conditions. First, it must suggest some way in which the theory can find empirical
verification. To proclaim that society must change is not
enough. That is too vague. The conditions under which
the social order changes must be indicated and the determinate possibilities of change at any moment stated.
Secondly, it must do justice to the consciousness of human beings that they actively participate in making
their own history. That is to say, when the determinate
possibilities of social change have been presented, the

probabilities that one direction will be taken rather than another, must be shown to be, in part at least, a function of class interests and purposes.

3. THE DIALECTIC OF SOCIAL CHANGE

Marx's own hypothesis that the development of the mode of economic production is the central but not exclusive causal factor of social and cultural change will be examined in detail later on. There are first to be considered certain problems of culture and knowledge confronting all philosophies of history. Marx's dialectical method really grew out of his reflection upon them.

One of the obvious facts which a philosophy of history must explain is the *continuity* between one culture and another. The continuity of culture can mean nothing else than the development of its institutions. Their development, indeed, their very functioning, implies the continuous activity of human beings. This activity has a two-fold aspect. It is conditioned by an antecedent state of affairs, and yet contributes either to perpetuating or transforming that state of affairs. The central problem of cultural change as formulated by Marx, is how it is possible for human beings conditioned by their cultural education and environment to succeed in changing that environment. The French materialistic philosophers had long since pointed out that human beings were over-determined by environment and education; but they could not explain in these terms how they themselves could be agitating for a revolutionary change to a different society.

"The materialistic doctrine," wrote Marx, "that men are products of their environment and education, different men products of different environment and education, forgets that the environment itself has been changed by man and the educator himself must be educated. That is why it separates society into two parts of which one is elevated over the whole.

"The simultaneity of both change in environment and human activity or self-change can only be grasped and rationally understood as revolutionary practice." (Third gloss on *Feuerbach, Gesamtausgabe,* Abt. I, Bd. 5, p. 534.)

Refusing to dissociate social experience into something which is only cause, the external world, and something which is only effect, consciousness, Marx tries to show how social change arises from the interacting processes of nature, society and human intelligence. From objective *conditions,* social and natural (thesis), there arises human *needs* and *purposes* which, in recognizing the objective possibilities in the given situation (antithesis) set up a course of *action* (synthesis) designed to actualize these possibilities. All change from one social situation to another, and from one social system to another exhibits (1) unity between the two phases, in that certain features are preserved (*e.g.,* the technical forms of socialized production under capitalism are preserved under communism); (2) difference, in that certain features of the first are destroyed (*e.g.,* the social relations of capitalist production, private property, etc.); and (3) qualitative novelty, in that new forms of organization and activity appear which change the significance of the old elements still preserved, and which cannot be reduced merely to a mechanical combination of them. The process of creative development continues for ever. There are no laws of social life which are invariant except the general schema of development. At a critical point in the complex interaction of (1) the social institutions from which we start, (2) the felt needs which their immanent development produces, (3) and the will to action which flows from knowledge of the relation between institutions and human needs, new laws of social organization and behavior arise.

The logic of the situation is not foreign even to natural phenomena At certain critical points in the varying temperature of water new qualities, ice and steam, emerge. But Marx is never weary of repeating that the distinctive character of social development as opposed to the natural processes of development lies in the fact that human consciousness is involved.

We can now see how undialectical it is for some pseudo-Marxians to maintain that communism involves a complete break with the past. The very fact that the same language would be used rich with the connotations of past experience, precludes the possibility of such discontinuity. The existence of the great cultural heritage of the past would always constitute a challenge to reinterpretation in and for the present. Change there must be, and *selective* change. The impact of selective change, to be sure, will necessarily be destructive. But only to religious values and attitudes which stress prayer rather than knowledge and action, to social values which in expressing the snobberies of birth, station, and eco-

nomic power, stultify the widest possible development
of creative personality—to all values which in exalting
the mastery of technique over life (machinery for machinery's sake, art for art's sake, science for science's
sake, philosophy for philosophy's sake) mistake the part
for the whole, sacrifice the organic connections between
one field and another, impoverish the world by cling-
ing to the tried and established, and oppose adventure,
experiment and growth. Nonetheless, communist culture is not merely destructive to the inheritance of the
past. It realizes that Socrates and Bruno and Rousseau,
conditioned by their time, were just as great rebels in
their day as Marx was in his; that Aristotle, Ockham
and Kant in relation to their past, were, at the very
least, the intellectual peers of Marx. Only undialectical
Marxists like Bukharin will speak of the "outspoken
black-hundred tendencies of Plato." Does this mean that
in accepting the heritage of the past communism accepts the theories of these men; fosters, for example, the
style of Michelangelo and encourages imitations of the
church music of Bach? Not at all. It reinterprets them
in a new cultural synthesis. The permanent, invariant
and universal aspects of human experience, as reflected
in art and literature, reappear in a new context so that
the significant insights of the past become enriched
through the reinterpretation of the present. The dialectic
of culture and history leads to the paradox that the past
is not something dead, a pattern congealed into an eternal rigidity, which may have beauty but not life. The
past grows whenever a new perspective in the present

enables us to look back and see what has grown out of it. And when we know what has grown out of it, we can without exaggeration say that we understand it better than it did itself.

Marx, himself, was well aware of the fact that the art or culture of an historical period, although reflecting a definite form of social development, can make an esthetic appeal which far transcends the immediate historical milieu in which it arose. Something, of course, is irretrievably lost when the persons for whom a work of art was originally created have disappeared and there is no way of fully reconstructing the prejudices and presuppositions which served as their criteria of esthetic appreciation. But human experience is sufficiently continuous to enable us to translate the significance of past artistic achievement into some present mood, emotion or faith. Often we are able to regard an ancient work of art as a specific expression, in local idiom, of a wider social or esthetic experience. In either case a critical discrimination results in making contemporary the significance of past cultural activity.

It was with this problem in mind that Marx wrote of the recurrent appeal of Greek art:

". . . the difficulty is not in grasping the idea that Greek art and epos are bound up with certain forms of social development. It rather lies in understanding why they still constitute with us a source of esthetic enjoyment and in certain respects prevail as the standard and model beyond attainment.

"A man cannot become a child again unless he becomes childish. But does he not enjoy the artless ways of the child and must he not strive to reproduce its truth on a higher plane? Is not the character of every epoch revived perfectly true to nature in child nature? Why should the social childhood of mankind, where it had obtained its most beautiful development, not exert an eternal charm as an age that will never return? There are ill-bred children and precocious children. Many of the ancient nations belong to the latter class. The Greeks were normal children. The charm their art has for us does not conflict with the primitive character of the social order from which it has sprung. It is rather the product of the latter, and is rather due to the fact that the unripe social conditions under which the art arose and under which alone it could appear can never return." (*Critique of Political Economy*, Kerr ed., pp. 311-312.)

The heavy overtones of German esthetic theory of the nineteenth century, especially Hegel's philosophy of art, can be heard in this passage; and its characterization of Greek art may, therefore, produce a comic effect upon the contemporary reader. Nonetheless, it strikes a clear note in behalf of the relative autonomy of the esthetic experience.

In discussing social change, Marx, however, presses the point of his dialectic a little deeper. Social institutions in the course of their own careers produce the means by which they are changed and generate the needs which ultimately inspire men to revolutionary action. Some important consequences follow. The conditions of extant social production must be accepted before they can be transformed. The evils generated by the private ownership of the means of production in an era of large-scale machine manufacture cannot be eliminated by rejecting the machine process and returning to hand industry, or to the soil, or, for that matter, to the bosom of the church. History may be reconstructed but it cannot be reversed. To attempt any such movement would result in more distress than originally called it forth. It could easily be shown, for example, that population, which is a function of the system of production, has grown to such an extent that its barest necessities could hardly be fulfilled to-day by a system of primitive hand manufacture and agriculture. It is not the machine which oppresses men but the social relations within which machine production is carried on. Periodic crises, unemployment and mass misery flow not from the former but from the latter. Consequently it is the social relations of production which must be changed. "But in every society," writes Marx, "the relations of production constitute a whole." If they are a whole, we cannot accept one aspect which we call good and reject another which we call bad. For the good and the bad are organically related to one another. We cannot preserve an open field for all business talent and economic initiative—the allegedly *good* side of capitalism—and eliminate overproduction—the *bad* side of capitalism; we cannot repudiate competition for the sake of a planned economy and at the same time accept the existing state. Here, one can achieve a genuine synthesis only by revolutionary action. It is the weakness of the reformer's ideology at this point to seek to mediate irreconcilables, just as at other points it is the incurable defect of his

Utopian half-brother, to break cultural and economic continuities. For one, all change is a slow evolutionary process upon whose lazy movement mankind floats forever forward; for the other, nothing develops but that it jumps. For Marx, however, revolution is the *political* mode by which social evolution takes place. When, where, and how, cannot be settled in advance. It is always a question of concrete specific analysis. But when it takes place the political contrast between the old and the new forms of government is stronger and sharper than between the old and the new forms of art, literature and philosophy.

4. The Dialectic of Social Psychology

We are now in a position to appreciate the profundity of Marx's social psychology. All social activity revolves around the gratification of human needs and wants. But those needs and wants are more than a schedule of biological impulses. They are social and therefore historical. We explain their character and variations in terms of the *productive* processes in which man as a member of a definite social system finds himself engaged. Production both in time and logic precedes consumption. Only late in his career does man begin with a ready made idea of what he wants. His consciousness is a slow reflection upon what he finds himself doing; only as a subsequent effect is there a reorganization of his activity. Anthropologists have shown that art production precedes art appreciation. That production usually precedes appreciation is true in other fields too. In social life,

Marx showed that production affects consumption and appreciation in three different ways. It furnishes the *objects* to be consumed; it determines the *manner* of consumption; and gives rise to *new wants* of consumption which, in turn, further other productive activities.

That production is necessary for continued consumption, in behalf of which it is undertaken, is too obvious to call for elaboration. But that production determines the manner in which human beings consume, the form and character of their wants, and often the highest reaches of their consciousness, runs counter to those social philosophies which draw a sharp distinction between man's nurture—which is social and variable—and his original nature—which is biological and constant. Marx was the first realistic sociologist to challenge this sharp disjunction without making man a purely passive agent in the social process. Whatever the drives and impulses which constitute his animal nature, man's *human* nature is revealed only in a socially determined context, in which the biological pattern functions as only one constituent element of the whole. And since the social context is historically conditioned, human nature, too, is an *historical* fact. "Hunger is hunger," writes Marx, "but the hunger that is satisfied with cooked meat eaten with knife and fork is a different kind of hunger from one that devours raw meat with the aid of hands, nails and teeth." Similarly, selfishness is selfishness, and power is power; but a selfishness and power that assert themselves in a system of commodity production, in which the legal right to prevent others from using land and machines means the material power to condemn them to poverty and death, are different kinds of selfishness and power from those which express themselves within a socialized economy, guaranteeing to all who are capable and willing to work, the right to life and subsistence.

Human nature is a complex of needs and desires. Man's productive activities, by giving rise to new needs and desires—whether it be the need for rapid locomotion unknown to our ancestors or the desire for romantic love whose vogue is comparatively recent—result in a significant development of human nature. Processes of social transformation are thus at the same time processes of psychological transformation. The dialectic principle explains how human beings, although conditioned by society, are enabled through *activity* to change both society and themselves. Intelligent social action becomes creative action. "By acting on the external world and changing it," says Marx, "man changes his own nature." (*Capital,* I, p. 198.) The normal individual, the natural individual who plays such a part in the writings of sociologists, is always a projection of the limited ideal of an historically conditioned society and of the dominant class in that society. Aristotle defined man as naturally a "political" animal (literally, a city-dwelling animal); Franklin as a "tool-making" animal. For Marx, man is all that and more. Once he acquires control of the conditions of social life, he can consciously make over his own nature in accordance with a morally free will, in contradistinction to man in the past whose nature has been unconsciously made over by the socially determined will of economic classes.

The emphasis which Marx placed upon the dialectic development of human nature and the possibilities of its growth has not prevented critics—even sympathetic ones —from charging him with a mechanical and rigid conception of its character. Almost at random I turn to a book which says:

"Karl Marx laid out a complete span of historical sequence on the basis of economic determinism in which he reckoned almost not at all with the possibilities of change in human nature." (Lindemann, *Social Discovery,* p. 46.)

One could fill pages with quotations to show how unjust such a characterization is. One single sentence suffices. Arguing against Proudhon, who, interestingly enough, seems to have come alive again in the modern petty-bourgeois socialism of public works and social planning, Marx exclaimed: "M. Proudhon does not know that the whole of history is nothing but the progressive transformation of human nature."

5. THE DIALECTIC OF PERCEPTION

Human nature does not change over night. It develops slowly out of the consciousness of new needs which, together with the limiting condition of the environment, determine new tasks and suggest new goals. But the new needs themselves do not emerge suddenly into human experience. They arise out of an attempt to gratify the old needs in a shifting environment and find conscious articulation only in the active practical process by which man both changes and adjusts himself to his environment. That is why the principle of dialectic, for Marx as for Hegel, finds expression in the active quality of individual perception and thought as well as in society and nature.

Marx did not work out his views in detail, but his criticism of Feuerbach's materialism contains suggestive hints of a dialectical theory of perception. This theory of perception was necessitated by his philosophy of history. If human beings are active in history, then, since all human activity is guided by ideas and ideals, human *thinking* must be an active historical force. That human stupidity is an historical force is a proposition which no one who has lived long can help believing sometimes. That human thought is active is a proposition which is characteristic of all philosophical idealism. But idealism is inadequate because it does not take into account the material conditions of intellectual activity, and the relation between thought and sensations. The materialists maintain that sensation depends upon something which is not thought. They swing, however, to a view which is the direct converse of the idealist error, and just as erroneous. They reduce thought to sensation; so that the ideas in a man's head are regarded as passive effects of an external world—as experiences which just happen to him in the same way that he gets electrical shocks. There is one short step from the view that consciousness is merely a product of forces acting from without, to Democritus' view that nothing exists but "atoms and

the void," to Hobbes' reduction of all psychic phenomena to "ghosts" and "apparitions," to Feuerbach's aphor-
ism, *"Der Nahrungstoff ist Gedankenstoff,"* and to
bring the variations in this record of absurdity down to
the present, to J. B. Watson's contention that there is
no such thing as consciousness at all.

After an early period of allegiance to Schelling and
Hegel, Marx threw his idealism overboard. But he
sought to save the idealist's insight that knowledge is
active. Otherwise his own historical materialism would
result in fatalism. Marx reasoned that if knowledge is
active and is organically related to sensation, sensation
itself must be something other than a passive experience out of which the world is built up by the psychological process of association and the logical process of
inference. Things are not revealed in sensation: sensations themselves arise in the course of man's activity
on things. The starting point of perception is not an
object on the one hand, and a subject opposed to it on
the other, but an *interacting process* within which sensations are just as much the resultant of the active mind
(the total organism) as the things acted upon. What is
beheld in perception, then, depends just as much upon
the perceiver as upon the antecedent cause of the perception. And since the mind meets the world with a long
historical development already behind it, what it sees,
its selective reactions, the scope and manner of its attention are to be explained, not merely as a physical or
biological fact but as a *social* fact as well. "Even objects

of the simplest 'sensory certainty' are given to man," writes Marx, "only through social development." All psychology, which is not a phase of biophysics or psycho-physics, thus becomes social psychology. For it is not perception alone, he adds, which is bound up with the practical material processes of social life, but the production of ideas and the higher forms of consciousness as well. Consciousness, therefore, is social before it is individual. And this is something which no mechanical, sensationalistic materialism can adequately explain.

"The chief defect of all previous materialism (including Feuerbach's) is that the thing—reality—sensation—has been considered only in the form of the *object* or of *direct apprehension;* and not as sensory human activity, not as practice, not subjectively. Therefore in opposition to materialism the *active* side was developed abstractly by idealism which naturally did not recognize real sensory activity as such. Feuerbach is willing to recognize sense objects which are really something other than objects of thought; but he does not conceive human activity itself as *objective* activity. . . . He therefore cannot grasp the significance of 'revolutionary,' of 'critical-practical' activity.

"The highest point to which sensationalistic materialism can reach, *i.e.,* the materialism which does not conceive sensation as practical activity, is the standpoint of the single individual and bourgeois society." (Marx-Engels, *Gesamtausgabe,* Abt. I, Bd. 5, pp. 533-535.)

6. The Future of Dialectic

A larger problem suggested by the social expression of dialectic is the question of what form the principle will take under communism. On this question a great deal of confusion prevails both in the camp of Marx's critics and in that of his friends.

The three leading principles of the Marxian doctrine are obviously historically conditioned in the sense that they hold only for class societies. Historical materialism, which explains the general character of social life in terms of the economic relations in which human beings find themselves and by which they are controlled; the theory of surplus-value, which teaches that the greater part of what the worker produces is filched from him by those who own the instruments of production; the theory of the class struggle, which maintains that all history since the downfall of early gentile society has been a struggle for state-and-social-mastery between different economic classes—these principles, of necessity, must be suspended in a collectivist society in which man makes his own social history, in which the total product of labor-power, although not returned to the individual worker, is disbursed and reinvested for the good of the commonalty, and in which economic classes have disappeared and only shifting vocational distinctions remain. Well then, what becomes of the possibility of social development under communism? What contradictions of social life provide it with driving force? Or is this the last word in human development, the idyll of the Kingdom-Come in which all evil, struggle and frustration disappear? (That is what professional critics of Marx, like Sorokin, charge Marx with believing!) What happens to dialectics? Hegel denied that it had any sway when it came to the Prussian state. When

Marx condemned him, did he mean to say, only, that Hegel should have waited for the communist society before he proclaimed the end of history?

As distinct from all other doctrines of Marx, the principle of dialectic still continues to operate in a communist society. It is not historically conditioned in the same sense as his other theories. It finds expression, however, on a more elevated plane. Although in advance no one can describe the detailed form it will take, it is clear that its general locus is individual and personal, and that whatever social change takes place, proceeds through coöperative conflict and not anti-social class struggles. The world still exists in incomplete process, and conflict ever remains at the heart of flux, but now, however, man wrestles not with the primary problems of social existence but with the more significant problems of personal development. Every social advance will create its own institutional abuses and problems, natural phenomena will still run their course indifferent to human welfare, and men will never be equally wise or beautiful. But the opportunities for the development of creative personalities will be more widespread than ever before. For it is a law of true creation that the mind flourishes best when the obstacles it has to overcome are not imposed upon it by material problems of subsistence but by the problems which arise in the course of the individual's intellectual, emotional and spiritual development.

Marx was not a utilitarian. Nowhere does he promise "happiness" in the future or fight for it in the present.

He condemns capitalism not because it makes people unhappy but because it makes them *inhuman,* deprives them of their essential dignity, degrades all their ideals by setting a cash value on them, and inflicts *meaningless* suffering. He would have approved of Nietzsche's savage thrust at Bentham: "Man does not desire happiness, only the Englishman does"; and he himself contemptuously remarks in *Capital* with an eye on the utilitarian bookkeeping of pains and pleasures that "with the dryest naïveté, Bentham takes the modern shopkeeper, especially the English shopkeeper, as the normal man."

This does not mean that Marx was opposed to human beings seeking happiness or that he denied the possibility of its existence. He felt quite rightly, however, that, of itself, utilitarianism could never serve as the basis of a fighting, revolutionary ethics. The reason is simple. Happiness arises through the gratification of needs, desires and ambition. It can therefore be attained either by increasing achievement in the way of effort or material goods, or by cutting down desire and ambition. Happiness comes, as William James somewhere says, either "by getting what we want or learning to like what we've got." There is nothing to show that honest Christians, and all other people for whom religion is an anodyne, are less happy than those who do not, "like the Camel and the Christian take their burdens kneeling." (Bierce.) But there is a great deal to show that those who are prepared to struggle for their ideals even unto death, who pit their intelligence and

strength against all remediable evils, who scorn the
cheap Philistine worldliness which will risk nothing
that endangers its fleshpots as well as the religious other-
worldliness which forsakes the most precious of all
human virtues—intelligence and courage—are noble,
even in their very defeat. Marx's own life with its ostra-
cism, grinding poverty, refusal to compromise truth and
revolutionary honor, is an illustration of what his ethical values were. He was surer that there were some
things that a human being ought to do than he was
that those things would bring pleasure and not pain.
Nowhere does Marx put this more strongly than in his
contrast between the revolutionary morality of the proletariat and the social morality of christianity:

"The social principles of Christianity preach cowardice,
self-contempt, abasement, submission, humility, . . . but the
proletariat, which will not allow itself to be treated as
canaille, regards its courage, self-confidence, independence,
and sense of personal dignity as more necessary than its
daily bread.

"The social principles of Christianity are mealy-mouthed;
those of the proletariat are revolutionary." (*Gesamtausgabe,*
Abt. I, Bd. 6, p. 278.)

In Marx as in Hegel the dialectic is, so to speak, the
philosophical rhythm of conscious life. The dialectic
method is a way of understanding this rhythm and participating in it. It expresses the tension, expansion and
growth of all development. It does not sanction the
naïve belief that a perfect society, a perfect man, will
ever be realized; but neither does it justify the opposite

error that since perfection is unattainable, it is therefore immaterial what kind of men or societies exist.

"Granted the principle of the imperfection of man, what then?" asks Marx. "We know in advance that all human institutions are incomplete. That does not take us far: that does not speak for or against them. That is not their *specific character*, their mark of differentiation." (*Gesamtausgabe*, I, 1, p. 201.)

For Marx as for Hegel cultural progress consists in transferring problems to higher and more inclusive levels. But there are always problems. "History," he says, "has no other way of answering old questions than by putting new ones." Under communism man ceases to suffer as an animal and suffers as human. He therewith moves from the plane of the pitiful to the plane of the tragic.

10

DIALECTIC AND TRUTH

ARX'S theories by his own admission are *historically* conditioned. They could have arisen only at a stage in social history where the dominant mode of production divides society, in the main, into two classes: those whose income is derived from the sale of their labor-power, and those whose income, in the form of profit, interest and rent, flows from their legal ownership of the social instruments of production. Not only are Marx's theories historically conditioned, they are also *class* conditioned in that they offer a survey of social life and a plan of social action in the interests of the international proletariat. But what does it mean to offer a survey in the interests of anything but the truth? To link truths, which are presumably general, objective and necessary, with class interests, which are limited, particular and subjective, is to create a chain of paradoxes. Marx certainly denied that economics, history and philosophy stand as impartial disciplines above the class struggle. Nor did he exclude his own theories. Speaking of his *Capital (A Critique of*

Political Economy) he says: "So far as such criticism represents a class, it can only represent the class whose function in history is the overthrow of the capitalist mode of production and the final abolition of all classes —the proletariat." His followers over the world refer to Marxism as a class theory. In what sense, then, is it an objective theory? Are its propositions relative truths dependent upon presuppositions which may legitimately be challenged from other class points of view? If so, what becomes of their objectivity?

1. OBJECTIVITY AND PRESUPPOSITION

The question of objectivity and presupposition is the most difficult one in the social sciences. Marx attempted to solve it by the use of the dialectical method. He believed that his theories were true. But what did he mean by a true theory? "The question whether human thought can arrive at objective truth is not a question of theory," he writes, "but a practical question. In practice man must prove the truth of thought." Suppose we examine, from this point of view, the traditional definition of truth against which Marx, together with Hegel, directed his shafts; *viz.,* that a true idea is one which reflects or corresponds with the external environment. In order to discover whether our ideas are true, we must act on them. In acting on them we change the external environment. The true idea, then, is one which is validated by the outcome of the interaction between our practical activity, which expresses the meaning of the idea, and the external object, which calls it forth. To be sure, in order to know how to act we must have some antecedent knowledge. But the reliability of that knowledge, again, can only be ascertained in practice. Whatever cannot be tested in action is dogma. But since, as the result of the activity of testing, some change has been introduced in the objective situation which we seek to know, the correspondence between idea and thing must be regarded as *prospective,* not retrospective.

Important consequences follow, if we bear in mind the distinction which Marx makes between the subject-matter of the physical sciences and the social and historical sciences. All human history is the result of the behavior of men in behalf of certain *ends, values* or *purposes.* Theories of history and society are themselves historical, *i.e.,* they are offered in behalf of some value or purpose which enters as an important factor in determining what information is relevant or irrelevant to the problem in hand. In so far as these theories claim to be *knowledge* they involve setting up activities in social life, *i.e.,* the introduction of those changes which are necessary for their experimental confirmation. In so far as they are offered in behalf of some purpose, they involve setting up changes in a certain *direction.* The direction in which we desire to travel determines the aspects of the existing scene to which we are attentive, the information we seek, the experiments we perform—in short, the criteria of relevance. Depending, then, upon the different ends or values in behalf of which theories have been projected, different modes of social action will be proposed. But in a class society, according to Marx, there can be no unanimity about the direction or goal which social organization should take. Different class interests express themselves in different goals.

To be sure, the possible goals that may be taken are always limited or conditioned by the state of the productive forces of society. But a choice is always possible, even if it be no more than one between the continuation of society or its destruction. The choices made by different classes are revealed in the social theories they accept. These social theories may contain a considerable amount of objective truth but from the point of view of one class the truths discovered by the other may be irrelevant. It would perhaps be more accurate to say that any social theory—the test of whose truth would involve a change in the existing property-relations or balance of class forces—will be denounced as a dangerous untruth by the class in power. That is why no true social experiment is possible in class society. As distinct from the experiment in the physical sciences, the criteria by which its success is judged will vary with the economic interests of the class which passes judgment. It is only in a metonymous sense that the Russian Revolution can be regarded as a social experiment. Those whom it swept from power, as well as their allies throughout the world, regarded the "experiment" as a failure when the first expropriatory decree was issued.

To say that knowing initiates a course of action which changes some aspect of the situation from which we set out; to say further that *social* knowledge is a guide to action in behalf of certain ends or values, and that the action becomes a factor in realizing the future state of affairs about which it professes to have the truth—all this does not imply that the causal connections which exist in the world of nature and history are created by men. This would mean subjectivism. The social laws which obtain in a capitalist economy, and the laws which obtain in a socialist economy, are not created by man; but whether the conditions are to exist, under which one or another type of law operates at certain historic moments, depends upon class will and activity. To deny this is to maintain that the laws of social life have the character of laws of nature. This expressed the pseudo-objectivism of the *laissez faire* economists, who, desiring to prevent the imposition of legal curbs upon the predatory expansion of capitalism, spoke of the laws of economics as natural necessities in order to deduce the convenient maxim that the government which interfered least was the best.

Marx's materialistic approach to problems of social development was always oriented with reference to his class allegiance and class revolutionary goal. That did not make his conclusions less objective, but it made them partial in their bearings and implications. Marx contended that all social thought, whether objective or not—especially when it became the "accepted truth" of its day—was similarly partial. On several occasions he suggests that "purely objective" descriptions of the social scene—even when they are true—have a tendency to degenerate into an apologia of the conditions they describe. This can be overcome only by inquiring into the possibility that these conditions may be changed by class activity. He was frank in his belief that every description of the social process must be completed by an evaluation. Judgments of fact as such are not judgments of value; but where the facts concern conflicts of class interests, Marx believed that no one could escape the necessity of passing a judgment of value upon them. And whoever refused to do so, from Marx's point of view, had therewith taken a position in virtue of the objective consequences of his refusal.

In an interesting passage, Lenin sharpens a distinction between the "objectivist" and the "materialist" which is quite faithful to Marx's meaning:

"The objectivist speaks of the necessity of a determinate historical process, while the materialist makes an exact investigation of the given socio-economic complex and the antagonistic relations which it produces. The objectivist, who tries to show the necessity of a determinate series of facts, continually runs the risk of degenerating to an apologist of these facts; the materialist lays bare the class oppositions upon which he proceeds to take a stand. The objectivist speaks of 'irrefragable historical tendencies'; the materialist speaks of the class which 'dominates' the given economic order and therewith calls forth determinate forms of opposition on the part of other classes. The materialist is therefore more consistent than the objectivist and manifests a deeper, completer objectivism. He does not restrict himself to indicating the bare necessity of the process but reveals what social and economic complex gives this process content, *what class* determines this necessity. . . . In addition, materialism involves a definite taking of sides in that it feels itself bound, when it evaluates events, to accept openly and clearly the standpoint of a definite social group." (Quoted by Deborin, in his article, "Lenin als Revolutionärer Dialektiker," in *Unter dem Banner des Marxismus,* Bd. I, p. 213.)

Like Marx Lenin also denied that it was possible to keep strictly neutral in analyzing the facts of class relationships and struggle. It is "the whole man" who knows. Although we must not let our values "cook" the facts—which is more easily avoided by recognizing our values than by pretending we haven't any—our values determine what facts we are looking for, and what we are going to do with them after we have found them. Arguing against those social scientists who proclaimed that it was unseemly for a student of class relationships to sympathize with one class or another, that it was his "duty" not to take sides, Lenin wrote:

"It is absurd in this connection even to speak of the duty not to take sides, for no living man, once he has understood the relationships and struggles between classes, can prevent himself from embracing the standpoint of one class or the other, exulting in its triumphs, lamenting in its defeats, becoming indignant with those who are hostile to it, and who retard its development by propagating mistaken views." (Quoted by Luppol, *Lenin und die Philosophie,* p. 144.)

Despite these passages, it would be completely misleading to speak, as some Marxists do, of *class truths.* Truth is above classes. What is meant is usually one of two things. Either that classes find it to their interest to discover or call attention to some truths and to conceal other truths; or that the real subject of discourse is *class values,* not class truths. In the first case, the truth or falsity of a proposition is utterly irrelevant to the class which discovers it; in the second, values cannot be characterized as true or false, and it is obvious nonsense to say that one value is "truer" than another when all that is meant is that a value is "more inclusive" or "intenser,"—or simply that it is *ours.*

The relationship between the class presupposition of Marxism and its claims to objective truth is sufficiently important to justify a restatement of the position from a different point of view. As a result of private owner-ship of the means of production, class struggles arise over the distribution of the social product. This strug-gle manifests itself not only on the economic field but in the realms of politics and culture as well. Each class develops ideals and programs of activity which, if acted upon, would involve loss, hardship or oppression for opposing classes. It develops a philosophy, a social and historical outlook which are congenial to its present rôle in the processes of production and to the rôle it desires to play in the future. It gathers facts and conducts analyses to justify its claims and to achieve its aims. Its doctrines cannot be impartial, for they express resolu-tions as well as descriptions, and therefore determine a course of social activity whose effects are prejudicial to one class in direct proposition as they are favorable to another.

Marxism, as the theory and practice of social revolu-tion, is the class theory of the proletariat. In this sense

it is a "partial" or "partisan" theory without ceasing to
be an objective expression of the interests of the proletariat. But whether the consequences of acting upon it
will really achieve the classless society—that can be
tested *without* further reference to class interests. Here
Marxism is either true or false. In taking note of the
conditions which must be fulfilled to achieve the classless society, in its descriptions of tendencies which render revolutionary action timelier, more likely to succeed,
etc., it again lays down propositions whose truth or
falsity is independent of class interest. For example, the
doctrine expressed in the preceding paragraph that class
conflicts give rise to conflicting ideologies is such a proposition. To accept this particular doctrine or any other
does not make one a Marxist unless one accepts the
class purposes which make these propositions relevant.

2. Is the Social Revolution "Inevitable"?

Let us test this exposition upon an important practical question—indeed, the central one of the socialist
movement, *viz.,* what does the advent of socialism depend upon? For one thing, upon the existence of large
scale, highly centralized production which is the result
of the accumulation of capital. But obviously this is only
a necessary not a sufficient condition. For the facts of
centralization and concentration in industry are recognized even by bourgeois governments, which, although
inexorably opposed to revolution have obligingly furnished the statistical figures from the days of Marx
down to the present. The existence of a class-conscious

proletariat is just as indispensable as any of the foregoing conditions. What does it, in turn, depend upon? On
the *need* and *want* produced in the course of the economic process. How much need and want? Can these
be accurately measured in any way? Certainly not. But
assuming that they can be, are they as inevitably produced, and produced in the same way, as industrial centralization and financial concentration? And does this
need, in turn, inevitably express itself in revolutionary
action? Merely to put these questions is to see the absurdity of the assumptions involved. For if these propositions were true, there would be no necessity to enunci-
ate them, no less to risk one's life for them. Certain
relatively independent factors enter into the situation.
The degree of enlightenment of the workers; what it
is that they regard as fundamental needs; "the consciousness of the class struggle and not alone its existence;" the presence of a political party which represents
the principle of revolutionary continuity from one crisis
to another—all these must be taken into account. They
are not automatic, simple functions of economic development; for as we shall see later, they are capable of
initiating, within limits, important changes in the economic order. Neither God, man nor the economic
process guarantees the final validity and certainty of
communism. Only the objective possibilities are given.
Whether they are realized is a political question. Economic development determines only the general period
in which communism is possible, not the specific time
of actual transition. "England possesses all the necessary

material conditions of social revolution," wrote Marx to Kugelmann in 1870, "what it lacks is universal outlook and revolutionary passion."

Marx counts upon need, or rather *consciousness* of need, to supply the active force in social change. But, as we have already seen, it is not biological need which determines the path and means of action. It is a social and ethical need. It is not those who are most brutalized by physical want who are the most revolutionary; but rather those who are most conscious of the disparity between the objective possibilities of material and cultural life, and what they actually realize in their experience.

"A house may be large or small, but as long as the surrounding houses are equally small, it satisfies all social requirements of a dwelling place. But let a palace arise by the side of this small house, and it shrinks from a house to a hut. The smallness of the house now indicates that its occupant is permitted to have either very few claims or none at all; and however high it may shoot up with the progress of civilization, if the neighboring palace shoots up also in the same or greater proportion, the occupant of the comparatively small house will always find himself more uncomfortable, more discontented, confined within his four walls. . . .

"Although the comforts of the laborer have risen, the social satisfaction which they give has fallen in comparison with these augmented comforts of the capitalist, which are attainable for the laborer, and in comparison with the scale of the general development society has reached. Our wants and their satisfaction have their origin in society: we therefore measure them in relation to society, and not in relation to the objects which satisfy them. Since their nature is social, it is therefore relative." (*Wage, Labour and Capital,* Kerr ed., pp. 35-36.)

The consequences we have drawn from these observations may appear commonplace. Yet the history of the Second International reveals how important commonplaces sometimes are. We are now in a position to understand what Marx really means when he speaks of the historic inevitability of communism. Communism is not something fated to be realized in the nature of things; but, *if society is to survive,* communism offers the only way out of the impasse created by the inability of capitalism, despite its superabundance of wealth, to provide a decent *social* existence for its own wage-earners. What Marx is really saying is: either *this* (communism) or *nothing* (barbarism). That is why communists feel justified in claiming that their doctrines express both the subjective class interests of the proletariat and the objective interests of civilization. The objectivity of Marxism is derived from the truth of the disjunction; the subjectivity, from the fact that *this* is chosen rather than *nothing.* Normally a recognition of the truth of the disjunction carries with it a commitment to communism. But the connection is not a *necessary* one any more than the knowledge that milk is a wholesome drink makes one a milk drinker. One might accept the economic analyses of Marx, recognize the existence of the class struggle, and apply historical materialism to the past. That does not make him a Marxist. Bourgeois thinkers have done so since Marx's day, and some even before. It is only when one accepts the first term of the disjunction—which is a psychological, and, if you please, an ethical act—that he has a right to the name.[1] The choice is intelligent only if it takes note of Marx's analyses; but once the choice is made, it *itself becomes an historical factor in making the revolutionary ideal come true.* How else can we explain why Marx's philosophy is itself an historical force in the world to-day, or understand his remark that "of all the instruments of production the greatest productive power is the revolutionary class itself?" The objective truth of Marxism realizes itself in the informed revolutionary act. Marxism is neither a science nor a myth, but a realistic method of social action.

[1] "The theory of class war was *not* created by Marx, but by the bourgeoisie *before* Marx and is for the bourgeoisie, generally speaking, *acceptable.*

"The one who *recognizes* only the class war is not yet a Marxist; that one may be found not to have freed himself from the chains of bourgeois reasoning and politics. To limit Marxist theory to the teaching of the class war means to shorten Marxism—to mutilate it, to bring it down to something which is acceptable to the bourgeoisie. A *Marxist* is one who *extends* the recognition of class war to the recognition of the *Dictatorship of the Proletariat.* In this is the main difference between a Marxist and an ordinary bourgeois. On this grindstone it is necessary to test a real understanding and recognition of Marxism." (Lenin, *The State and Revolution,* Eng. trans., Vanguard Press, 1926, p. 141.)

11

THE MATERIALISTIC CONCEPTION OF HISTORY

OF ALL Marx's theories, the materialistic conception of history has been most widely misunderstood. This is attributable not only to the ambiguity of some of its central terms, but to the fact that whereas Marx projected it as a *method* of understanding and making history, his disciples have tried to convert it into a *system* of sociology. Because of this the flexibility it possesses in the writings of Marx and Engels is sacrificed for unverifiable dogma in the works of the epigoni. Depending upon the class loyalty of the critics, the theory of historical materialism has been regarded as a commonplace, or an absurdity, or as the most powerful instrument available for investigating the origins of social thought. Marx, himself, sketched the theory only in general outline, but regarded the whole of his writings—in history, economics, and philosophy—as an exhibition of its meaning and a test of its truth.

The theory can best be expounded in terms of Marx's own intellectual development and in relation to the evolution of social and economic forces of the nineteenth century. Considerations of space, however, forbid this. For the purpose of the present analysis, it will be sufficient to state its central propositions in schematic form, discuss the criticisms and misunderstandings to which it has been subjected, point out where it has been fruitful and what problems remain to be solved. We may profitably begin by blocking the theory off from other theories with which it has been associated or identified.

1. MARX'S CONCEPTION OF HISTORY

What does Marx mean by history? For Marx, history is not everything which has happened. Many happenings, like the birth of a planet or the disappearance of an animal species, are not historical in any sense which concerns him. Nor is history the records or chronicles of social life. For these are the result of history—the materials which must first be explained and interpreted to become significant. History is a process—and it is distinguished from all other natural processes in that "it is the activity of man in pursuit of his *ends.*" (*Gesamtausgabe,* I, 3, p. 265.) The fact that human behavior is undertaken in behalf of ends or ideals distinguishes the subject-matter of history from that of physical nature. But the difference between the two is not so great that a realistic method cannot be applied to historical activity.

Although no historical activity is possible without ideals, historical *effects* cannot be explained in terms of ideals alone. For the interests and drives which move men in daily life are very diverse and conflicting. Each man reaches out to serve himself and yet each one finds himself caught up on the actions of others. The upshot of the complex interaction of individual wills is different from what each one has willed. Engels puts this very effectively in his *Feuerbach*:

"The history of social development is essentially different in one respect from that of nature. In nature—in so far as we disregard the reaction of man upon it—there exist only unconscious, blind agents which influence one another and through whose reciprocal interplay general laws assert themselves. Whatever occurs . . . does not occur as a consciously willed end. On the other hand, in social history the active agents are always endowed with consciousness, are always men working towards definite ends with thought and passion. Nothing occurs without conscious intent, without willed end. But this difference, important as it may be for historical investigation . . . does not alter the fact that the course of history obeys general laws. For here, too, on the surface, despite the consciously willed ends of individuals, chance seems to rule. Only seldom does that occur which is willed. In most cases the numerous ends which are willed conflict with or cut across one another, or they are doomed from the very outset to be unattainable, or the means to carry them out are insufficient. And so, out of the conflicts of innumerable individual wills and acts there arises in the social world a situation which is quite analogous to that in the unconscious, natural one. The ends of actions are willed; but the results, which really flow from those actions, are not willed, or, in so far as the results seem to agree with the willed ends, ultimately they turn out to be quite other than the desired consequence." (Duncker ed., p. 56.)

The crucial question, which every philosophy of history must face, is whether or not there are any factors which determine the historical resultant of the interaction of individual wills. Is it possible even without having knowledge of the content of innumerable wills to predict what will take place when, say, the density of population increases or the level of real wages falls? Or is the unexpected historical resultant—the whole record of what has happened—itself a matter of chance? There are some philosophers who have made the problem easy for themselves by denying that there is any determinate causation in history, that everything which has happened could have happened differently, that no rhyme or reason can be discovered in the direction of history save what the poets, prophets or fanatics read into it. They have pointed to the rack and ruin of past cultures, to needless blood and misery which have accompanied change from one social order to another, to the unrelieved tragedy and injustice of visiting the historical sins of one generation upon the heads of its descendants —as supplementary evidence that the surface appearance of chance is not, as Marx and Engels believe, a reflection of an inner law but is rather an expression of the stark irrationality of the historic process. The historical resultant, they say, has been determined by the interaction of many wills, and nothing else. And since these work at cross-purposes with one another, the arbitrary character of the historical pattern is explained.

There are at least three good reasons why this hypothesis of wholesale chance in history must be rejected. First, there are some events that have taken place which seem to us to have been necessitated by a whole chain of antecedent circumstances, although all the links in that chain may not be clear. No one can seriously maintain to-day that either the World War or the recent invasion of Manchuria was a chance phenomenon. To be sure, chance elements entered into them, but they were not decisive. The exact date of the World War, the type of men at the head of their respective governments, the thousand and one details with which the war burst upon the world, could never have been deduced in advance. Nonetheless the event itself, the period within which it occurred, its most important consequences, were not only determined by the conflict between the imperialist powers for world hegemony—they were actually foreseen. They were not, however, pre-determined, in the sense that they could not have been different even if antecedent conditions had been different. Had the international proletariat been both sufficiently organized and genuinely Marxist, it might have transformed the World War into an international civil war and fought its way to socialism. But the fact that the international proletariat was not prepared to do this was itself not a chance event, but followed, as we have already seen, from a whole constellation of other social forces.

Secondly, to take seriously the hypothesis that chance alone rules in history would involve the belief that anything could have happened at any time. This is the favorite assumption of all rationalist constructions which try to show that if only reason and intelligence had guided human behavior, mankind would have been spared most of its evils. If only free-trade had been introduced at the time of the crusades, they say, hundreds of years of oppression would have been avoided; if slavery had only been abolished by the Church in the early centuries of Christendom, there would have been no civil war in America in 1861; if the crowned heads of Europe had only listened to Owen, we would all be living to-day in a communist commonwealth. Now just as it is true that there are chance elements in history, so is it true that many things in the past could have turned out differently from what they did; but only within a narrow range of possibilities conditioned by an antecedent state of affairs. Booth might very well have missed when he fired at Lincoln, but it is extremely improbable that Lincoln would have been able to carry out his reconstruction policy. The Church might have remained faithful to its primitive communism even after it had entered into concubinage with the Roman Empire, but it would have been no more able to arrest the course of economic development in Europe than its condemnation of all interest as usury was able a thousand years later to prevent the rise of capitalism.

Not only are the possibilities of development of material culture limited by determinate social forces, whose character we shall examine in detail below; even the autonomous creation of the mind, the flights of fancy by which men often think they transcend the limits of space and time—art, religion and philosophy—obey an order, in addition to their own, which is imposed upon them from without. Once they come into the world, they often exhibit relatively independent careers, but they cannot come into the world at any time and at any place.

"Is the view of nature and of social relations which constitutes the basis of Greek phantasy and therefore of Greek art, possible in an age of automatic machinery, railroads, locomotives, and electrical telegraphs? Where does Vulcan come in as against Roberts & Co.; Jupiter as against the lightning rod; and Hermes as against the Credit Mobilier? All mythology masters and dominates and shapes the forces of nature in and through the imagination; hence it disappears as soon as man gains real control over the forces of nature. What becomes of the Goddess Fame side by side with Printing House Square? . . . Or from another angle, is Achilles possible side by side with powder and lead? Or the Iliad with the printing press and printing machines? Do not singing and reciting and the muses necessarily go out of existence with the appearance of the printer's bar; and do not, in consequence, the necessary prerequisites of epic poetry disappear?" (Marx, *Introduction to Critique of Political Economy,* Eng. trans., pp. 310-311.)

The third reason for not surrendering the field of history to the realm of the unknown and unknowable is that despite the enormous variation in the motives of human conduct, there are certain statistical constants which are observable in all mass behavior. Not only are life insurance companies able to reap a harvest by safe betting on the death rates of different groups of people, but all other social institutions can function only by

presupposing certain large regularities of human behavior. We build schools for children who are not yet
born and jails for people who have not yet committed
crimes. What act is more supremely personal than
suicide? Yet it is possible to tell within narrow limits
how many people will take their lives next year, and
what percentage will be men or women, Jew or Gentile,
married, single or divorced. And where the rates of
death, suicide, marriage and divorce change—and they
do, of course—it is often possible to find variations in
other social phenomena with which to correlate them.
These correlations often suggest, although they do not
necessarily involve, causal connections. What accounts
for the recurrence of these regularities? It is not even
necessary to assume as did Karl Liebknecht in his revision of Marxism,[1] that there are *"average material motives"* behind human behavior which express nothing
but economic interests. For the greater the diversity of
motives of human behavior, the more impressive is the
statistical regularity which results, and the more probable it is that if an explanation of this regularity is to
be found, it will not lie in any of the schedules of invariant psychological forces, dispositions or desires so popular among latter day sociologists.

2. Alternative Conceptions of History

So far we have shown only that there are definite
patterns in history which all philosophies of history

[1] *Studien über die Bewegungsgesetze des gesellschaftlichen Entwicklung*, p. 181.

must recognize. In terms of what principle can the succession of these patterns be explained? We must now distinguish between two generic theories of history and civilization—the idealistic and materialistic—before the differentiating character of Marx's theory can be grasped.

Idealistic theories of history explain the ordered sequence of events in terms of purpose—divine or natural—and refuse to go beyond the will or intelligence of the men who make history or of the God who controls it. Whatever order is discovered to exist, must be for them a teleological order attributable to good or bad purposes, to intelligence or stupidity. The future of civilization depends upon man's willingness and ability to purify his heart or improve his mind—as the case may be.

Supernatural idealism may be dismissed with a word. It can never explain why anything happens. It can only bestow its blessings upon an event *after* it has happened. Whether the appeal is to God's will, Plato's Form of the Good, Plotinus' One, Hegel's Absolute, Schopenhauer's Will, E. von Hartmann's Unconscious or Bergson's *élan,* it cannot predict or make intelligible a single historical occurrence. Hypostasis, rationalization, and fetishism are its intellectual techniques; quietism and the narcosis of resignation its political consequences. Every practical step it takes is at the cost of a logical contradiction. The pious man who prays, "O Lord, Thy Will be done," in a church whose steeple flaunts a lightning rod to correct that will if it absentmindedly strikes in the wrong place, expresses only more dramatically the confusion of the idealistic philosopher who proclaims that the immediate pain of the part is the ultimate good of the whole and then practically translates this sentiment into the proposition that the slavery of one class is necessary for the leisure of another.

Psychological idealisms which look to the ideas and emotions of human beings for the final causes of social and historical change are legion. An adequate discussion of them would require a separate volume. Their common defect may be briefly indicated. First, in appealing to psychological entities like ambition, sympathy, love of domination, fear or whatever it is that is taken as central in the historical process, something is being invoked which, although existent, is not easily observable. The specific mechanism by which it presumably transmits its efficacy is rarely given, so that its influence appears to be highly mysterious. When mechanisms are constructed or discovered on the basis of the biological analogy of the nervous system, a greater difficulty presents itself. These psychological attitudes which the hypothetical mechanisms make possible are either constant or variable. If they are constant, how explain the enormous variety in the social patterns out of which those attitudes—since they are never found in a pure form—are analyzed? Man may be a loving animal, a playful animal, a fighting animal. But how explain in these terms the differences in the *way* man loves (*i.e.,* the forms of the family), the *character* of his play (contrast the primitive dance and the modern cinema), and the *manner* of his contests (socialist competition and nationalist war). Assuming, now, that these psychological attitudes are variable and that they are correlated with varying social relations, the more urgent question asserts itself as to what determines this change in their character. *When, where* and *to what extent* do they flourish and become dominant? These questions cannot be explained without introducing some material conditioning factors, since, as we have seen, the variations in the motives of individual behavior are too extreme, the motives themselves—fear, love ambition, hate—too ambiguous in meaning, to warrant using any specific psychological element rather than another as the key term in explaining the character of historical effects.

If human motives are subjected to material control from without, *i.e.,* by changes in nature or economic organization, are these latter, too, of a purposive character? Do they fall into the teleological order so essential to all idealism? He would be a hardy man to assert it, for he would have to read will, feeling, and reason, which are specifically characteristic of individual men, back into the social and physical conditions out of which the life of man arises. No, we must conclude that ideas do not make history, for whether they are accepted or are not accepted depends upon something which is not an idea; that, although there can be no history without psychologically motivated behavior, the particular emotional set which asserts itself from out of the whole gamut of emotional life is selected by factors which are not psychological but social.

Materialistic philosophies of history turn away from the quest for objective meanings, spirit, and purpose in the historical process and seek for its controlling conditions in some observable aspect of the physical and social environment. Before Marx, most materialist philosophies took a physical, chemical or biological approach to cultural life. Hobbes, for example, laid down a theoretical program according to which it should be possible to deduce from the mathematical laws of motion and the positions of material particles in space and time, all political and social life. Feuerbach, that suggestive but too impressionable thinker, was so carried away by the primitive food chemistry of his day that he tried to summarize the political difference between England and Ireland as a difference between roast-beef and potatoes. This might have been a starting point for a social analysis, but Feuerbach remained stuck in his chemistry. The result was that the same man who produced the most fruitful hypothesis of the nineteenth century in the psychology of religion, offered the most ludicrous revolutionary theory ever devised by attempting to base his politics upon food-chemistry. Feuerbach actually believed that the revolution of 1848 had ended with the triumph of reaction because the poorer elements of the population had been made sluggish by their potato diet. "Potato blood (*träges Kartoffelblut*) can make no revolution!" he cried.

"Shall we then despair?" he inquires. "Is there no other food-stuff which can replace potatoes among the poorer classes and at the same time nurture them to manly vigor and disposition? Yes, there is such a food-stuff, a food-stuff which is the pledge of a better future, which contains the seed of a more thorough, even if more gradual, revolution. It is beans." (*Sämtliche Werke,* herausg. von Bolin und Jodl, Bd. X, p. 23.)

To be sure, not all chemical determinists were guilty of such excesses. But the same methodological absurdities were committed by the racialists and later by the social-Darwinists, who regarded all social life as a resultant of a biological struggle for existence.

The attempt has recently been made, especially by Ellsworth Huntington, to revive the geographical interpretation of history, already suggested by Herder and Montesquieu in the eighteenth century and more explicitly stated by Buckle in the nineteenth. It is asserted that there are certain climatic pulsations and shiftings of the climatic zone which can be correlated with the rise and fall of cultures. The nature of the evidence for these climatic changes is highly questionable. Uncontrolled extrapolations have been made from one region of the world to another—and from the present to the past. There is not the slightest ground for believing that the climate of Greece has varied in any appreciable way from the sixth century B.C. to the first A.D.—a period of tremendous social change. And even where periods of extreme climatic stress have been observed, as in the great floods and cold of the fourteenth century, no plausible connection has been established between these facts of climate and the profound subsequent changes in European material and ideal culture. Sometimes the effects attributed to natural forces are really the effects of social factors. For example, the devastation produced by periodic floods in China is not always the result of uncontrollable natural disasters but is due to the fact that the Chinese war lords divert to military purposes the tax money raised to keep the elaborate system of dikes and canals in repair.

There is no climate that cannot support different cultures; while similar cultures often flourish in different climates. The same arguments apply to the racial interpretation of history, especially where differences between the races are explained by differences in the climate and the selective effect it has had upon man. Were the wildest claims concerning the correlation of climate and cultural change to be accepted, still, in the absence of any knowledge of the specific ways in which climate affects creative impulses, we should have to look for more relevant social causes to explain the rise and fall of ideas.

The chief defect of all these materialistic philosophies is the attempt to reduce the social to merely a complicated effect of the non-social, and the consequent failure to observe that new types of relations arise in the associated behavior of men which are irreducibly distinctive. In addition to the fundamental objection that the reduction of the specific qualities and laws of social behavior to categories of physics and biology is not intelligible, the evidence points to the fact that in any given area these physical and biological factors are relatively constant while social life shows conspicuous variations. So much even Hegel, the idealist, had pointed out. Marxists admit that climate, topography, soil and race are genuine *conditioning* factors of social and historical activity; they deny that they *determine* the general character of a culture or its historical development. They claim that a truly historical philosophy must do greater justice to the activity of man upon all phases of cultural life than is provided for in the theories of the physical and biological determinists. Engels writes in his *Dialektik und Natur:*

"Natural science as well as philosophy has completely neglected the influence of the activity of man upon his thinking. They know only nature on one side, thought on the other. But it is precisely the *changes in nature brought about through men,* and not nature as such alone, which is the most essential and primary foundation of human thought. In proportion to the extent to which man learned to change nature, his intelligence developed. The naturalistic conception of history, found, *e.g.,* more or less in Draper and other natural scientists according to which it is nature which exclusively acts upon man, and natural conditions which exclusively determine his historical development, is therefore onesided. It forgets that man can react upon nature, change it, and create new conditions of existence. Of the "natural conditions" of Germany as they existed when the German tribes came in, mighty little has remained. The surface of the soil, climate, vegetation, fauna, man himself have gone through infinite changes, and all in virtue of human activity. On the other hand, the changes that have taken place in the natural aspects of Germany in which human beings had no hand, is incalculably small." (*Marx-Engels Archiv,* Bd. II, p. 165.)

3. The Theory of Historical Materialism

In the remainder of this chapter we shall state briefly the central propositions of the theory of historical materialism, following Marx as closely as possible and leaving difficulties and problems for the succeeding chapters. We shall begin the exposition by stating Marx's theory of social organization and then go on to his theory of social development. They constitute respectively the (*A*) static and (*B*) dynamic phases of historical materialism.

A—1. Every society for Marx is a structurally interrelated cultural whole. Consequently no material or ideal aspect of that whole, whether it be its legal code, methods of manufacture, educational practices, religion or art, can be understood as an isolated phenomenon. It must be taken in relation to the way in which the system functions as a whole. Traditional elements may exist within it but they have been readapted to harmonize with the dominant patterns of thought and action. For example, Christianity in America is a traditional religion, but the specific character it exhibits to-day as distinct from the past, and in America as distinct from, say, Bavaria, is a reflection of the American frontier life with its alternations between drab experience and emotional release, American exhibitionism, philosophical optimism, go-getting tactics in business, etc. These in turn reflect the influence of American religion. But although cultural elements exist in some functional connection, they are not so organically related with one another that a change in one produces a change in all at the same time or to the same degree. Even in such a highly organized system as the human organism—though the whole organism is involved in the functioning of any of its parts—a change in some of the organs will not produce an immediate effect upon others and may leave still others comparatively unaffected. Similarly, no one can seriously contend that the latest refinements in philosophical logic must necessarily affect fashions in women's dresses. Nonetheless important changes in fashions of dress and fashions of ideas reveal not only a development peculiar to their own fields, but changes outside of them. When women took to wearing breeches and abandoning corsets in the twentieth century and philosophers stressed race or national ideas in rewriting their histories, it was not because of any immanent logic within the fields of fashion or philosophy, but rather because of the impact of certain social and political forces from without. Or even more obviously, looking at the legal systems of Rome, the medieval church and twentieth century Europe, we can see that, despite the similarity of some of the concepts, these systems did not grow out of one another, but out of deep social changes. A significant history of law—or even an analysis of law—then, would have to include an account of the social and cultural changes which found expression in formal and legal concepts. A knowledge of only the logical interpretation of these concepts would tell us more about logic than about law. Interestingly enough, the starting point of the development of Marx's theory was the philosophy of law. In sketching his own intellectual history, he tells us that even earlier than 1844, in the course of a criticism of Hegel's philosophy of law, he had become convinced "that legal relations as well as the forms of the state could neither be understood by themselves nor explained by the so-called progress of the human mind, but that they are rooted in the material relations of life."

What is true for one phase of ideal culture is true for all. And if true for all, we can understand Marx's paradoxical remark that, from his point of view, there is no history of ideas *as such,* but only a history of societies. That is to say, just as it is possible to regard the thoughts of an individual as events in his life—the proper history of their succession involving, therefore, his biography—so the rise and fall of leading ideas (their truth is another question) may be regarded as social events to be properly grasped only as part of world history. This was Hegel's great empirical insight, overstated and obscured by a too inclusive organic determinism, but corrected and developed by Marx. To what extent this is compatible with pluralism will be considered in the succeeding chapter.

2. Within any civilization law exercises an influence upon education, education upon religion, religion upon economic organization, economic organization upon politics, and vice versa. This is apparent to all but those who would build life out of one block. But to recognize that the cultural process is one of multiple reaction and interaction does not help us understand why the general

character of one civilization is distinct from another, or in what direction a particular civilization has developed and will develop. To stop at the recognition of the complexity of the factors involved is eclecticism. Neither Hegel nor Marx was an eclectic. Both sought for a key which, allowing for the reciprocal influences of the parts of a culture upon each other, would provide a general explanation of the whole process. Hegel maintained that "political history, forms of government, art, religion and philosophy—one and all have the same common root—the spirit of the time." (*History of Philosophy,* Vol. I.) We have already seen that this is theology. Whether it has any meaning or not, its truth cannot be tested.

According to Marx's hypothesis it is the material "relations of production" (*Produktionsverhältnisse*) which condition the general character of cultural life. "The sum total of these relations of production constitutes the economic structure of society—the real foundations, on which rise legal and political superstructures and to which correspond definite forms of social consciousness." The economic structure of society, the *Produktionsverhältnisse,* includes, but cannot be identified with, the forces of production (*Produktivkräfte*) such as technology, existing skills, both physical and mental, inherited traditions and ideologies; nor is it the same as the conditions of production (*Produktionsbedingungen*) such as the natural supply of raw material, climate, race, population. The "relations of production" express the way in which productive forces and productive conditions are organized by the social activity of man. They constitute the mode of economic production. Property relations are their legal expression. For Marx it is the relations of production, not the forces of production and not the conditions of production, which are the basis of the cultural superstructure. Later we shall see how important these distinctions are. At any rate it should be clear that it is only the *relations* of production that can properly be described as feudal or bourgeois. We cannot speak of feudal or bourgeois forces and conditions of production except in a metonymous sense.

3. Relations of production are indispensable if processes of production are to continue. The only question which can be intelligently asked about them is whether any given set of relations is still compatible with the continuance of production. Whatever set of relations exists is independent of the will of those who participate in production. A man finds himself an employer or employee, a feudal lord or serf, a slave or a slave holder. Some few individuals may succeed in changing their status, but no class as a whole can do so without revolutionizing the existing system of social relations. Such a revolution cannot be undertaken at any time, nor if undertaken, succeed, save under certain determinate conditions, all of which are necessary for victory but no one of which is sufficient. Since a class is defined by the objective rôle it plays in the organization of production, the sources of the antagonism between classes flows not from the consciousness (or lack of it) of individual members of the class but from the divi-

sion of the fruits of production. To insure the system of division against discontent, to facilitate a greater appropriation of the product, the property relations which are the formal expression of the relations of production must be backed up by extra-economic power. The state is the institution and instrument through which the legal relations receive their moral and physical sanctions. No class can dominate production unless it controls the state. All political life and history, then, since it revolves around struggle for the mastery of the state power, is to be explained in terms of the class conflicts generated in the process of production.

4. The division of society into classes gives rise to different ways of looking at the world. This is in part determined by the character of the actual work done, but even more so by the desire to preserve the existing order or to transform it. The political, ethical, religious, and philosophical systems—no matter how high their summits tower—are reared on values that may be universal in form but never in fact. Analysis reveals that they all turn out to be relevant to the struggle for social power, even when they profess not to be concerned with it. A struggle for survival and domination goes on between ideas no less than between classes. Since those who control the means of production also control, directly or indirectly, the means of publication—the church, press, school, cinema, radio—the prevailing ideology always tends to consolidate the power and strengthen the authority of the dominant class. "In every epoch," wrote Marx, "the ruling ideas have been the

ideas of the ruling class." It does not follow that ideological indoctrination is always deliberate or that those who embrace a doctrine can themselves distinguish between what is true in their belief and what is merely helpful in achieving their political purposes. In every system the deepest and most pervasive kinds of cultural conditioning are never the results of a mechanical inculcation. In the course of his life-career the individual imbibes the values and attitudes which are accepted as natural by those who surround him. A system of checks and approvals controls conduct at every step—not only on those rare occasions when an individual rises from one social level to another but even within his own class. The tone and model of behavior, the very objects of ambition, are set by those who wield power or who serve those that wield it. In every age the prevalent conception of the "ideal man" summarizes the virtues and celebrates the status of the ruling group. Aristotle's "magnanimous man," Castiglione's "courtier," the medieval "fighting monk," the English "gentleman," the early American "log-cabin president," and the late American "captain of industry," inspired a pattern of feeling and action among the ruled as well as the rulers.

B—1. We now turn to the dynamic phase of the social process. If this is the way a culture is organized, how does it come about that it changes? In every social system a continuous change goes on in the material forces of production. In early societies, where production is primitive, these changes are often produced by natural phenomena such as the desiccation of rivers or the exhaustion of soil. Usually, however, and more particularly under capitalism, this change takes place in the development of the instruments of production. At a certain point in the course of their development the changed relations in the forces of production come into conflict with existing property relations. At what point? At a point when it no longer becomes possible on the basis of the existing distribution of income to permit the available productive processes to function to full capacity; when the great masses of human beings, out of whose labor all social value and capital have come, cannot be sustained by their own institutional handiwork. It then becomes recognized that "from forms of development of the forces of production the relations of production turn into their fetters."

2. The class that stands to gain by modifying the relations of production becomes revolutionary in order to permit the forces of production to expand. It asserts itself as a political force and develops a revolutionary ideology to aid in its struggles for state power. Sometimes it masks its class interests in the guise of slogans of universal appeal as did the French bourgeoisie in the eighteenth century when it declared for freedom from all oppression but fought only for the freedom to buy cheap and sell dear; sometimes it dresses itself up in the borrowed robes of antiquity or echoes the prophets, or, like Cromwell's men, marches into battle to the song of hymns; but at all times, its doctrines are patterns of social action which function instrumentally

137

to rally a frontal attack against the enemy, or by insidious criticism operate to undermine his morale. A class is not always critically conscious of what it really is fighting for. It is the shock and consequence of the struggle which brings it to self-consciousness. Strictly speaking it is only in the absence of self-consciousness that a set of ideas becomes an ideology.

". . . the distinction should always be made," writes Marx, "between the material transformation of the economic conditions of production which can be determined with the precision of natural science and the legal, political, religious, esthetic, or philosophic—in short, ideological forms in which men become conscious of this conflict and fight it out. Just as our opinion of an individual is not based on what he thinks of himself, so can we not judge of such a period of transformation by its own consciousness."

The most important task of historical materialism is to criticize cultural and social doctrines in order to lay bare their social roots and presuppositions, to expose the contradiction between their avowed program and their class allegiance, and to discover the social incidence which practical activity in their behalf will probably take.

3. Viewed in the light of contemporary experience, all history since the disappearance of primitive communism may be regarded as a history of class struggle. A class, it will be remembered, is any group of people which plays a definite rôle in production. This is not to say that all history is *nothing but* class struggles. As we shall see later, it only asserts that no other form of

human association, whether it be of struggle or of co-operation, can be intelligibly regarded as the moving agent of social change. Every class struggle is at the same time a political struggle, for the state is never really neutral in class conflict, and a class struggle carried to successful completion is directed towards the overthrow of the existing state. Every ideal struggle, in so far as it bears in any way upon the class struggle, has political repercussions, and may be evaluated from a political point of view without prejudice to its own specific categories.

4. The struggle between the capitalist and proletarian classes represents the last historic form of social opposition, for in that struggle it is no longer a question of which class should enjoy ownership of the social functions of production but of the existence of private ownership as such. The abolition of private ownership in the means of production spells the abolition of all classes. This can be accomplished only by the revolutionary dictatorship of the proletariat. Political power is to be consolidated by the proletarian state during a transitional period in which the last vestiges of anti-social activity will be rooted out. When this is accomplished the proletarian state, to use Engels' phrase, "withers away," *i.e.,* its repressive functions disappear and its administrative functions become part and parcel of the productive process of a society in which "the free development of all is the condition for the free development of each."

This in bare outline is what historical materialism means. In the next chapter we shall dissociate it from what it is often interpreted to mean, and then proceed to a discussion of its validity.

12

WHAT HISTORICAL MATERIALISM IS NOT

$\mathbb{S}$O WIDESPREAD are
the current misinterpretations of historical materialism
that a chapter is necessary to show how they arise from
a one-sided emphasis upon different phases of the doctrine. Such a discussion will also contribute to making
the fundamental concepts of the theory more precise.

1. TECHNIQUE AND ECONOMICS

The commonest misinterpretation of historical materialism, and one shared by many who regard themselves
as Marxists, is the identification of the social relations of
production with the technical forces of production, and
the consequent transformation of the materialistic interpretation of history into the technological interpretation
of history. According to the technological interpretation
of history, all social life depends upon the nature of the
tools employed in production and upon the technical
organization of their use in mines, fields and factory.
The hoe and the rake, the pick and the shovel, will
produce one society; the steam plow and tractor, the

pneumatic hammer and the steam derrick another. The difference between the tenth century and the twentieth may be expressed as the difference between the individual hand-tool and the standardized machine-tool. All other cultural differences are derivative from this central fact.

Marx often said that the development of technology could serve as an index of the development of society; but that is an altogether different thing from saying that we must look to the development of technology as the cause or independent variable of social change.[1] For Marx, technique was only *one* of three generic components of the productive process. The other two were nature and the social activity of man. When he speaks of the economic foundations of society, he means the whole complex of relationships which arise from the specific ways in which these three elements are organized. Machinery as such, he reminds Proudhon, "is no more an economic category than is the ox which draws the plow. It is only a productive force."

The social relations of production (which are synonymous with the expressions "the property relations," and "the economic foundations of culture") cannot therefore

---

[1] This fundamental error runs through and vitiates the essential portions of Bukharin's *Historical Materialism*. A representative example of his analysis is the statement on p. 143 (Eng. trans.) that "the combinations of the instruments of labor (the social technology) are the deciding factor in the combinations and relations of men, *i.e.*, in social economy." Marx proved in *Capital* that just the converse of this was true. Bukharin's position is closer to that of the mechanical materialists of the eighteenth century than it is to dialectical materialism.

be regarded as the automatic reflection of technology. On the contrary, the development of technology is itself often dependent upon the system of social relationships in which it is found. The direction that technical invention takes is determined by needs which are not themselves narrowly technical but economic or social. Indeed, the important question as to whether any specific invention is to be utilized or scrapped is normally decided not by the inventor or by the logic of his creation but by its compatibility with the underlying rationale of production. To-day, for example, the decisive consideration is whether or not it will contribute to diminishing production costs and to increasing profits. This does not mean that whenever a social need exists, some invention will arise to fulfill it. Think of all the many crying needs of industrial and social life which still remain unfulfilled. Nor does it mean that whatever technical invention does arise is always directed towards realizing some improvement in production, for thousands of ingenious devices have come from the mind of man which have had no bearing upon production or have been permitted to lie unused. What is asserted is only that the *selective application* of technical invention is determined by the existing relations of production and not vice versa. The primitive technology of antiquity was in large part due to the character of a slave economy which found it easier to use human beings as machines than to make more efficient their labor. This was indirectly reflected in the attitude which prevailed among the leisured classes, who possessed a monopoly

143

of the science of the day, that it was degrading (slave-like) to apply theoretical knowledge to material and practical subject-matter. Whenever, as under capitalism, the continuous improvement of all technical forces leads ultimately to the paralysis of the productive process, the cause is to be sought not in the *forces* of production but in the *relations* of production (the property system) which, by their very nature are compelled to call into being those productive agencies that turn out to be its own nemesis. It is not technology—or what soft and romantic thinkers call the "curse of the machine"— which causes the downfall of capitalism. In a larger sense, capitalism is the source of its own downfall. It comes into the world bearing the seeds of death at its heart. The logic of its growth compels it to develop its productive limbs to a point where it can no longer co-ordinate its movements. Or more concretely, it is compelled to reinvest capital to produce further means of production without being able to guarantee the consumption of the commodities produced.

Not only does the character of technology and the direction of its development depend upon the social relation of production; it is even more obvious that the *social consequences* of technological invention can never be deduced from technological considerations alone. Otherwise how account for the fact that mechanical inventions, far from lightening the toil of the masses, freeing them from age-long burdens of drudgery, and opening opportunities for creative leisure, have instead intensified labor and reduced the worker "to an appendage of the machine." The only promise of leisure the progressive mechanization of industry holds out to the modern wage-worker to-day is the enforced leisure to starve.

One of the most interesting claims made for the technological interpretation is that it accounts for the final elimination of chattel slavery from Western Europe in the twelfth century. The reputed causal change in technique was a simple one. Until that time, cattle had been yoked by the neck (*traction par la gorge*) which winded them easily and made possible an average load of only half a ton even for relatively short distances. Production was necessarily limited, hardly more than enough to feed the families of both master and slave. Someone discovered, however, that yoking cattle by the shoulders (*collier d'épaules*) increased their pulling strength many times over and did not exhaust them so easily. As a result, productivity increased and man was able to provide his master with sufficient supplies in approximately half the working time that had been previously consumed. He now cultivated the rest of his patch in the remaining time and enjoyed a higher standard of living as a serf than had been possible to him as a slave.

The difficulties with this specific application of the technological theory are typical of all others. First of all feudalism was a full-grown system of production long before the twelfth century. Secondly, there is no assurance that yoking cattle by the shoulders was unknown in slave-holding antiquity and in parts of Asia.

Thirdly, and most important, it is hard to see how the whole system of land tenure, with its specific codes of mutual obligations and services, could be derived from the shift from one method of yoking to another. Finally, it is not clear why the enhanced productivity of labor could not have been retained within a slave economy; for there was always the possibility of using slave labor on huge public works as had been done in Egypt and Greece, and of equipping armies for the purpose of conquest and pillage. The decline of slavery must be sought elsewhere than in the gradual improvement of productive technique.

For further evidence that technique of itself does not determine the mode of economic production, one need but point to the use of large-scale machinery in such different economies as prevail to-day in the U.S.A. and the U.S.S.R.

A technological interpretation of history which separated technique from antecedent social need in search for a measurable *first* cause of social change, would have to surrender its materialistic starting point just as soon as the simplified logic of that procedure were pressed against it. For no technical change is made without a leading *idea* in the mind of the technician or inventor. Even if it be true that no great invention has ever been the sole creation of one mind, nevertheless the machine is projected in thought before it is embodied in stone and steel. The cause then would be some bright idea or happy thought in the mind of one or more persons, and we would be back to a thoroughgoing idealistic philosophy of civilization.

2. ECONOMIC CONDITIONS AND ECONOMIC SELF-INTEREST

Perhaps the most unjustified of all misinterpretations to which Marx's doctrine of historical materialism has been subjected is its reduction to a theory of personal motives. According to this conception Marx believed that all human beings are activated by a desire to further their own personal self-interest, and that this self-interest is inevitably expressed in a desire for economic gain. The materialistic interpretation then means that all behavior is guided by material consideration, that every act has a cash value and every man has his price. Ideal motives—esthetic, religious, moral—are just rationalizations of economic drives.

The amazing thing about this interpretation is that it cannot support itself by a single text from any chapter of Marx or from the open book of his own life. Yet it is found in high academic places. It arises in part from an ambiguity in the term "materialistic" and from the resultant confusion between ethical materialism and historical materialism. Ethical materialism is *egoism;* it assumes that the object of every desire is the attainment of pleasure or the avoidance of pain; and that the life of reason is an organization of natural impulses to secure for *oneself* the maximum amount of pleasure over pain. Historical materialism, however, is a theory which tries to explain when, where and why egoistic and non-egoistic motives arise. Marx was the first one to denounce the cheap cynicism which denies the *sincerity* of ideal behavior whether it be sacrifice for one's cause, religious piety, patriotic fervor or disinterested attachment to truth and beauty—a cynicism which cloaks itself in the sophisticated doctrine that all the large interests which sway individuals are constructed out of petty interests. Only a petty person generalizing from his own case could project such a theory. Already as a young man Marx had maintained that, even if it were true that the object of every desire fulfilled some interest of the self, it by no means followed that the interest was a selfish, no less a pecuniary one:

"It is known that a certain psychology explains greatness out of a multitude of small causes in the correct intuition that everything for which man struggles is a matter [*Sache*] of his interest. But from that it goes on to the mistaken notion that there are only 'small' interests, interests only of stereotyped selfishness. It is also well known that this kind of psychology and human science [*Menschenkunde*] flourishes particularly in cities where, in addition, it is regarded as a sign of subtle intellect to see through the show of the world, and to glimpse behind the cloud of ideas and facts completely petty, envious, intriguing mannikins stringing the whole of things on their little threads. But it is well known that when one peers too closely into a mirror *one bangs against one's own head*. The knowledge of the world and the knowledge of men of these clever people is primarily a mystifying bang into their own heads." (*Werke*, I, 1, pp. 218-219.)

Marx attacked both Bentham and Stirner precisely because they conceived man on the pattern of an egoistic and self-centered petty bourgeois shopkeeper who keeps a profit and loss account of his feelings and whose every act is determined by calculation of the possibilities of personal gain. It is not commonly known that Marx answered Max Stirner's *Das Einzige und sein Eigentum* —the most extreme gospel of super-sophisticated worldliness ever penned—with a work which was even lengthier than Stirner's own. In it he shows that the common defect of Stirner's glorious pseudo-paganism and of the sentimental Christian morality of Feuerbach (and Hess) to which it was opposed, is a disregard of the social and historic context of all ideals. He charges them—one, for his "I, me, myself," the other, for his "Love your neighbor, for you are your neighbor and he is you,"—with committing the same religious hypostasis in the field of morality which they had both accused the metaphysicians of committing in the realm of knowledge.

For Marx, the motives which guide individual man are quite various. And it is only the rare individual who knows what his motives really are. But Marx is not in the least concerned with the motives of *individuals* as such except in so far as they typify a class attitude. His problem is to explain why certain ideals prevail at one period rather than at another; and to discover what factors determine the succession of ideals for which men live and die. His hypothesis is that economic conditions (in the wide sense indicated above) determine which ideals are to flourish; and that the locus of all effective ideals is the class struggle. It thus becomes easy to show that economic conditions cannot be identified with economic self-interests, for the prevalence or absence of the latter is explained in terms of the former. In any given society, economic interests, as motives of conduct, will be much weaker among those classes which need pay little attention to economic processes, than among those classes which do not enjoy the same measure of economic security. The careless lavishness of the American captain of industry does not prove that he is inherently more unselfish than his tight-fisted Yankee ancestors. It merely reflects the difference between early commercial capitalism, in which thrift was a virtue because of the part it played in production, and late finance capitalism, in which conspicuous waste has the same function.

3. Is Marxism a Monistic System?

The most unfortunate characterization that historical materialism has received—and this at the hands of its followers—is the "monistic conception of history." Monism is a highly ambiguous term. It may mean that the stuff of history, that is, *what* must be explained, consists only of actions of one kind. Marxian monism would mean that history is nothing but economic activity—the most monstrous distortion ever fathered upon a critical thinker. Or historical monism may mean that only one kind of *explanation* is valid and that all historical events can be explained in economic or social terms. Some "Marxists" believe this, but Marx never did. Or finally, it may mean that there is a *continuity* between the phases of historical life and that no branch of culture, be it ever so abstract, is heaven born; that all the arts and sciences have arisen from the stream of social life and that they bear the marks of their origin irrespective of their subsequent development. But this is a tautology, for it is involved in the very meaning of the historical approach. If anything cannot be *historically* approached, *i.e.,* studied in the light of its continuities, it simply is not part of history. The question whether anything exists in the external or internal world which is not a part of history is a question of metaphysical analysis and is outside the province of the historian. If everything is historical, it is clear that several senses of the term must be distinguished.

Marx's concrete historical analyses show better than any exegesis possibly can what he conceived his method to be. He introduces the mode of economic production as the fundamental conditioning factor of only the general and most pervasive characters of a culture. He does not overlook what is specific and unique to each country and to each of its historical situations. Tradition, accident of personality, consideration of the formal possibilities of development, all enter as important variations upon the fundamental *Grundton* of economic production. In the hands of his uncritical "monistic" followers, his method has often led to the attempt to explain *specific* cultural facts or historical events in terms of *general* economic conditions whose existence is often just as compatible with the absence of what is to be explained as with its presence. It is obvious that the explanation, for example, of any specific form or expression of contemporary American culture, *e.g.,* its contemporary religion, science, law, or popular music, cannot be adequate unless it contains more than a treatment of the economic conditioning circumstances. For at any given time the mode of economic production would be invariant for all aspects of culture, and unless other traditional or formal factors were brought into the situation, we could not distinguish between the specific effect which economic organization has on American religion and the specific effect it has on American law or American science. It should not be overlooked that the difference between American law and American science may be considered as a difference between two aspects of one underlying economy. But that is not the only difference between them. There is a *formal* difference between jural relationships and scientific propositions which cannot be reduced to anything else but which must be regarded as defining autonomous domains with logical relationships uniquely their own. This is not denying that legal and scientific activities arise out of the social processes and reflect every important change in many other domains—especially in the relation of production. But it calls emphatic attention to the fact that (*a*) each field reflects such basic social changes in its own characteristic way; (*b*) each field has a limited independent development of its own which must be explained in terms of its own technique, *e.g.,* in law, by the necessity of establishing a logically coherent body of rules; in science, by the necessity of accounting for all known phenomena on the basis of the simplest set of verifiable assumptions; in art, by the necessity of exhibiting some psychological pattern which unifies all details; and finally (c) the autonomous development within these fields under certain circumstances set up important counter-effects in the social process as a whole and in economic life particularly. Illustrations of this last abound on all sides. Herz's discovery of electro-magnetic waves was the direct consequence of the quest for experimental confirmation of Maxwell's equations; its profound influence upon cultural life and especially upon economic activity, by making wireless telegraphy and the radio possible, is as incalculable as it is indisputable. In law many rules of procedure adopted to facilitate the disposition of cases, *e.g.,* in bankruptcy, have become responsible for the increase of those very practices they had set out to correct.

There is a formal element in all cultural activity to whose existence Engels in later life felt it necessary to direct the attention of his followers:

"Just as soon as the new division of labor makes necessary the creation of *professional jurists,* another new independent domain is opened which for all its dependence upon production and trade in general still possesses a special capacity to react upon these fields. In a modern state, law must not only correspond to the general economic situation and be its expression; it must also be a *coherently unified expression* and free from glaring internal inconsistencies. In order to achieve this, the fidelity with which the law directly reflects economic conditions becomes less and less.

This is all the truer in those rare cases where the legal code expresses the harsh, unrelieved and naked fact of class rule." (From his Letter to Schmidt. Cf. Appendix.) ". . . one point . . . which Marx and I did not sufficiently stress and in relation to which we are equally to blame. We both placed and *had to place* the chief weight upon the *derivation* of political, legal and other ideological notions, as well as the actions they led up to, from fundamental economic facts. In consequence we neglected the formal side, *i.e.,* the way in which these ideas arose, for the sake of the content. . . . It's the old story. In the beginning the form is always neglected for the content." (From a Letter to Mehring. Cf. Appendix.)

In addition to the formal elements of culture, there are traditional elements. In stressing the preponderant influences of the mode of economic production upon the general character of social life, Marx never failed to indicate that in every particular case tradition played an important part in modifying the rate of change in the non-material aspects of culture. "The tradition of all dead generations," he writes in the *Eighteenth Brumaire,* "weighs like a nightmare on the brain of the living." Sooner or later family relationships, religion, art and philosophy will reflect the new social equilibrium produced by changes in the economic order. But at any given time an analysis of their nature will reveal a lag both in the way they function and in the structure of their organization. This is another way of saying that no culture is organic through and through. From the vantage point of a long-time perspective, the phenomena of cultural lag may not appear significant; but from the point of view of short-scale political operations, they are of great importance. To disregard, say, the peculiar character of local and sectional religious traditions in the United States may spell disaster even for such enterprises as organizing trade unions or successfully conducting a strike.

Tradition, of course, is never of itself a sufficient explanation for the existence or survival of any cultural trait, otherwise we could not explain why some traditional influences and practices have survived while others have not. It may even be granted that any cultural practice or belief which common usage uncritically refers to as traditional, *e.g.,* the wearing of marriage rings, or the prevalence of Platonic and Hegelian idealism, has some functional relation to the contemporary process of social life. Nonetheless all cultural traits have their traditional aspect. An adequate social analysis must reveal these features and show how what they are at any moment is the resultant of what they once were and of the changes produced by a changing social environment. For example, the revival of the Platonic and Hegelian philosophies in Western Europe and their contemporary vogue may be partially accounted for by the easy formulae they supply to cover up the great social problems generated by imperialist expansion and war. The perfect state as one in which all classes collaborate under the rule of the intellectually elite, the perfect society as a *Schicksalsgemeinschaft* of capital,

155

labor and state officials [2]—what could be more in consonance with the corporative ideology of Fascism by which finance capital denies the existence of a class struggle in order to make its own class rule more secure? Nonetheless, the fact that it was the Hegelian and Platonic philosophies which were revived and not others sufficiently similar in type to serve the same social functions, demands an explanation in the light of academic and religious traditions as well as of certain standing philosophical problems. That these traditions and problems in their original form in some way reflected their contemporary economic and political milieu, does not alter the hopeless logical confusion which results from regarding the *original* cause of a tradition to be also the cause of the survival of that tradition. This fallacy vitiates the work not only of men, like Eleutheropoulos, who have clung to a simplistic economic approach, but also of their Marxist critics, men like Kautsky and Plechanov. Plechanov, we may note in passing, did most to give currency to the phrase, "the monistic conception of history."

The source of the monistic fallacy in its refined form is the attempt to explain all specific cultural phenomena in terms of factors which are admitted to be plural but among which one—the economic—is always assumed to be predominant. Let us take some illustrations from Plechanov's own writings:

[2] For an unwitting confession of the real secret of the Hegel Renaissance in Germany, especially the Hegelian philosophy of law, see Binder, J., *Archiv für Rechts-und-Wirtschaftsphilosophie*, Bd. XXII, 1929, p. 313.

"If we want to understand a dance performed by Australian Aborigines, it suffices that we should know what part is played by the women of the tribe in collecting the roots of wild plants. But a knowledge of the economic life of France in the eighteenth century will not explain to us the origin of the minuet. In the latter case we have to do with a dance which is an expression of the psychology of a non-productive class. . . . We must not forget, however, that the appearance of non-productive classes in a society is itself the outcome of the economic development of that society. This means that the economic factor remains *predominant,* even when its activity is overlaid by that of other factors." (*Fundamental Problems of Marxism,* p. 61, Eng. trans. Italics mine.)

"If you try to give a direct economic explanation of the appearance of the school of David in French painting at the close of the eighteenth century, you will certainly talk non-sense. But if, on the other hand, you regard this school as an ideological reflection of the class struggle which was going on in French society, on the eve of the great revolution, the problem will assume an entirely new aspect. Then certain qualities of David's art which might have seemed to have no connection with social economy, will become perfectly comprehensible." (*Ibid.,* p. 63.)

Now these highly selected illustrations are obviously quite favorable to the Marxian point of view which Plechanov is defending. In challenging Plechanov's explanation we are not calling Marx's method into question but Plechanov's application of it. How valid are his explanations?

Suppose we begin with the minuet. The minuet as well as the gavotte, generally associated with it, was originally a peasant dance. It antedated not only the court of Louis XV but even of Louis XIV. As a rustic dance it was gay and lively; as a court dance it was stately and artificial. Consequently it is not its origin which can be explained in terms of the psychology of the non-productive class but at best its peculiar development. But now, what necessary connection exists between the psychology of a non-productive class and the mincing gravity of the minuet? The gavotte was a little more animated and was tacked right on to the minuet. Could not a debonair and tripping step convey the psychology of a non-productive class just as well as the minuet? Indeed, cannot one say that wild and licentious dances could just as readily have expressed the psychology of a non-productive class in the eighteenth century? And if these dances had been in vogue, the same formula could easily be invoked to explain their existence. No matter what dances had been performed, it would be easy to attribute their character to the fact that the dancers were not directly concerned with production. The class psychologies of non-productive classes are not all the same. Why was *this* particular dance associated with *this* particular non-productive class? And why could not the minuet have expressed the psychology of a productive class? As a matter of fact, there is evidence to show that the minuet was a national dance and not merely a court dance, and that its local variations were just as pronounced as the difference between its original rustic form and later court development. Further, how are we to explain, on Plechanov's theory, the rapid spread of the minuet through all of Western Europe among productive and non-productive classes alike? How are we to explain in terms of the psychology of a non-productive class the fact that Beethoven developed the minuet into the scherzo? But Plechanov's crowning error is to reason that because the minuet was the outcome of the psychology of a non-productive class, and because the appearance of a non-productive class was itself the result of economic development, therefore the minuet is the result of economic development. The logic would be similar to the argument that since Mr. X's suicide by shooting was made possible only by the existence of fire-arms, and since fire-arms depended upon the application of science to industry, therefore the real cause of Mr. X's death was science and capitalism. In any case, even if it be granted that the minuet had an origin in the economic life of the past, that economic life could by no known canon of logic or scientific method be regarded as a cause of the presence of the minuet in the economic life of a later day.

Similarly it can be argued that the style of David was not produced by the ideological struggles of eighteenth century France, but that during and after the Revolution it was *selected* by republican France because of the definite political import of its imitation of the rugged virtues of Roman and Greek antiquity. As a matter of fact, definite departures from the rococo style had already been made before David. Independently of the whole movement of neo-classicism in France, the German, Winkelmann, had proclaimed that "The sole means for us to become—if possible—inimitably great, is the imitation of the ancients." It must be remembered that David was a member of the Convention and that his studies of the assassinated Lepelletier and Marat were political commissions. His technique in those pictures was no different from the technique he later employed in his *Coronation* which glorified Napoleon. Nor was it appreciably different from the technique of his greatest pupil, Ingres, who used it to celebrate the voluptuous beauty of nudes in a Turkish Bath.

All this suggests an important distinction between the *origin* of any cultural fact and its *acceptance*. In art, for example, all sorts of stylistic variations or mutants appear in any period. The social and political environment acts as a *selective* agency upon them. The dominant style selected may in turn exercise a social and political influence. When we say that the style which is accepted "expresses" the social interests or political aspirations of a class, we may mean one of two things. We may mean either that the technical elements of a work have grown out of a new social experience or that technical elements already in existence have been fused in a new way or filled with a new content. This is not a hard and fast distinction, but all interpretation of culture demands that it be made. In literature this distinction is hardest to draw, in painting it is less hard and in music easiest of all. But even in literature it is clear that some formal elements, *e.g.*, the sonnet form, reportage, the autobiographical novel, may be used indifferently to express disparate political and social interests.

In painting, realistic technique may serve revolutionary or non-revolutionary purposes. In music, the same tunes are often the battle songs of Fascists in Germany and of Communists in Russia.

The tentative conclusion we have reached is that although each specific expression of a culture is socially conditioned, its pattern of development may depend upon certain relatively irreducible, technical factors, and that for some purposes, an explanation in terms of these technical factors may be valid. The extent to which the social environment enters as a constitutive element in this pattern is a subject of empirical investigation. Nothing significant can be inferred from the truism that without some form of social organization the cultural fact in question could not exist. Where the social environment influences a cultural phenomenon it may do so in two distinct ways which must be distinguished in analysis even though they may not be separated in fact. It may provide the technical *materials* out of which new forms develop. For example, the manufacture of inflated duralumin tubes may make possible new variations in architecture, the discovery of poison gas and aeroplane warfare may revolutionize the art of military science and strategy. The second way in which the social environment may influence a culture trait is by the *use* to which it is put. Inflated duralumin tubes may be used to construct more profitable skyscrapers or may be used to build more livable homes for the working population in intelligently planned cities. An army which is knit together by a revolutionary, democratic

[*236*]

faith will develop new forms of warfare impossible to an army which is only discipline bound. The *use* to which materials and techniques are put is in the larger sense of the words, political and moral. It is bound up with the class struggle and with the different objectives and paths of action which flow from it. The class character of any art is unmistakably revealed not so much in its materials and techniques—save derivatively—but in its objectives.

If the foregoing analysis is sound, a genuine Marxian criticism of culture will never be guilty of the monistic reductions which have only too often masqueraded in its name.

13

PROBLEMS OF HISTORICAL MATERIALISM

A PROPER test of the claims of historical materialism could be made only by applying its propositions to the rich detail of politics, law, religion, philosophy, science and art. This would require not a chapter but an encyclopedia. We must consequently restrict ourselves to a discussion of certain fundamental problems which arise in every field in which historical materialism is applied.

The upshot of the discussion will show that Marx's historical method is organically connected with his revolutionary purpose and activity, that it does not attempt to explain all aspects of present and past social life but only those that have bearing upon the conditions, direction and technique of action involved in social change, that the explanations he does offer were never projected as final, and that the concept of causation which underlies the theory of historical materialism is practical and not theoretical.

For purposes of convenience the points around which the discussion will center will be (1) the rôle of per-

sonality in history; (2) the larger question of objective
chance and objective necessity which that particular
problem suggests; (3) the importance of the admission
of reciprocal influences between multiple factors; (4)
the Marxian theory of the practical character of social
causality which takes the place of a theory of measurement; and (5) the nature of historical intelligibility,
i.e., what it means to understand human behavior in its
historical aspect.

1. The Rôle of Personality in History

Because he opposed that ever-fashionable theory that
all history is the biography of great men, Marx has been
criticized for underestimating the significance of personality in history. His historical analyses, however, are
full of brilliant characterizations of individuals, and in
view of his constant emphasis upon the creative activity
of man in history, it is a little hard to see why this
notion should have arisen. Probably this is due to the
all too common failure to distinguish between the contradictory of a proposition and its contrary, so that the
two statements, "It is not the case that all history is
the history of great men," and "No history is the history of great men," have been identified. But the chief
reason for the misinterpretation, it seems to me, is that
most of Marx's disciples have actually agreed with his
critics—not perhaps in so many words—but as far as the
objective intent of their interpretation goes.

In terms of Marx's philosophy of history it is easy to
make short shrift of any conception such as Carlyle's

which sees in the development of civilization nothing but the deeds of heroes and the thoughts of genius. We may begin with the crushing consideration that the very meaning of "greatness" in social and political matters is not something fixed but is historically conditioned. Each society not only has its own economic organization, its own law of population and its own art-styles; it has its own criterion of greatness. The saint of one age is the fool of another; the strong man of to-day may be the criminal of to-morrow. In politics and religion the "great man" is the man who can get himself *believed in*. To get people to believe in him, he must in some way gratify or fulfill their *need*. The need and the possibilities of fulfilling it are often so patently present that no special endowment is required to mount from obscurity to renown. In such cases—and this is the stuff of which it is most often made—greatness is thrust upon a man; it is not achieved. A Charlemagne, a Mahomet, a George Washington or a Frederick II boasted the possession of no qualities so unique that other men could not have easily been found to lead the movements whose titular heads they were. To-day the same can be said of Hitler or Gandhi. It is no exaggeration to maintain that if they had not been what they were, then, historically speaking, others would have been what they were. Now, if the stature of the great men of history were no higher than that of those enumerated, then we could hold that there would have been little appreciable difference in world history if they had never existed. Of all of them we could say as we can of

165

Columbus: if he had not discovered America, someone else would have. "Every society," writes Marx, "needs its great men, and if it does not find them it creates them, as Helvetius said." (*Klassenkämpfe im Frankreich,* p. 69.) Such men owe their greatness not to pre-eminent capacity but to historical necessity.

The crucial question, however, is whether all the great men of history are of this dimension. Could we say of Pericles, Caesar, Cromwell, Napoleon, Marx and Lenin what we have said of Mahomet or George Washington? Before we answer this question, let us turn to other fields where the relationship between individual greatness and social needs is a little different—the fields of science and art.

Looking at the history of science as a systematic organization of knowledge (which, we are aware, is an abstraction but which we are justified in making for the purpose of analysis), can we say that if Archimedes, Galileo, Kepler, Newton, Clerk Maxwell, and Einstein had not lived, the history of science would have been substantially the same? He would be a rash man who would unqualifiedly assert it. Take Newton from whom all the subsequent developments of science branch out. It is granted that he did not begin from the beginning, that many of his problems were common problems of his time, that neither his activity nor his results would have been possible without the existence of the permissive conditions of the society and politics of his day. But for that matter neither would his work have been possible without the permissive conditions of the weather, his own birth, and the existence of the world in general. There is no theoretical limit to the number of necessary conditions which had to be fulfilled before Newton could have achieved what he did. Nonetheless all of these permissive or necessary conditions are irrelevant to the real problem at issue which is whether in the absence of Newton (supposing he had died of croup in childhood) his discoveries, which not only revolutionized theoretical science but profoundly influenced the development of industry and capitalism, would have been made by others. To retort that Leibnitz was the co-discoverer of the calculus and that no great scientific discovery has been made by one man is to reveal a pathetic inability to grasp the issue here. Any man who could have solved Newton's problems had to be of the same intellectual stature as Newton. Let us grant, contrary to fact, that every one of Newton's discoveries were independently made by other men. Let us assume that not only did Newton and Leibnitz discover the calculus independently of one another, but, for good measure, that two others did so too. The question at issue is whether if all of these *four* great men had not existed (a supposition not beyond the pale of probability), the calculus would have been invented anyhow. What possible evidence is available bearing upon this point? Only the fact that attempts had been made to solve certain problems of the circle and the cube from the time of Archimedes down, and that Galileo and Bernouilli puzzled over difficulties which involved functions. Loosely speaking, all we can say is that a scientific problem existed. And we can even grant that this and other problems were set, not only by the immanent development of mathematics and science, but by certain practical problems of warfare, industry and commerce. But by what mystical assurance can one assert that all these problems, no matter how and why they arose, *must* find solutions? This is not to suggest that any problem is insoluble or unknowable. It simply asserts that there is no logical, scientific or social necessity that every problem find its solution.[1]

If it is true that the presence of great men has had an irreducibly significant influence upon the development of science, how much truer is it for the development of art and literature. Here, too, the social environment has provided both the opportunity and the materials for creation. In contradistinction, however, to the political illustrations considered above, society has not been able to bestow greatness but only to select it. Lacking a Shakespeare or a Goethe, mankind "would have been shorter by a head." To object by saying that society "produced" Shakespeare in one case, and Newton in another, is to use very confusing language. Unless it could be shown that the actual biological birth of Shakespeare was involved in the literary development of England in the sixteenth century, and the birth of Newton in the scientific development of the seventeenth, we cannot in any sense claim that these men were produced by their

---

[1] If it be claimed that a problem clearly stated is a problem implicitly solved, then what the above means is that there is no cosmic or social necessity that the problem be explicitly solved.

environments. But to assume such an organic connection between the realm of biology and the realm of society is on the face of it absurd. What "social" or "literary" necessity guided the union of the sperm and egg out of which the child Shakespeare was born? If Shakespeare hadn't been born would someone else have been Shakespeare? Mystic connections of this sort can be asserted only by the philosophy of absolute idealism, not by dialectical materialism.

Men of art and science, it will be objected, no matter how great they may be, do not affect history. Very well, then, we return to the rôle of great personalities in social history and politics. Would the Russian Revolution have taken place in October, 1917, if Lenin had died an exile in Switzerland? And if the Russian Revolution had not taken place when it did, would subsequent events in Russia have taken the same course? [2] Would the history of Europe have been different if Napoleon had lost his life in the first Italian campaign? If Cromwell early in his career had carried out his threat to sell his estate and quit the country, would the Roundheads have been victorious anyhow? If Sulla in addition to depriving Julius Caesar of his property and priesthood in 82 B. C. had not listened to the intercession of the Vestal Virgins and had proceeded with Caesar's scheduled execution, would Rome have arisen to the heights of world empire? These questions cannot be answered

[2] Compare Trotsky's interesting discussion of this problem and his ambiguous answer, *History of the Russian Revolution*, Eng. trans., Vol. I, pp. 329-330.

dogmatically in the affirmative. They are ticklish problems and the historical evidence does not give determinate solutions. Instead of leaving those questions open to be decided by elaborate analysis of historical possibilities, most of the disciples of Marx have settled all the difficulties *in advance* by a rigid and mechanical application of historical materialism. We may begin with Engels:

"That a certain particular man, and no other, emerges at a definite time in a given country is naturally pure chance. But even if we eliminate him, there is always a need for a substitute, and the substitute it found *tant bien que mal;* in the long run he is sure to be found. That Napoleon— this particular Corsican—should have been the military dictator made necessary by the exhausting wars of the French Republic—that was a matter of chance. *But in default of a Napoleon, another would have filled his place; that is established by the fact that whenever a man was necessary he has always been found: Caesar, Augustus, Cromwell."* (From his Letter to Block. Cf. Appendix. Italics mine.)

Karl Kautsky, who has been called the "old war-horse of Marxian orthodoxy," writes on the same theme:

"Had it not been Cromwell or Napoleon, it would have been someone else. Due to the revolutionary origin of the armies which raised Cromwell and Napoleon to power, all the fighting instincts and capacities among the revolutionary sections of the population had been aroused, and at the same time a path was cleared to the highest places for those among the whole nation who were gifted in military matters. Everyone remembers the saying that every soldier of the revolutionary army carried a marshal's baton in his knapsack. In this way there was built in the armies of the English and French republic a high minded and superior corps of officers who would have easily selected another military dictator if Cromwell or Napoleon had not succeeded in coming to the top." (*Die Materialistische Geschichtsauffassung,* Vol. 2, p. 703.)

Plechanov,[3] Cunow,[4] and Bukharin,[5] on this question, play the game of follow your master with amazing fidelity.

With all due respect, this position seems to me to be arrant nonsense. Its most intelligible expression would involve the abandonment of Marx's naturalistic materialism and a surrender to idealistic mysticism. To argue that if Napoleon had not lived someone else and not he would have been Napoleon (*i.e.,* would have performed Napoleon's work) and then to offer as evidence the fact that whenever a great man was necessary he has always been found, is logically infantile. For how do we know when a great man is needed by society? Surely *not after* he has arisen! The need for him must be antecedent to his appearance. But, then, did society need great men *only* at those periods when Caesar, Cromwell, Napoleon, and others came to the fore? That would be like saying society needed great thinkers only when Aristotle, Aquinas, Kant, etc., lived. Would it not be truer to say that society always needs great men? Why then are not great men always at hand? Where

[3] Plechanov, *Fundamental Problems of Marxism,* p. 68ff.
[4] Cunow, *Die Marxche Geschichts-Gesellschafts-und Staats-Theorie,* Bd. 2, p. 220.
[5] Bukharin, *Historical Materialism,* p. 97.

was the great man at the time when the Tartar hordes overran Russia and arrested its development? Why did not a great man arise to unify India against foreign imperialism in the nineteenth century, and China in the twentieth? Where was the great leader hiding when Italy was objectively ready for revolution in 1921 and Germany in 1923? Was he not needed then? And granted that there was a need for a Napoleon, a Marx, a Lenin when they arose. What is the source of the assurance that that need *had to be* fulfilled, if not by these men, then by others fully as great as they? The pious Christian can fall back upon the will of God. But the militant revolutionist who permits the automatic, economic development of society to perform the same logical function in his system as the will of God in the system of the believer, has committed intellectual suicide. When, under pressure of the argument, he throws overboard the notion of the automatic development of society, he is logically compelled to surrender the notion that whenever a great man is necessary he must be found. There are no musts in history; there are only conditional probabilities.

Marx's own view is more sober and Engels on other occasions was faithful to it. We shall discuss it in conjunction with the larger problem of the rôle of chance in history.

2. CHANCE IN HISTORY

In a previous chapter we have examined and rejected the theory of wholesale chance in history. But to go from the denial that "not all history is a chance affair" to the statement that "there are no chance elements in history" is an altogether different matter. That is precisely what some Marxist historians have done. Pokrovsky, for example, in his *History of Russia* (Vol. I) states that "to appeal to chance in history is to exhibit a certificate of poverty." In this simple way of disposing of the problem, he is at one with most bourgeois historians who have neglected the dialectical approach to the question of law and chance in history.

What is a chance event? This is both a metaphysical question and an historical question. Here we are only concerned with chance events in history. A chance event, first of all, is not merely an event of which we are ignorant. For a great many events of which we are ignorant may turn out to be historically determined. At one time we were ignorant of the causes of the First Crusade and translated that ignorance into the phrase *un fait écclessiastique*. That did not make the Crusades a chance event; an historian with proper knowledge of the social and economic history of Europe in the latter half of the eleventh century need not have invoked chance or the will of God in his account.

Nor is a chance event in history one that is uncaused. Whether all events, of whatever nature, have a cause, is a question outside of the province of the historian. His problem is whether all events which have *historical effects* have themselves *historical causes*. An earthquake is a natural event which has definite *geological* causes. It has, however, definite *historical* effects. An historian treating of the socio-economic development of a country would have to regard the *occurrence* of the earthquake as a chance event. Why? Because he could not deduce or explain its happenings on the basis of any of the historical and social material available to him. The *causes* of the earthquake are historically irrelevant; its *effects* are not, for the social consequences of an earthquake will be different in one economic situation from what it will be in another. A chance event in history is one which although it has historical consequences has no historical causes. The historian could no more predict an earthquake on the basis of historical data than the geologist could predict the *social* consequences of an earthquake on the basis of his geological laws alone.

Not all events which have historical effects are easily classifiable into those whose causes are purely physical or biological and those whose causes are purely social. The continued dependence of the relations of production upon the supply of natural raw materials, etc., preclude the possibility of drawing hard and fast divisions. But they do not exonerate the historian from trying to evaluate the degree of chance which is operating; and distinguishing chance events, whose effects and causes are historically irrelevant, from those chance events whose causes are historically irrelevant but whose effects are not. Marx, in a famous letter, pointed out the sense in which objective chance was present in history, and what the consequences were of denying it:

"World history would indeed be a very easy thing to make were the struggle to be carried on only under conditions of unfailingly favorable chances. Its nature would have to be of a very mystical kind if 'accidents' played no rôle. These accidents naturally fall within the general path of development and are compensated by other accidents. But the acceleration and retardation of events are very largely dependent upon such 'accidents' among which must be reckoned the character of the people who stand at the head of the movement." (To Kugelmann on the *Paris Commune,* April 12, 1871.)

Marx does not mean to suggest that the character of any leader is uncaused and that a biologist and psychologist could not offer a perfectly satisfactory explanation of its nature. He merely points to the fact that something, which the historian cannot altogether explain, may have a decisive influence upon a great historical event. It is in this way that Marx propounds the solution of the specific problem from which we started. The presence of a great man means the presence of great historical effects. *Vide* Marx himself. But is the presence of a great man the effect of an historical cause? Only partly. His biological endowment, from the historical point of view, is a matter of chance. The specific cultural expression of it is not. World history is the resultant effect of two relatively independent series of phenomena—the biological (or the physical as the case may be) and the socio-political in which the latter is more decisive because it supplies the content and materials of personal expression.

What does Marx mean by the statement that world history would have to be of a "mystical" character were there no chance events? He means that, once chance were ruled out, all causal connections which were involved in an historical event, whether they were physical or biological, would have to be regarded as *organically* related in one *meaningful* historical whole. It would mean that if anything were different in this whole, everything would be different; that the particular conjunctions of series of events, no matter how trivial, are necessary, and could be deduced, if we had sufficient knowledge, before they actually occurred in time. This could only be true if the world were either one absolute totality outside of time, as Hegel conceived it to be, or one great complex machine in which all parts were given at once, as the metaphysical mechanists assumed. Both views are equally fatalistic and share the same theological prepossessions.

3. HISTORICAL RECIPROCITY

Once it is recognized that all historical events have chance aspects, which in most cases may be safely disregarded, the way is cleared for a consideration of the related problem of the reciprocal interaction between social factors. No process can ever be explained in terms of one factor. For all activity whether it be of man or nature presupposes some material to be acted upon. The character of both the activity and the material must be reflected in the resultant effect. Where the activity continues to be the same and the materials differ, differences in the result will be attributed, for all practical purposes, to the causal influence of the material; where the material is the same and the activities are different, differences in the result will be explained by differences in the nature of the activity. Now in a large sense, history in the making, *i.e.,* in the rich qualitative immediacy of the present, is a resultant product of *one* material and of *one* activity. That material is the whole complex of tradition and institutions which each generation finds at hand; the activity is the pursuit of ideals, conditioned by the traditional civilization—an activity which results in changing those conditions. Closer analysis, however, shows that neither the material of history nor historical activity is one; the material has *many* aspects, the activity, *many* forms. It is the same civilization which expresses itself in its architecture as in its songs, but a history of song is not a history of architecture, although there may be points of contact; the quest for truth in a laboratory and the quest for empire are both historical activities—but chemistry is not military strategy although they may, of course, be related.

The explanation of any specific situation, then, demands some conception of what is *relevant* and what is *irrelevant* to it. If all the material aspects of history and all forms of historical activity were related to every situation, then the explanation of one situation would be identically the same with the explanation of any other. Indeed, there would be no way of distinguishing one situation from another. The problem then is to discover what is relevant and what is irrelevant to any cultural phenomena to be explained. Just as it is possible to admit that the whole history of the solar system is involved in the existence of any individual on earth, and yet rule out the internal constitution of the sun as irrelevant in analyzing the personality of John Smith (or for that matter even his anatomy), so it is possible to admit that the mode of economic production is involved in every cultural fact, and rule it out as irrelevant in an analysis of a *specific* work of art. In a *total* explanation, it would be relevant; but no one is interested in total explanations, and it is questionable whether the phrase has a meaning.

The problem of cultural reciprocity must be recognized by anyone who realizes two things. First, that historical activity which includes all forms of social effort, although it arises from the conditioning social environment, reacts upon it in some concrete way. And second, that the different forms of historical activity— scientific, legal, artistic—will often influence one another by reacting upon their common social conditions. For example, a new invention in building materials, adopted as profitable, may give rise to a mass housing project and influence architectural style; the aeroplane made possible commercial airways which, in turn, necessitated new legal developments. The refusal or inability of some Marxists to do justice to cultural phenomena of this kind led hostile critics to maintain that historical materialism suffered from a primitive monism according to which all efficient causes in history were material, never ideal. Before he died, Engels was compelled to take the field against them:

"The political, legal, philosophical, religious, literary, and artistic, development rests upon the economic. But they all react upon one another and upon the economic base. It is not the case that the economic situation is the *sole active cause* and everything else only a passive effect. There is a reciprocal interaction within a fundamental economic necessity which *in the last instance* always asserts itself." (From Letter to Starkenberg. Cf. Appendix.)

"According to the materialistic conception of history, the production and reproduction of real life constitutes in the *last instance* the determining factor of history. Neither Marx nor I ever maintained more. Now, when someone comes along and distorts this to mean that the economic factor is the *sole* determining factor, he is converting the former proposition into a meaningless, abstract, and absurd phrase. The economic situation is the basis. But the various factors of the superstructure—the political forms of the class struggles and their results, *i.e.*, constitutions, etc., established by victorious classes after hard won battles, legal forms, and even the reflexes of all these real struggles in the brain of the participants, political, jural, philosophical theories, religious conceptions which have been developed into systematic dogmas—all these exercise an influence upon the course of historical struggles, and in many cases determine for the most part their form. There is a reciprocity between all these factors in which, finally, through the endless array of contingencies (*i.e.*, of things and events whose inner connection with one another is so remote, or so incapable of proof, that we may neglect it, regarding it as non-existent) the economic movement asserts itself as necessary. Were this not the case the application of the theory to any given historical period would be easier than the solution of a simple equation of the first degree." (From Letter to Bloch. Cf. Appendix.)

"What all these fellows lack is dialectic. They see only cause here, only effect there. They do not at all see that this method of viewing things results in bare abstractions; that in the real world such metaphysical polar opposites exist only in crucial situations; that the whole great process develops itself in the form of reciprocal action, of very unequal forces to be sure, but in which the economic movement is far and away the strongest, most primary and decisive. They do not see that here nothing is absolute and everything relative. For them, Hegel has never existed." (From Letter to Schmidt.)

4. The Marxian Theory of Social Causation

In all of the foregoing citations the phrase, "in the last instance," is crucial. It is synonymous with the expressions, "the real basis of society" and "the most decisive factor." When it is declared that the mode of economic production is any one of these things, the natural question to ask is: What do these expressions mean and how can we test the truth of what they assert?

Whenever anything is characterized as *in the last instance* determining something else, it must be borne in mind that a certain point of view is involved *from which* the analysis is projected. The meaning of "in the last instance" (or "in the last analysis") is not something absolutely given and fixed for every point of departure. It depends rather upon the position we want to prove. And where social activity is involved, it depends upon the practical interest which lies at the heart of that position. *Real* and *decisive* in this connection are, also, relative to a contemplated program of activity, and can only be tested in that activity. It is here that the direct connection lies between Marxism as the theory and practice of social revolution in the era of capitalism, and historical materialism as a theory of social change. What justifies Marx and Engels in holding that the mode of economic production is the *decisive factor* in social life is the revolutionary will of the proletariat which is prepared to act upon that assumption. It is a will strengthened by knowledge of the *limiting* conditions which affect the success of their effort. But it is the revolutionary act containing both the risk of failure and the promise of success which is essential not only to social advance but, at times, even to the acquisition of social knowledge. It is as necessary as any or all of the other limiting conditions. It is this faith in *action* which makes of Marxism a critical hypothesis, instead of a dead dogma or a romantic myth. It is only because we want to change the economic structure of society that we look for evidence of the fact that in the *past,* economic change has had a profound effect upon all social and cultural life. Because we want to change the economic structure of society, we assert that this evidence from the *past* together with our revolutionary act in the *present* constitutes a sufficient cause for believing that the general proposition, "in the last instance the mode of economic production determines the general character of social life," will be true in the near *future.* In other words, the test of the truth of historical judgments about the past is to be sought in the concrete historical activities of the present, and their future results.

The real test of causal connection in the social realm —whatever may be the case for physics—is human activity. It is only in so far as we can produce things, or bring certain situations to pass, that we can conquer the well known Humean difficulties about causation. *What* we want to produce, and when we want to produce it, cannot be derived from the general want or desire to action; for they are socially conditioned. But neither can the want*ing* or desir*ing* be deduced from the actual or possible objects of desire; for human activity is an irreducible constituent of the social process. By its action it does not make or create laws but it helps to realize the conditions under which one of several possible types of causal connection operates.

Engels generalizes this practical conception of causality to hold even for the natural world:

"The first thing that strikes us when we consider matter in motion is the connection between the individual motions of individual bodies with one another, their mutually *conditioned* character. However, not only do we find that one motion follows another, but that we can produce a certain motion by establishing the conditions under which it occurs in nature. Indeed, we can even produce movements which do not take place in nature at all (industry), or at least not in the same manner, and we find that these movements can be given a definite direction in advance. *In this way, through the activity of man* is grounded the idea of *causality*—the idea that one movement is the *cause* of another. The regular succession of certain natural phenomena can indeed give rise to the idea of causality: *e.g.,* the light

and heat associated with the sun. But this succession constitutes no proof and thus far Humean-scepticism is justified in saying that the regularities of *post hoc* (after this)
will never prove *propter hoc* (because of this). It is only
through the activity of man that the test of causality can
be made." (*Dialektik und Natur, Marx-Engels Archiv*, II,
p. 164.)

It is the practical reliability of causal connection which
concerns man and not its rational necessity. Whoever
responds that the reliability of causal connection upon
which our action depends, and in *social* situations which
our action helps to enforce, is itself conditioned by antecedent necessities in the nature of things, is converting
probabilities into unverifiable certainties. This question
is involved with the most fundamental problem of metaphysics and logic that one can raise, to wit, what does
it mean to *understand* anything, what is the criterion of
an *intelligible* explanation. The three great canons of
intelligibility have been derived from the fields of
geometry, psychology and history. Their explanatory
categories have been, respectively, logical necessity, psychological plausibility, and successful action. For Marx
and for those of his followers who have been faithful to
his revolutionary ideal, it is history and action that are
the matrix of intelligibility. There are some things that
cannot be established as true merely by argument. "But
before human beings argued," wrote Engels, "they
acted. *Im Anfang war die That.*"

To understand is to act. To act successfully means to
construct.

5. The Nature of Historic Intelligibility

If practice and successful action are criteria of intelligibility, then critical intelligence may be defined as an awareness of the technique, procedures and instruments involved in all directed activity. There is no directed activity outside of the realm of history. All genuine problems become problems of ways and means, and although there is no assurance that they can be solved, the necessary conditions of their solutions are already known. With this approach the whole of life becomes secularized. Only difficulties remain, but no mysteries. For whenever we are confronted with a mystery, we have not yet become conscious of the rationale of our technique, we have not yet realized what we are doing.

"All social life is essentially *practical*. All mysteries which cause theories to turn to mysticism find their rational solution in human practice and in the awareness [*Begreifen*] of this practice." (Marx, *Gesamtausgabe*, I, 5, p. 535.)

In so far as science is a part of human activity, Marx's gloss holds true of all of its many "mysteries" which have so often occasioned flights to theology and superstition. For science, too, is a practical affair. Not in a vulgar commercial sense but in that it involves, at crucial points, a changing and arranging of material things. When one looks for a solution of the many "mysteries" (as distinct from the difficulties) which have multiplied with the contemporary analysis of the structure of the atom, resort must always be to the techniques by which certain empirical effects have been observed, to the apparatus and presuppositions of measurement, and to the methods of interpretation. From this standpoint it becomes forever impossible to bootleg transcendental and religious moonshine *a la* Eddington, Jeans, Millikan, *et. al.,* into the equations of mathematical physics.

In social and political life, it is more obvious that what is declared to be "inexplicable" or "mysterious," such as the source of moral and political obligation, or the origin of profit, is to be explained in terms of the actual way in which human beings behave. The task of the revolutionary philosopher is to bring social classes to an awareness of what it is they are doing and of the historical conditions of their activity. When a class attains consciousness of what it is doing, of the rôle it plays in production, it discovers the secret of the whole society of which it is a part. It can now understand itself and not wait for some future historian to distinguish between the real meaning of its acts and the fancied meanings which were the pretexts or excuses for action. Its ideology becomes a realistic philosophy. Because it understands itself, it is free. But full understanding and social freedom can come only after classes have been abolished. For only then will the fundamental dualism between social ideas and social conduct disappear.

"The life process of society, which is based upon the process of material production, does not strip off its mystical veil until it is treated as a production by freely associated men, and is consciously regulated by them in accordance with a settled plan." (Marx, *Capital*, I, p. 92. Eng. trans. All references are to the Kerr edition.)

It is dangerous to close on the paradox that the history of class society can never be fully understood except in retrospect, and that only the history of classless society, because it is freely made, can receive complete rational explanation. It is dangerous because it suggests that the human freedom of the future will not be bound or conditioned at all. The truth is, however, that the very possibility of human history, and the range within which human history can be made, will always be conditioned by natural necessities in whose existence man can have but a minor part. Man's freedom will lie in the *conscious* choice of one of the many possible careers set for him. That choice will be a unique and irreducible expression of his own nature. Marx, himself, puts this in a passage in *Capital* as follows:

"The freedom in this field cannot consist of anything else but the fact that socialized man, the associated producers, regulate their interchange with nature rationally, bring it under their human control, instead of being ruled by it as some blind power; that they accomplish their task with the least expenditure of energy and under conditions most adequate to their human nature and most worthy of it. But it always remains a realm of necessity. Beyond it begins that development of human power, which is its own end, the true realm of freedom, which, however, can flourish only upon that realm of necessity as its basis." (Vol. III, Eng. trans., p. 954.)

14

MARX'S SOCIOLOGICAL ECONOMICS

M ARX'S economic doctrines are the result of the application of historical materialism to the "mysteries" of value, price and profit. The solution of all mysteries, Marx taught, was to be found in social practice. And it is his analysis of the *social* character of all economic traits and categories which represents Marx's distinctive contribution to political economy.

Traditional economics had approached the objects of political economy in the same way that a physicist approached a steel bar or a chemist a dye. Economic relations were not derived from the way in which things entered into the social process, but were regarded, on the analogy of the physical sciences, as intrinsic properties of things. They were as much in evidence in the solitary domestic economy of a Robinson Crusoe, and in the primitive economy of the savage horde, as in the complex economy of a modern society. It was therefore not necessary, orthodox economists assumed, to take into account the distinctively historical contexts in which the economic properties of things were discovered. Further, all attempts on the part of the state to regulate prices, wages, or capital investment could be denounced as absurd and pernicious attempts to interfere with the natural functioning of economic laws. No room was left for normative judgments. From this abstract unhistorical point of view gold was regarded as *naturally* money, instruments of production *naturally* capital, human labor-power *naturally* wage-labor, the soil, and not society, the *natural* locus of rent. What for Marx was the outcome of a socio-historical process was taken as the natural precondition of that process. The historical expressions of a set of relations of production were turned into fixed things; and human behavior in all its economic ramifications was explained as controlled by things.

The upshot of this unhistorical approach corresponds to the actual consciousness of those who live in a commodity-producing society and have not yet penetrated to the secret of commodity production. The rise and fall of the market, periodic glut and scarcity, small-scale and large-scale panics, are taken as natural events bestowing blessings and calamities, like the fortunes of the weather, upon the just and unjust, the wise and the unwise. The social relations between human beings are "thingified" into impersonal, automatic laws while the material instruments of life are "personified" into the directing forces of human destiny. Man finds himself ruled by the products (commodities) of his own hands. The relationships between these products "vary continually, independently of the will, foresight and action of the producers. To them, their own social action takes the form of the action of objects, which rule the producers instead of being ruled by them." (*Capital,* I, 86.) The whole of bourgeois economy consists of a process in which things carry on, so to speak, behind man's back. It is a process which makes a mockery of man's strivings for security, comfort and peace by producing unemployment, want and war. It diverts human relations from their human form, and by casting a shadow of mystery on human affairs generates mysticism, superstition and religious obscurantism. Instead of the instruments of production being utilized by human beings for human purposes, in bourgeois society human beings are utilized as instruments to serve machines. It is not only in Samuel Butler's satiric Utopia that human beings are the instruments of production used by machines for the manufacture of bigger and better machines. That is what they are in the practice and theory of commodity-producing societies. This is what Marx means when he calls bourgeois society a "fetishism of commodities" and the orthodox "science" of political economy, its theology.

Although the marginal utility school came into its own after Marx, its unhistorical character is just as marked as that of the classical school. In its most developed form it regards its task to be the study of "human behavior as a relationship between ends and scarce means which have alternative uses." Pure economics would result in the statement of formal laws—

invariant relations—derived from the general empirical fact that many things are wanted which are mutually incompatible. The character of the psychological incentives and aims involved in human behavior, the social institutions which provide its framework, are ruled out of the scope of economic inquiry while the propositions of pure economic science—which are really empirical—are paraded as analytic deductions from first principles. Changes in evaluation, which flow from altered psychological and social conditions of economic behavior, are regarded as brute irrational data. No attempt is made to show how economic laws change with a developing society, for by definition, economic laws are eternal. Only their historical expression can change, not their meaning and validity. From this point of view, the laws of economics are the same for all societies— feudal, capitalist and communist. An analysis which refuses to investigate the way in which formal relationships are affected by material context, cannot escape, for all its disavowal of value judgments, the air and manner of subtle apologia for the *status quo*. To maintain that propositions such as "the share of income which is received by land, labor and capital is exactly proportionate to their specific, marginal productivities," are *expressions* of eternal, economic laws without further distinguishing between the formal, skeletal economic elements which are presumably invariant, and the concrete historical situation which provides the flesh and blood of significance, is to encourage the uncritical belief that the economic system is rightly ordered be-

cause, from a strict economic point of view, it can be
no other than what it is.

Not all non-Marxian theories of economics are guilty
of overlooking the specific historical and social context
of the economic relations they submit to analysis. But
the question which arises concerning those schools which
adopt a genetic and functional approach—like the historical school of the nineteenth century and the institutional school of the twentieth—is: to what extent are
they really theories? The task of a theory is to organize
the empirical propositions of its subject-matter into some
systematic connection, so that the consequences deduced
are either compatible with observed phenomena or capable of serving as a guide to the discovery of new
phenomena. Descriptions of mechanisms and processes
can only supply the raw material for theoretical elaboration. The historical school cannot do justice to the
present tendencies of economic development unless it is
guided by a theory. Although its starting point is
diametrically opposed to the abstract, analytical school,
its practical upshot is the same: the acceptance of *what is*
as the norm of what *should be.*

It would be a mistake, however, to contrast Marx's
sociological economics with the economic systems of
those who begin with price, or demand, or cost, or welfare as fundamental, and then to inquire which of the
two systems is truer. For they are not concerned with
the same problems. The empirical findings of the various contemporary schools can be taken over by Marxists
as the indication of certain correlations in the fetishistic

expression of the movement of commodities. But what distinguishes Marx's economic analysis from all others is its fusion of the historical and analytic moments of capitalist production in the interests of a practical program of revolutionary activity. His refusal to consider political economy as an independent science, his evaluation of the significance of the historic tendencies of capitalist accumulation in the light of the totality of the social relations of production, which includes the specific historical context, the politics, psychology, and legal relations of the day, enables him to incorporate in a concrete synthesis what is sound in both the historical and analytic approach. What Marx is really offering is a philosophy of political economy based upon all of the important observable facts and suggestive of a method of fundamentally transforming the existing order. His theory of political economy cannot be used as a guide to play the market or make safe investments any more than a treatise on the fundamental causes of war can be used as a manual for military operations on the field of battle.

The "immediate" aim of Marx's economic analysis is to discover the laws governing the production and distribution of wealth in *capitalist* societies. Wealth in capitalist societies presents itself as "an immense accumulation of commodities whose elementary form is the single commodity." Not every product is a commodity and not all wealth is capital. These are *historical* categories. Societies exist in which things produced are not commodities and in which wealth is not capital. A commodity is a product which can be *exchanged* for other products—it is something which normally can be bought or sold; capital is wealth used for the production of more commodities. Capital may exist in the form of money or means of production; but no matter what the form of its embodiment, "it is not a thing, but a social relation between persons established by the instrumentality of things." The social relations between persons, under which the wealth used for the production of more wealth is known as capital, are expressed in that mode of economic production called capitalism.

What is capitalism? Capitalism is private ownership of the social means of production carried on for private profit, and employing *workers who are formally or legally free to sell their labor-power*. The italicized phrase distinguishes capitalism from all other forms of production (including what is sometimes mistakenly called ancient capitalism) and stamps it with a definitely historical character. Since the decline of genteel society, there has always been private ownership of the means of production; and the profit motive is as old as the traders of antiquity. But it is only when the quest for profit is carried on with "free" wage-labor that the capitalist system emerges. Wage-labor under capitalism is free "in the double sense that neither they [the free-laborers] themselves form part and parcel of the means of production, as in the case of slaves, bondsmen, etc., nor do the means of production belong to them, as in the case of peasant proprietors; they are therefore free from, unencumbered by, any means of production of their own."

This point is important because Marx maintained that the wages of labor constituted the chief "mystery" of capitalist production, and that the solution of the mystery would reveal that the laborer, for all his freedom, was still being exploited as his forbears had been under feudalism and slavery. Why is the exploitation of labor, if it exists, any more of a mystery under capitalism than it was under previous forms of society? [1] To answer this we must glance for a moment at the relations of production as they existed in feudal and slave times. Here everything is as clear as daylight. The serf who works three days on his own field and three days on his lord's field can distinguish between the work he does for himself and the unpaid work which he does for another. He does not have to infer the existence of this difference; the difference is visible in space and time. The parcels of land are generally separate from each other and the days which he must allot to the lord's land are already assigned. Or, where he must pay his tithe in products, he can divide into two piles that which he may keep and that which he must turn over. Under slavery all labor is unpaid and the very food which the slave receives as fuel for his body seems to come as bounty from his master. In none of these cases is there any mystery about the fact of exploitation, and where and when it takes place.

Under wage-labor the case is quite different. For all

[1] *Capital*, I, p. 591.

of the labor, both what is strictly necessary to keep the laborer in condition and the surplus produced over and beyond this necessary minimum, seems to be paid for. The laborer, say, is hired to work by the day. He does not stop at that point where the value of what he has produced equals the value of the money or commodities he receives as wages. There is no clear physical or temporal division between the work for which he is paid and the work for which he is not paid. At the end of the day, his wage payment is ostensibly for the whole day's work. Now it may be asked how is it known that there is any portion of the day's work for which the laborer is unpaid? Isn't the assumption that the worker creates more value in the form of goods and services, than what he receives in wages, an arbitrary one? Marx's answer is that if there were no difference between the value of what the worker produced and the value of what he received, there would be no profit, or interest or rent.

There is no mystery about the *existence* of profit, interest and rent. It is their origin which is in question. In contradistinction to all other economists before or since, Marx contended that these forms of income were all derived from the unpaid labor of those actually engaged in production. That the origin of profit and interest constituted a problem was sure to strike anyone who inquired by whose largess those unproductive classes in society which neither toiled nor spun were fed and clothed and housed. And as for the huge profits often made by entrepreneurs who participated in pro-

195

duction, it was unplausible, on the face of it, to attribute it all to wages of superintendence. How, then, did profit arise? Before we examine Marx's own theoretical construction, it would be well to see on what grounds he rejects the current theories of the origin of profit.

1. Does profit arise in the course of the ordinary exchange and circulation of commodities? The normal situation in the circulation of commodities is the exchange of *equivalent* values. This does not mean that the use-values of the commodities exchanged are equivalent, for then there would be no motive for the exchange. So far as *use* is concerned both sides gain in the transaction. But in respect to the exchange-values of the commodities, their combined price—which is the rough index of their exchange-value—is the same immediately before and immediately after the exchange. Consequently, no new value has been produced. In circulation, a buyer may take advantage of a seller or vice versa, in which case we say there was no honest bargain. This only means that existing values were redistributed, not that new value was created. The circulation of commodities, however, in a competitive market, cannot take place through a series of dishonest bargains. The seller may tack on a capricious surcharge to the value of his commodity. But in order to keep on selling, he must be a buyer, too. The seller, from whom *he* buys, reasons that what is sauce for the goose is sauce for the gander, and places the same overcharge upon his goods. The result is that only nominal prices increase. In a society where buyers are sellers and sellers are buyers, it is absurd to explain

profit as something created by the sale of commodities above their values. And if they are exchanged at their values, the world is not the richer by any new value. It is true, however, that even if profit is not *created* in exchange, it may be *realized* through exchange. But the real question is, What is the *original* source of profit?

2. Does profit arise from the use of machines or instruments of production? This is a view originally proclaimed by J. B. Say, the French economist. It has been revived by those who have noticed that other things being equal, a plant working with a great deal of machinery (say $9,000) and with little wage-labor (say $1,000) shows a rate of profit at the end of the year which is the same as that produced by a plant with relatively little machinery (say $2,000) and much wage-labor (say $8,000). If it is true, as Marx claimed, that the source of profit is the unpaid labor or surplus-value produced by the worker, then the second plant should have shown a much greater profit than the first, since a larger portion of its total capital consisted of wage-labor. In addition, if profit is exclusively derived from labor-power, how account for the eagerness of capitalists to replace labor-power by machines? We shall consider these problems in further detail in the following chapter. Here the question must be asked: What specific character do machines possess which enable them to confer more value upon their products (we are not speaking of use-values) than they themselves possess? Assuming there is no monopoly, the value produced by the machine upon the total annual product of goods, according to

Marx, is no more than its annual depreciation. The business man in fixing the price at which he is to sell his commodity, just as his accountant does in drawing up his profit and loss statement, adds an amount derived by dividing the original cost of the machine by its average life. The machine transfers value, which it itself has, to its products; but it cannot produce new value. Where monopoly conditions permit prices to be charged which are higher than the real value of the commodity, it is not the machine which is the source of the additional profit so made but the social conditions of monopoly production.[2]

3. Is profit and interest on capital the reward of abstinence? Senior regarded profit as the natural reward for not immediately consuming capital, as a return for the sacrifice involved in accumulating capital in order to get a higher return later. The "waiting" or "deprivation" of the capitalist in the present was regarded as part of the cost of production and had to be paid for. What is called abstinence, however, by itself never produces any new value; at most, it only permits a situation to develop under which the new value is produced. Whether the capitalist class as a whole accumulates or consumes its wealth, does not depend upon its own free will but upon the necessities of capitalist production.

---

[2] "However useful a given kind of raw material or a machine or other means of production may be, though it may cost £150, or say 500 days labor, yet it cannot, under any circumstances, add to the value of the product more than £150. Its value is determined not by the labor process into which it enters as means of production, but by that out of which it has issued as a product." (*Capital*, I, p. 229.)

This is true with certain qualifications even of the individual capitalist. So long as he desires to make a *profit,* the amount he consumes and the amount he reinvests in his plant are settled for him by the market. If he does not desire to make a profit, there is no less and no more abstinence involved on his part than if he does. The choice of either one of two possible acts open to him involves on his part an "abstinence" from the other. Why, then, should some kinds of abstinence result in a profitable reward?

4. Does profit arise from the fluctuations of supply and demand? If this were so, the prices at which commodities are exchanged would have to be the resultant of the interacting forces of supply and demand. That prices varied with supply and demand, Marx did not deny. The clue to the price of a particular commodity at a particular time in a particular place must always be sought in the local schedules of supply prices and demand prices. But Marx was interested in the direction in which prices moved, in the conditions by which supply and demand were themselves limited. Although the final price of a commodity in the absence of monopoly is dependent upon the higgling of the open market, the seller already knows what its market value approximately is before he offers it for sale, indeed, before he even produces it. Otherwise why should he risk everything in production? Business may sometimes be a gamble; but it is not yet a game of pure chance. If the answer is made that the seller is guided by knowledge of the past schedules of

supply and demand for the commodity in question, it can be pointed out that where a brand new commodity is put on the market its price is determined long before the demand has begun to make itself felt. In fact, the demand for it can be treated in part as a function of the price, *i.e.,* as a dependent variable.

The accidents of the market will determine whether a commodity is sold above or under its "real value," and in this way profit may partly depend upon the fluctuation of supply and demand. But in order to make his profit the seller need only dispose of the commodity at its real value. What determines the real value of a commodity? According to Marx it is the amount of *socially necessary labor-power* involved in its production. Are commodities ever sold at their real values? Rarely, if ever. When would they be? If the organic composition of capital were equal. Are they equal? No. Is there any sense, then, in saying that the prices of commodities *tend* to equal their "real values"? Yes, as much sense, as we shall later see, as there is in saying that bodies in motion *tend* to remain in motion unless acted upon by an external force, even when we know that there is no body which is not acted upon by the external force of gravitation.

We return now to a more straightforward exposition, reserving the analysis of Marx's methodology until the next chapter.

Under capitalism labor-power appears on the market like any other commodity. Its value is determined in the same way and it is subject to the same variations of supply and demand. Under the ideal or typical conditions of capitalist production, the worker receives in exchange for his labor-power a sum of money equivalent in value to the means of subsistence necessary to sustain him—food, clothing, and shelter for himself and family. Like all commodities the use-value of labor-power is different from its exchange-value. But in one respect it is absolutely unlike other commodities. Its specific use-value lies in the fact that it creates more exchange-value than it is itself worth. If labor-power produced no more exchange-value than what it receives in money wages, then the value of the commodities produced would be equal merely to the value of the raw material, machinery and labor-power which entered into its manufacture. Where would profit come in? The capitalist might just as well close up his shop, for the only income he could receive under such circumstances would be the exchange-value of his own labor-power, provided he did work in his own plant. But why should he stay in business to give himself a job, when, without risking his capital, he might take a job elsewhere? He can remain in business only so long as there is a difference between the value of the labor-power he has purchased and the values which that labor-power creates. Profit is possible only when the value of the second is greater than the value of the first.

Marx calls that portion of the working day in which the worker produces commodities whose exchange-value (as distinct from the exchange-value of the raw materials, etc.) is equivalent to the exchange-value of his own labor-power, *necessary labor time;* anything over and above this is *surplus labor time.* What is produced during this latter time is surplus-value for which the worker receives no return whatsoever. The ratio between surplus-value and wages (the value of labor-power) Marx calls the *rate* of surplus-value or the rate of exploitation. The profit of capitalist production is derived solely from surplus-value; and the progress of capitalist production consists in devising ways and means by which surplus-value may be increased. There are two generic methods of doing this. One is by prolonging the length of the working day. In this way *absolute* surplus-value is derived. Another generic method of increasing surplus-value, more in evidence under modern capitalism than in early capitalism, is by increasing the productivity of labor and curtailing the necessary labor time. In this way, even when the length of the working day remains constant, the difference between necessary labor time and surplus labor time increases, and therewith the rate of surplus-value and exploitation. By this means *relative* surplus-value is derived. Surplus-value is not appropriated in its entirety at the point where it is produced, but in the course of the whole process of capitalist production, circulation and exchange. The distribution of the total surplus-value at any time is determined not only by the operation of immanent economic laws but by the *political struggles* between entrepreneur, landowner and bankers; between entrepreneurs themselves even when production has become monopolistic; and, above all, between the entrepreneur and the wage-earners.

Marx divides the capital of a manufacturing concern into constant capital and variable. Constant capital consists of what orthodox political economy calls fixed capital, such as buildings and machinery, and part of what it calls circulating capital, *i.e.,* power and raw materials. Variable capital consists of wages, which non-Marxian economists regard as only part of circulating capital. The division of capital into constant and variable is made in the interests of Marx's analysis according to which the value of constant capital is only reproduced in the manufactured products, whereas wages, or variable capital, always creates some new value over its own cost of reproduction. The ordinary distinction between fixed and circulating capital reflects the entrepreneur's assumption that the source of profit is not only wage-labor but inanimate instruments of production as well. He, therefore, computes his rate of profit upon the whole of the capital he has sunk into his project and not upon the amount he has advanced as wages. This accounts for the disparity between what is called the rate of profit and the rate of exploitation. For example, in a $1,000,000 concern, $900,000 will represent investment in machinery and raw material (which Marx calls *constant* capital C) and $100,000 wage payments (*variable* capital V). If profit (which is called surplus-value S, since all profit, according to Marx, is produced during surplus labor time) is $100,000, then the rate of profit is S divided by C plus V, which is 10 per cent. The rate of surplus-value, however, is S divided by V, which is 100 per cent. The larger the rate of surplus-value (which is always being increased by either one or both of the two ways indicated above), the greater the absolute *amount* of profit produced. The total profit is not consumed for personal purposes but a large part of it is reinvested in constant capital; modernization and rationalization is made necessary by the pressure of competition and the quest for ever larger profits. The total amount of capital in use grows. In order, however, to keep the *rate* of profit constant, since the total amount of capital has been enlarged, the *amount* of profit and therewith the rate of surplus-value (the rate of exploitation) must be increased. The yearly increment of profit which is added to the capital investment grows together with that to which it is added. The constant capital of to-day is nothing but the unpaid labor of yesterday. Relatively to the increase in the magnitudes of constant capital, the amount of variable capital employed in production diminishes. The diminution of the amount of variable capital is attended by a demand for relatively fewer laborers and by a substitution of unskilled for skilled. Wages fall and an industrial reserve army comes into existence.

The rate of profit, as we have seen, is determined by the ratio between surplus-value and the total capital invested. With the increase in the organic composition of capital (*i.e.*, the ratio of constant to variable capital) the rate of profit falls even when the rate of exploitation, or surplus-value, remains the same. The desire to sustain the rate of profit leads to improvement of the plant and to increase in the intensity and productivity of labor. As a result ever larger and larger stocks of commodities are thrown on the market. The workers cannot consume these goods since the purchasing power of their wages is necessarily less than the values of the commodities they have produced. The capitalists cannot consume these goods because (1) they and their immediate retainers have use for only a part of the immediate wealth produced, and (2) the value of the remainder must first be turned into money before it can again be invested. Unless production is to suffer permanent breakdown, an outlet must be found for the surplus of supplied commodities—a surplus which exists not in respect to what people need but to what they can buy. Since the limits to which the home market may be stretched are given by the purchasing power of wages—which constantly diminishes in virtue of the tendency of unemployment to increase with the increase of the organic composition of capital—resort must be had to export.

The first things to be exported are consumption goods: say, Boston shoes to South America, if we are an American manufacturer, and Lancashire textiles to India, if we are English. There was a time when natives had to be taught to use these commodities. But having learned how to use them, they soon desired to learn how to make them. In this they are helped by the manufacturers of shoe machinery in New England and textile machinery in Manchester who naturally desire to dispose of their *own* commodities. The raw materials are right at hand—

Argentine hides in the one case, Egyptian and Indian cotton in the other. They are relatively cheaper than in the mother country because (a) transportation costs are lower; (b) where land is cheap its products—hides and cotton—are cheap; and (c) the working day is longer. Before long, Argentine shoe plants are underselling the Boston factories and India is "spinning its own." The Manchester looms lie idle and the New England manufacturers clamor for a tariff even while their stocks remain unmoved. But this is an ever-continuing process. Having learned how to use shoe and textile machinery, what is more natural than that the colonies should wish to learn how to manufacture it? In this they are helped by the manufacturers of *machine tools* in America and England who desire to dispose of their *own* commodities. Before long there is a shoe machinery factory in the Argentine, and India is manufacturing her own looms. Later on, representatives of the U. S. Steel Corporation will be convincing the South Americans and Indians that it would be more profitable to import iron and steel and other materials which enter into the manufacture of machine tools than to buy them ready made. Or natural resources may be discovered which will invite exploitation. A New York or London banking house will advance the money necessary for this capital outlay as it did for the other plants. Interest and profit will be considerable but none of it will turn a wheel in the many idle factories in New or Old England. If there is a glut on the colonial market, and interest payments cannot be met, the governments of the United States and Great Britain will step in to save their national honor and protect life and property.

This process is accompanied by periodic crises of over-production. They become progressively worse both in local industries and in industry as a whole. The social relations under which production is carried on, and which make it impossible for wage-workers to buy back at any given moment what they have produced, leads to a heavier investment of capital in industries which turn out production goods than in industries which produce consumption goods. This disproportion between investment in production goods and investment in consumption goods is permanent under capitalism. But since finished production goods must ultimately make their way into plants which manufacture consumption goods, the quantities of commodities thrown on the market, and for which no purchaser can be found, mounts still higher. At the time the crisis breaks, and in the period immediately preceding it, the wage-worker may be earning more and consuming more than usual. It is not, therefore, underconsumption of what the worker *needs* which causes the crisis, because in boom times his standard of living is generally higher than in slow times, but his underconsumption in relation to what he *produces*. Consequently, an increase in the absolute standard of living under capitalism, since at most it could only affect the rate and not the tendency to overproduction, would not eliminate the possibility of crisis. That can only be done by the elimination of capitalism as such. Although the standard of living may be higher as production goes from the crest of one boom to another, once the crisis begins, the standard of living declines at an accelerated rate.

The anti-social consequences of the contradiction between the tendency towards ever-expanding forces of production under capitalism and the relatively progressive limitations upon consumption finds its crassest expression not merely in the existence of crises but in the way they are overcome. Despite the crying want of millions of human beings commodities are deliberately destroyed and basic production systematically curtailed. Even war is sometimes welcomed as the best means of disposing of surplus stocks of commodities—and of the surplus population which the normal progress of capitalism produces. The historical tendency of capitalist production is to go from small-scale organization to large; from the exploitation of wage-labor to the expropriation of the capitalist, from isolated action against individuals to the organized overthrow of the system. No one can improve upon Marx's own graphic recapitulation:

"As soon as this process of transformation has sufficiently decomposed the old society from top to bottom, as soon as the laborers are turned into proletarians, their means of labor into capital, as soon as the capitalist mode of production stands on its own feet, then the further socialization of labor and further transformation of the land and other means of production into socially exploited and, therefore, common means of production, as well as the further expropriation of private proprietors, takes a new form. That which is now to be expropriated is no longer the laborer working for himself, but the capitalist exploiting many laborers. This expropriation is accomplished by the action of the immanent laws of capitalist production itself, by the centralization of capital. One capitalist always kills many. Hand in hand with this centralization, or this expropriation of many capitalists by few, develop, on an ever extending scale, the coöperative form of the labor process, the conscious technical application of science, the methodical cultivation of the soil, the transformation of the instruments of labor into the instruments of labor only usable in common, the economizing of all means of production by their use as the means of production of combined socialized labor, the entanglement of all peoples in the net of the world market, and therewith the international character of the capitalist régime. Along with the constant diminishing number of the magnates of capital, who usurp and monopolize all advantages of this process of transformation, grows the mass of misery, oppression, slavery, degradation, exploitation; but with this too grows the revolt of the working class, a class always increasing in numbers, and disciplined, united, organized by the very mechanism of the process of capitalist production itself. The monopoly of capital becomes a fetter upon the mode of production, which has sprung up and flourished along with, and under it. Centralization of the means of production and socialization of labor at last reach a point where they become incompatible with their capitalist integument. This integument is burst asunder. The knell of capitalist private property sounds. The expropriators are expropriated." (*Capital*, I, pp. 836-837.)

15

THE PHILOSOPHY OF POLITICAL ECONOMY

Most of the criticism of Marx's economic theories, both favorable and unfavorable, concerns itself with the truth of specific propositions in his analysis. At best it considers the connections which exist between one proposition and another, but it overlooks the further double connection between (1) the entire set of propositions contained in *Capital* and Marx's methodology of abstraction, and (2) the relation between his economic analysis and the political and economic struggles of the working class.

In what way does the method of abstraction enter into Marx's analysis? For Marx the social process is a developing whole in which man and the conditions of human activity are in continuous interaction. An analysis of any aspect of the social process, *e.g.*, its economic organization, will necessarily seem to involve tearing certain institutional aspects of social life out of their living context and transforming them into self-acting agencies. Over any given period of time, other social factors, in the interests of the analysis, will have to be

regarded as constant even though everyone knows—
and no one more than Marx—that they are not constant. A further distortion, however, enters when the
analysis of the economic organization of society begins.
For economic life is not made up of discrete and hap-
hazard activities which are fully intelligible in their
own immediate context; they are organic parts of a
process, too—a process in which the material needs of
society, whether it be as ends or means, are gratified.
The simple economic act, then, with which Marx begins
Capital—commodity exchange—involves a two-fold abstraction, once from the whole complex of social activity,
and once from the specifically economic process which,
in relation to the social process, is itself an abstraction.
This double initial abstraction is necessary to any analysis which seeks to disclose the complicated rhythm of social life, and to discover why it takes the direction it
does.

The methodological difficulties involved in this approach may be clarified by expanding an analogy which
Marx himself employs. The system of human needs and
activities which Hegel called civic society, Marx refers
to as a social organism. Political economy, he calls the
"anatomy" of that organism. Now, it is clear that the
anatomy of an organism may be studied independently
of its nervous, vascular and digestive systems, as well
as of its embryology and comparative history. Nonetheless, its function within the organism can be properly
understood only in relation to these other processes. A
detailed study of the bone structure—its composition,

rate of growth, etc.—reveals that the anatomy, too, is a process to be explained in the light of other aspects of the organism as a whole, and that it has a history which is illuminated by a study of the skeletal structure of other animals. The more we learn of the way in which the body functions as a whole, the more we may be compelled to modify our conclusions about the nature of anatomical structure. But we can only study the organism as a whole by beginning with an analysis of its parts. What is true of the relation between anatomy and the organism as a whole, is true of the relation between the anatomy as a whole and any part of it. Whether we take as the anatomical unit, the bone cell, or the mechanical configuration of a limited area of the skeletal structure, the knowledge derived by analyzing the unit in isolation will have to be modified as other aspects and areas are considered. Just as the organism as a whole cannot be studied unless parts are abstracted from it, so here, too, the anatomy as a whole can only be studied by beginning with a relatively isolated unit and showing how the larger system of interrelations is involved within it. This will involve modifying some of the conclusions arrived at in the preliminary analysis of the isolated unit.

Marx was interested in the analysis of capitalist production as a whole. But he necessarily begins with an analysis of a part—its tiniest part, the economic cell-form—the value-form of the commodity. In ordinary life no one can see this economic cell; it is embedded in a huge structure. "But the force of economic abstraction replaces the microscope." Marx attempted in the course of his analysis to show how all the characteristic phenomena of economic activity are already involved in this simple cell-form. "In the value-form of the commodity there is concealed already in embryo the whole form of capitalist production, the opposition between capitalists and wage-laborers, the industrial reserve army, the crisis." [1] The leading assumptions of Marx's analysis are such as to permit him to derive all the known phenomena he was interested in. *Practically,* it was necessary for Marx to begin his analysis with the simple abstraction—the unit of commodity exchange; *theoretically,* it would have been possible to begin anywhere, for the nature of capitalist production is revealed in all economic phenomena. Similarly, in the interest of analysis, he was compelled to assume, at the outset, that the exchange of commodities took place under a system of "pure" capitalism in which there were no vestiges of feudal privilege and no beginnings of monopoly; that the whole commercial world could be regarded as one nation; that the capitalist mode of production dominates every industry; that supply and demand were constantly in equilibrium; that having abstracted from the incommensurable use-values of commodities, the only relevant and measurable quality left to determine the values at which commodities were exchanged, was the amount of socially necessary labor-power spent upon them.

Marx's distinctive contribution to economic theory was not the labor theory of value, nor even the application of the labor theory of value to the commodity of

[1] Engels, *Anti-Duhring,* 12th ed., p. 336.

labor-power—all this is already found in Adam Smith—but his claim that the use-value of the labor-power purchased by the entrepreneur was the source of more exchange-value, under normal conditions of demand, than what the labor-power itself possessed, and that out of the difference between the exchange-value of labor-power and the exchange-value of what labor-power produced was derived profit, rent, and interest. Marx "proves" his claim by showing that *if* there were a system of "pure" capitalism, and *if* we were to disregard for a moment the presence or absence of revolutionary action of the proletariat (which as we shall show Marx never really does), then his theory of labor-power, together with the labor theory of value, play the same logical rôle in the explanation of the mechanics and dynamics of the economic system as, say, the Copernican hypothesis in the explanation of the movements of the solar system. To say that Marx's assumptions play the same logical rôle as the Copernican hypothesis is not to say that they play the same rôle. For in one case, our knowledge and our activity make no difference at all to what is going to happen, while in the other case, they decidedly do; in one case, the reliability of prediction is overwhelming, in the other, only tendencies and directions can be charted; in the first, the occurrence of *new* phenomena can be inferred, in the second, nothing not already known can be inferred, so that fundamental assumptions take on the character of elaborate *ad hoc* hypotheses; as a consequence, in the first, no laws are historical, in the second, all laws are.

By pure logic alone no one can prove or disprove any theory of value. In this respect theories of economic value may be compared to theories of geometry. The same relations of physical space may be described by many different geometries. Here, no matter what the deliverances of experience are, so long as we retain a narrowly theoretical view, spatial experience can be described in either Euclidean or in one of the many varieties of non-Euclidean geometry. The deliverances of experience can never refute a geometry, if we resolve to cling by it. It can only make it more complicated. Of course, *experimentally,* it makes considerable difference whether experience *compels* us to complicate our geometry or not. The "true" geometry, for the physicist, is the one that, on the basis of his experimental findings, he need complicate least. But where experimental control is not in question, the geometer may save all the appearances by introducing subsidiary assumptions and spin out his theories in any geometrical language he chooses. The same may be said of theories of economic value.

Indeed, the analogy between the different theories of value and different theories of geometry may be pressed further. Just as it is possible to translate any description of a physical relation, written in terms of Euclidean geometry, into the language of non-Euclidean geometry, so theoretically it is possible to re-state any explanation of an empirically observed economic phenomenon offered from the point of view, say, of the labor theory of value into the marginal utility theory of value and vice versa. In the instance in question, this is all the easier because both the Marxian and the marginalist schools allow that both utility and labor-cost enter into determination of price but differ in their assignments of relative primacy to the two factors involved. The marginalists, although insisting that labor-costs must ultimately be derived from price, admit that price may be affected by supply, which, in turn, is controlled by labor-costs. Marx, in consonance with the classical school,[2] insists that price must ultimately be derived from labor-cost; but in qualifying labor-cost by the phrase, *socially necessary,* he admits the powerful influence of demand.[3]

Subsidiary hypotheses play even a larger part when a theory of value is applied to economic phenomena than they do when theories of geometry are applied to physical existences. That is why no theory of value can be refuted by pointing to alleged contradictions. These contradictions can always be regarded as difficulties to be solved by introducing special conditions or assumptions. The latter may be additional analytical principles or particular historical data. The much heralded contradiction between the first and third volumes of *Capital* may be taken as an illustration. Instead, however, of introducing

[2] "Possessing utility, commodities derive their exchangeable-values from two sources: from their scarcity, and from the quantity of labor required to obtain them. . . . Economy in the use of labor never fails to reduce the relative value of a commodity. . . ." (Ricardo, *Principles of Political Economy and Taxation,* pp. 5, 15, Everyman ed.)

[3] Emphasis on this point is one of the distinctive merits of Lindsay's interesting volume, *Karl Marx's Capital,* p. 78*ff.*

a subsidiary hypothesis to solve the difficulties, all Marx did was to point to the fact that the abstract and ideal conditions postulated as holding in the first volume did not actually exist.

Let us look a little closer at the contradiction. It arises as follows. The source of profit is surplus-value. Surplus-value can be produced by labor-power alone. The wages of labor-power represent the variable capital of the concern. If the same total capitals are involved, and if the rate of exploitation is the same, the larger the variable capital, the greater should be the profit, and the greater the *rate* of profit. Let A represent a concern whose total capital is $1,000,000, of which $900,000 is invested in constant capital C, and $100,000 in variable V. The rate of exploitation being 100 per cent, the profit or surplus-value S will be $100,000. The rate of profit, which is given by S divided by C plus V, will equal 10 per cent. Let B represent a concern whose total capital is $1,000,000, of which $700,000 is invested in constant capital C' and $300,000 in variable capital V'. The rate of exploitation being 100 per cent profit or surplus-value, S' will be $300,000. The rate of profit which is given by S' divided by C' plus V' should be 30 per cent. Is it? It is not. The rate of profit is independent of the organic composition of capital.

It was Marx himself who pointed out the apparent contradiction and it was he who offered an explanation of it. In this connection, one can say of him what has been said of Darwin, that there was hardly a single criticism directed against his theories which he himself had not already anticipated and stated. In his chapter on "Different Composition of Capital in Different Lines of Production and Resulting Differences in the Rates of Profit," he writes:

"We have demonstrated, that different lines of industry may have different rates of profit, corresponding to differences in the organic composition of capitals, and, within the limits indicated, also corresponding to different times of turnover; the law (as a general tendency) that profits are proportioned as the magnitudes of the capitals, or that capitals of equal magnitude yield equal profits in equal times, applies only to capitals of the same organic composition, with the same rate of surplus-value, and the same time of turnover. And these statements hold good on the assumption, which has been the basis of all our analyses so far, namely that the commodities are sold at their values. On the other hand there is no doubt that, aside from unessential, accidental, and mutually compensating distinctions, a difference in the average rate of profit of the various lines of industry does not exist in reality, and could not exist without abolishing the entire system of capitalist production. It would seem, then, as though the theory of value were irreconcilable at this point with the actual process, irreconcilable with the real phenomena of production, so that we should have to give up the attempt to understand these phenomena." (*Capital,* Vol. III, pp. 181-182.)

How does Marx account for the fact that in the normal processes of production and exchange an average rate of profit would result from varying rates of profit in different industries? By assuming that the variations in the rate of profit would give rise to competition for larger returns between capitals of varying organic composition, producing in this way an average rate of profit. At any given time, the price of a commodity is determined not by the amount of socially necessary labor-power contained in it but by its cost of production plus the average rate of profit:

"Now, *if* the commodities are sold at their values, then, as we have shown, considerably different rates of profit arise in the various spheres of production, according to the different organic composition of the masses of capital invested in them. But capital withdraws from spheres with low rates of profit and invades others which yield a higher rate. By means of this incessant emigration and immigration, in one word, by its distribution among the various spheres in accord with a rise of the rate of profit here, and its fall there, it brings about such a proportion of supply to demand that the average profit in the various spheres of production becomes the same, so that values are converted into prices of production." (*Capital*, Vol. III, p. 230. Italics mine.)

It is clear that Marx's explanation implies that commodities, as a matter of *fact*, are never actually exchanged on the basis of the amount of socially necessary labor-power contained in them, but always over or under this norm. The analysis of the economic cell-form in the first volume of *Capital* was not an empirical description of what actually took place in the observable world, but an attempt to discover the tendencies of capitalist production *if* variations in supply and demand could be ruled out, *if* no monopolies existed, *if* the organic composition of all capitals was the same, etc. It is only under the latter presuppositions that the theoretical analysis of exchange would correspond to the actual empirical practice, that the price at which a commodity was sold would correspond with its true value. But Marx was not interested in the variations of price. He could accept any of the orthodox psychological theories from Jevons to Pareto which concern themselves with price *variations* from one moment of time, to another not far removed from it. When it came to explaining the pattern of price variations over a long period of time, psychological notions were irrelevant.

The significant point to be made here, however, is that no matter what the deliverances of market experience are, the labor theory of value can be saved. But why save it? Some have claimed that it should be saved for the same reason that any other scientific hypothesis should be saved, that is to say, because of its power to predict. *Yet neither the labor theory of value nor any other theory of value can predict anything which is not already known in advance.* War and crisis, centralization and unemployment, were already quite familiar phenomena when Marx reformulated the theory of value. He could show that their existence and increasing frequency were compatible with that theory and that the most significant phenomena of economic life could be described in its terms. It is a mistake to believe, however, as, for example, Bukharin does, that one can predict anything *specific* on the basis of the labor theory. That wars and panics will occur and capitalism break down are propositions too general to be enlightening;

for unless these events are given *specific temporal co-efficients,* it can be shown that they follow just as readily from economic assumptions other than those used by Marx. To counter in the familiar way by saying that economic phenomena are too complicated to permit of prediction is to concede the point at issue, for it is to admit that the theoretical assumptions are not adequate to what one has started out to explain; that no method of measuring the degree of relative indeterminacy in the conjunction of events exists, and most important of all, that *no specific guide to action* can be derived from these allegedly true general propositions. Theories of value have no predictive power.

Why, then, save the labor theory of value? Save it, say some radical thinkers who in their hearts are convinced of its scientific untenability, because it is a good rallying cry to stir the proletariat into action. It teaches the worker that he is being robbed of what he has produced, that exploitation is as natural and automatic in social life as expansion and contraction of the lungs in breathing. It is one of those necessary myths that arise to gratify the universal need for a doctrine which will fortify by logic the heart's immediate demand. Karl Liebknecht,[4] Helander, Beer, and the theoreticians of

[4] Liebknecht, however, offers his own economic construction in which wages do not represent the exchange value of labor, but *always* less than its value, so that the worker is cheated not only of the surplus exchange-value which results from the use of his labor-power, but of the actual price of reproducing that labor-power. (*Studien über die Bewegungsgesetze der gesellschaftlichen Entwicklung,* p. 259.)

the syndicalist movement throughout the world, represent this view.

This position has nothing to recommend it but its simplicity. It involves an un-Marxian theory of the nature of a myth and of the relation between the myth and the environment in which it functions. If we were to assume that a social myth is tacked on to a movement merely for purposes of helping its propaganda along, any one of a half dozen myths which painted the worker as the incarnation of all virtue and the entrepreneur as a personally wicked oppressor would be an improvement upon the labor theory of value and surplus-value. If we were to assume that a social myth owes its efficacy to the poetic way in which it ritualizes the fighting demands of a group, then the theory of value with all its analytical curlicues would have to be discarded as an esthetic blasphemy. From a Marxian point of view, a myth is an element in a general system of ideology. It consequently reflects in a distorted form its social environment, and the activities and purposes which develop within that environment. No large myth which grips millions of people can be an arbitrary creation.

The theory of value and surplus-value in its specifically Marxian form is neither an arbitrary intellectual construction nor a myth. It is not even an ideology. For it is not an unconscious reflection of class activity. It is rather the self-conscious theoretical expression of the practical activity of the working class engaged in a continuous struggle for a higher standard of living— a struggle which reaches its culmination in social revolution. It states what the working class is struggling for and the consequences of its success and failure. In this respect it is no different from the whole of Marx's doctrines which he himself tells us in the *Communist Manifesto,* "only express in general terms the circumstances of an actually existing class struggle." In its full implications it can be grasped only by one who has accepted the class struggle from the standpoint of the working class and thrown himself into its struggles. To the extent that economic phenomena are removed from the influences of the class struggle, the analytical explanations in terms of the labor theory of value grow more and more difficult. The labor theory of value is worth saving if the struggle against capitalism is worth the fight.

This may seem a cavalier way of settling the problem; but anyone who has read Marx closely will see that the whole theory of value and surplus-value bears upon its face the marks of this continuously experienced struggle between those who own the social means of production and those who must live by their use. Every struggle between capital and labor expresses a conflict between two theories of value—one which would leave the distribution of the social product of collective labor to the brutal historic fact of legal possession and the operation of the laws of supply and demand, and the other which would distribute the social product in accordance with some social plan whose fundamental principle is not the accumulation of capital for private profit but its intelligent use in behalf of mankind. Every

223

struggle of the working class is an attempt to wrest surplus-value from the control of the propertied classes and to apply it to its proper social use. The final victory in the conflict for the possession of surplus-value can be won only by political means. Meanwhile every concrete economic struggle is also a theoretical struggle between economic principles. Speaking of the victory of the English working classes in carrying the Ten Hours' Bill, Marx said:

"This struggle about the legal restrictions of the hours of labor raged the more fiercely since, apart from frightened avarice, it told indeed upon the great contest between the supply and demand laws which form the political economy of the middle class, and social production controlled by social foresight, which forms the political economy of the working class. Hence the Ten Hours' Bill was not only a great practical success, it was the victory of a principle; it was the first time that in broad daylight the political economy of the middle class succumbed to the political economy of the working class." (*Address to the International Workingmen's Association,* 1864.)

The practical import of the theory of value is clearest in its bearing upon wage-labor. However it may be with other commodities, the value of wage-labor, in the strictest economic sense, depends to a large extent upon the class struggle. According to Marx, the value of labor-power is determined by the value of the means of subsistence necessary to sustain the laborer. What is necessary to his sustenance? At least the gratifications of his natural wants. Are his natural wants fixed and determined by nature? Marx writes:

"The number and extent of his [man's] so-called necessary wants, as also the modes of satisfying them, are nevertheless the product of historical development, and depend therefore to a great extent on the degree of civilization of a country, more particularly on the conditions under which, and consequently on the habits and degree of comfort in which the class of free laborers has been formed. *In contradiction therefore to the case of other commodities, there enters into the determination of the value of labor-power an historical and moral element.*" (*Capital,* I, p. 190. Italics mine.)

The historical and moral element which enters into the determination of labor-power is measured by the intensity of the class struggle. Its existence explains the continuous transformation in the "meaning" of a subsistence wage. It is the living link between economics and politics. The outcome of to-day's class struggle affects the measure of value to-morrow. When crisis comes or war or unemployment, their social and political consequences are not merely a matter of economic laws inevitably working themselves out, but of the presence or absence of working-class activity. This is what Marx means when he says that man is at the basis of production and all the laws of production. The portion of surplus-value which goes to the entrepreneur, the landowner, the banker on the one hand, and to the proletariat, on the other, is not only an economic fact, but a political and moral one as well. It is a moral fact not because it depends on an abstract theory of justice, but on the concrete practice of struggle in behalf of class needs and interests. Marx's revolutionary outlook

225

was not something which he "added on" to his economic analysis. It was involved in his economic analysis.

The fundamental deviations from Marx's economic theories on the part of international reformism are not to be sought in the substitution of different explanations of the economic process, but in its refusal to carry on a fundamental struggle against the domination of capital. This is the root deviation from Marxism.

The philosophy of Marx does not involve fatalism either in the metaphysical or economic sense. Social institutions exhibit a definite structure in the course of their organic growth. But the pattern of this structure never realizes itself in its pure form. Within limits, human beings are able to redetermine its development. Indeed, it was Marx himself who insisted that the activities of human beings were the material basis of all social institutions. Knowledge of the ways in which man can react upon the social conditions which seem to control him, brings power and freedom!

"Man himself is the basis of his material production as of everything else he established. All institutions (*Umstände*) in which man, the subject of production, expresses himself, modify more or less all his functions and activities including those concerned with the production of material wealth —commodities. In this connection it can easily be proved that all human relationships and functions influence material production and exercise more or less of a determining effect upon it." (Marx, *Theorien über den Mehrwert*, Bd. I, p. 388.)

16

THE CLASS STRUGGLE AND SOCIAL PSYCHOLOGY

A LETTER to the author from a union organizer active in New England, who is interested in revolutionary theory, reads in part as follows:

"I have had many and quite intimate contacts with trade unions. I know for instance that in Haverhill, Mass., where I tried to run a union for some time, the decisive factors in the working population, sex, religion, nationality, etc., are so strong that while they are all shoemakers, they have no common characteristic. They will act much more readily as men and women—the women get more work than the men—as Irish, Greek, Italian, and as Catholic and Protestant and Jew than as a working class."

This is not an uncommon experience. It poses some crucial problems. If the class struggle is the central doctrine of Marxism, it is important to know whether the class struggle is a theory or a fact, whether there is one class struggle or many, whether it derives from other Marxian doctrines or they from it.

227

We may begin by pointing out the organic connection which exists between the theory of the class struggle
and the theories of historical materialism and surplus-
value. The theory of historical materialism holds that
the different rôles which different classes play in the
process of production give rise to a conflict of needs and
interests. Out of this conflict there crystallizes opposing
modes of thought and practice which express themselves
in different reactions to a common situation, and, where
the conflict is carried on within a common historical
tradition, in different emphases and interpretations of
supposedly common doctrines. The widening rift between the expanding forces of production and the fixed
property relations under which production is carried on,
leads to an even sharper differentiation in social philosophy and practical struggle. For this conflict to be
historically resolved, classes must identify themselves
with, and become the carriers of, conflicting social relations. The march of history is forced by class action not
by the dead instruments of production, nor by isolated
individual acts. We have already seen how integral the
class struggle is to Marx's economic theories. The division of the surplus social product is never an automatic
affair but depends upon the political struggles between
the different classes engaged in production. The truth
of the theories of historical materialism and surplus-
value presuppose, therefore, the existence of the class
struggle. If the facts of the class struggle can be successfully called into question, the whole theoretical construction of Marx crashes to the ground.

Some definitions are in order. What is a class? Logically, in any universe of discourse, a class consists of a collection of elements all of which have a common characteristic not shared by some other elements. When we speak of human beings, any group of men constitutes a class if each one of its members possesses some distinctive property not shared by other men. Any member of such a class may also be a member of some other class. If x is a member of the class of red-heads, he may also be a member of the class of fathers, the class of tall men, the class of Irishmen. Marx, however, is not interested in classes *as such* but in *social* classes. Not in every type of social class but only in those social classes which are defined by the rôles which different groups of men play in the processes of economic production, *i.e.,* in economic classes. Social classes—taken in the broadest sense—are bound up with the existence of any type of society in which there is division of labor; economic classes, however, represent the fundamental social divisions in those societies in which private property in the means of production exists. In what sense economic classes represent "fundamental" social divisions will be indicated below.

In *Capital* Marx distinguishes between three different economic classes—capitalists, landlords and wage-earners. Their respective source of income is profit, ground-rent and wages. No contemporary society, however, exhibits this stratification of classes in a pure form. There are intermediate, transitional and vestigial groups within and between these classes. In one country there are

[*304*]

remnants of a feudal class, in another a large *lumpen,* or slum, proletariat, and almost everywhere, pauperized peasants, professionals, hand-workers and an officialdom. But already in the *Communist Manifesto* Marx contended that the normal development of capitalist production would result in "splitting society more and more into two great hostile classes . . . bourgeoisie and proletariat," and in *Capital* he shows how this results from the tendency towards centralization of industry and concentration of wealth. In the era of monopoly capitalism, the interests of large landholders are so closely involved with the interests of the capitalists at many points in the financial and marketing structure, that both groups may be regarded, for all their rivalry, as wings of substantially the same economic class.

In the interests of political action, however, at no time is the economic schema of class divisions to be abstractly applied in a way to suggest that all classes or groups outside of the proletariat constitute "one reactionary mass." For one thing, what these classes have in common may at certain times be obscured by their differences. Then again, the composition of classes as well as their impending future is continually changing as the limits imposed by the processes of production narrow. In the fifties of the last century it may have been possible to exploit the antagonism between the English landowners and capitalists to win the Ten Hour Day. At the present time no antagonism between these groups is so great that it will not be overlooked in the common defence against the working class. During the last century, although the working class made common cause with the continental petty bourgeoisie and peasants to win certain political reforms, it could not overcome the bitter hostility of these classes to its socialist program. To-day, in the face of the impending transfer of large sections of these classes into the ranks of the unemployed or pauperized proletariat, they may be won over for revolutionary social action. This necessitates the use of a broader conception of what constitutes a class—and *who* constitutes it. So far as history in the making is concerned, the political potentialities of a class are not simply and unequivocally determined by its economic status—though this is basic—but by a whole complex of socio-psychological forces as well. That is why one cannot infer the political future of a country if one has knowledge only of its economic set-up and the numerical strength of its classes. Marx begins by locating an economic class by its rôle in production and then, by analysis of the particular *historical* situation, discovers its specific socio-psychological attitude. In the *Eighteenth Brumaire of Louis Napoleon,* as in all other of his political writings, Marx uses the concept of class in this wider socio-psychological sense, but in every case it is based on the functions which a group plays or has played in production.

"In so far as millions of families live in economic circumstances which distinguish their mode of life, their interests, and their culture from those of other classes, and made them more or less hostile to other classes, these peasant families constitute a class." (Eng. trans., p. 133.)

If classes are defined with reference to their productive functions, it follows that the source of their antagonism must be sought in the processes of production. According to Marx, in any society in which a class has a monopoly of the instruments of production, an inevitable opposition, not necessarily conscious, arises over the distribution of the total social product. The more one class appropriates, the less remains for the other. The best will in the world cannot alter the fact that where a finite amount of goods must be distributed in a society in which there exists potentially unlimited wants, the division must take the form of an inverse relation.

The inverse relation in the distribution of the product does not of itself define a class antagonism although it must always be present wherever class antagonisms are present. For a great many social antagonisms, which are not yet class antagonisms, may arise from the same general social situation. For example, the more electric power is consumed, the less coal will be bought: the public utilities trust, therefore, will find itself in opposition to the coal producers. Orange growers may find that the more tomatoes are sold, the less will be their own sales. The prosperity of the one group may mean the ruin of the other. In certain industries, the higher the wages of the skilled workers are, the lower are the wages of the unskilled. And it is clear that in any human society, so long as some goods or privileges do not exist in sufficiently large quantities to provide everyone with as much as he wants (and it must be remembered that wants and needs are variables, which have no upper limit) there will always be an objective basis for social opposition and conflict. None of these forms of social opposition, from Marx's point of view, constitutes a class opposition. Why not?

In the first place, the oppositions between different groups of capitalists may in time be ironed out by mergers, combines and trustification. The railroad companies absorb or come to an understanding with the auto-bus companies, the public utilities with the mines, one association of farmers with another. Where this does not take place and one group actually goes under, the *opposition* is not *reproduced* as is the case with the *continuous* opposition between worker and capitalist— an opposition which is a natural consequence of the fact that the social instruments of production are owned and controlled by a class other than that which uses them. Secondly, viewing capitalist production as a whole, all the employers have a common interest against all the workers in that the lower the average wage rate, the higher the profit. Thirdly, oppositions between different vocational groups within capitalist society, as well as the social oppositions which may arise outside of capitalist society, are not oppositions in which one group is exploited by another. This is the key difference between social oppositions which are class oppositions and those which are not. *In all societies in which the instruments of production are not held in common, the process of*

233

production is at the same time a process of human exploitation. The class opposition which is essential to capitalist production is more important than any other social oppositions, such as are generated in the higgling of the market or in the competition between different industries or in disagreements between different groups of workers. For class oppositions cannot be resolved without changing the structure of society, whereas the other social oppositions are continually being resolved within the unaffected framework of the capitalist mode of production. The most fundamental of all the necessary objective presuppositions of social revolution, therefore, is a *class* antagonism and not the other social oppositions which are present as contributory factors. Many of the latter, upon analysis, appear to be derived from the former.

So far we have only spoken of class opposition, not of class struggle. Struggle involves consciousness, and not all class opposition is accompanied by class consciousness. Many Negro slaves before, and even during, the Civil War, accepted their lot, if not contentedly, nonetheless without active protestations. Class struggles arise when men become *aware* of the nature of class antagonisms. This awareness does not come all at once. It grows slowly out of actual participation in a dispute about some immediate issue. It becomes deeper in the face of the severer repressions which the first signs of revolt call forth. It may be expressed in allegiance to abstract ideals. It is always sure to see in the realization of a specific set of class needs the most effective and most equitable method of realizing the needs of the community.

Do class oppositions automatically produce class struggles? Obviously not. Certain factors operate to prevent the existence of class opposition from becoming a self-conscious opposition. The most important of these factors are other *social* oppositions which conceal the basic class opposition and often lead to an alliance of a section of a class with its class enemy against other sections of its own class. These social oppositions may be the opposition between the skilled and unskilled, the rich and poor, Negro and white, Catholic and Protestant, employed and unemployed. The social and economic history of Europe and America is rich in illustrations of the way in which these and other varieties of social opposition have served as counteracting forces to arrest the growth of consciousness of class antagonisms. The history of the English Labour Party, and to a considerable extent of the American Federation of Labor, is a history of successive alliances between the highly skilled workers and their employers against the unskilled. Manufacturers have been known in America to foster labor troubles in the plants of richer and more powerful competitors in order to gain for themselves a temporary economic advantage. In the basic American industries, employers have for many years played upon race and national prejudice to divide the ranks of the workers and to recruit an army of strike breakers in case of industrial disturbance. The Belfast Port Strike was lost because of the religious dissensions created between Protestant and Catholic workers. In the division of the German working class after the war into four types of trade unions, religious differences played an appreciable part. Since 1929, in some industries controlled by conservative unions, employers have been able to cause the employed and unemployed to fall out with each other by offering workers a choice between either reducing wages and spreading work or upholding wages and restricting work.

The simple and undeniable fact is that every member of society is not only a member of a class but a member of other groups as well. In the clash of group loyalties is it necessary and inevitable that loyalty to one's class will triumph over, say, loyalty to one's church or to one's country? Let us listen to Marx apropos of the division in the ranks of the English and international working class:

". . . The English bourgeoisie has not only exploited Irishmen in order to reduce the standard of living of the English working class by compelling the Irish poor to emigrate; in addition, it has split the proletariat into two hostile camps. The revolutionary fire of the Celtic worker does not unite itself with the powerful but slow moving strength of the Anglo-Saxons. On the contrary, in all the great industrial centers of England there prevails a deep antagonism between the Irish and English proletariat. The ordinary English worker hates the Irishman as a competitor who depresses his wages and living standards. He feels a national and religious antipathy towards him. He regards him almost in the same light as the poor whites of the Southern States of North America regard the black slaves. This opposition between the English proletariat is kept alive and artificially nurtured by the bourgeoisie. It knows that the true secret of the conservation of its power lies in this division.

"This antagonism repeats itself on the other side of the Atlantic. The Irishmen who are driven from hearth and home for the sake of oxen and sheep [enclosures] find themselves in America where they constitute an appreciable and ever growing part of the population. Their only thought, their only passion is hatred of the English. The English and American governments—that is to say, the classes which these governments represent—feed these passions, in order to perpetuate the international oppositions which hinder every earnest and honest alliance between the working class of both sides of the water and consequently their common emancipation." (From Letter to Kugelmann, March 28, 1870.)

The key questions, then, are (1) under what conditions does the common class opposition which unites the whole of the proletariat against the whole of the bourgeoisie focalize itself in consciousness and struggle, and (2) under what conditions does class consciousness triumph over divisive ties of racial, religious or national consciousness? No final and synoptic answers to these questions can be given; or more accurately, the answers depend on a peculiar complex of social, economic and traditional factors which vary from situation to situation. At best only the most general necessary conditions can be indicated.

Class opposition develops into class struggle whenever in the course of production an exploited class finds that it can no longer sustain itself at the level to which it has been accustomed. The development of the productive forces of society continually widens the gap between those who have property rights to the production forces and those who live by toiling at them. Cultural disparities grow with the differences in material comfort and security. The rapidity with which an oppressed class locates the source of its exploitation and the extent to which its consequent class consciousness triumphs over its other loyalties are functions of a peculiar set of historical circumstances. In one country, due to the accidents of natural wealth and free land, the illusion that every man with initiative can win a living may still prevail even when the original conditions have vanished. In another country, a low standard of living may make for acquiescence. In one country, the population may be divided into opposing races and religions, and a fall in the standard of living may exacerbate their differences instead of uniting them. In another country, a strong revolutionary tradition may result in turning every industrial conflict into an armed battle.

The existence of political groups or parties is just as necessary for the growth of class consciousness as is the development of productive forces. The political party is the agency by which the socio-psychological obstacles to class consciousness are removed. It formulates a class philosophy to express the class needs already dimly sensed in the daily antagonisms of economic life and in the occasional conflicts into which those antagonisms burst out. The political party makes explicit as a program what is implied in the struggle of the masses. It

agitates for action on the basis of ideals, helps organize
the masses, and seeks to convince all progressive elements in society of the desirability and practicality of
its social ideas. It prepares for the conquest of power.
The course of preparation is a course of education in
which the religious, national and racial oppositions within the class it represents are overcome. Class struggles
are possible without a political party. But of themselves
they can never become revolutionary struggles unless
they are transformed from sporadic and undirected ex-
plosions of pent-up misery into the starting and con-
tinuing points of one long campaign. The political
organization serves as the active principles of revolutionary continuity. Marx and Lenin realized that left to
itself the working class would never develop a socialist
philosophy. Its intermittent class struggles would be
regarded as only *one* kind of social opposition among
others and not the most crucial of all social oppositions.
The programs of most conservative trade unions
throughout the world proclaim an essential unity, not
an antagonism, between the interests of the employer
and the wage-earner.[1] A revolutionary socialist philos-

[1] For example, Par. 10 of the constitution of the *Federation of
Conservative Trade Unions of Berlin,* organized in 1913, reads: "The
trade unions see in the employer not an economic enemy of the
worker but a *collaborator* in the processes of production. It follows
from this conception that the interests of the workers and employers
far from being always antagonistic are, on the contrary, in most cases
in harmony with each other." (*Correspondenzblatt,* Oct. 11, 1913,
p. 627, quoted by Michels, *op. cit.*) The theory and practice of the
American Federation of Labor is too well known to need documentation.

ophy does not flow from the same source as the primitive class struggle of trade unionism. It must be introduced literally into the trade-union movement, although without the existence of such a movement, socialism would have no revolutionary meaning. Only when the working class becomes imbued with the knowledge of the causes of its own existence, and fired with the ideals suggested by this knowledge, can it be called, in a truly radical sense, class conscious.

This emphasis upon the *conscious* activity of the political party, far from representing an idealistic deviation from Marxism, as most mechanical Marxists imagine, is central to Marx's revolutionary position. The opening sections of Parts II and IV of the *Communist Manifesto* make this clear to all who read it. Plechanov's epithet of "heretic" to the contrary notwithstanding, Lenin was in direct line with the Marxist tradition when he condemned the attitude of those who held that the spontaneous movement of the working class would result in revolutionary class consciousness:

". . . subservience to the spontaneity of the labor movement," he wrote, "the belittling of the rôle of the 'conscious element,' of the rôle of Social Democracy, *means whether one likes it or not, growth of influence of bourgeois ideology among the workers.* All those who talk about 'exaggerating the importance of ideology,' about exaggerating the rôle of the conscious element, etc., imagine that the pure and simple labor movement can work out an independent ideology for itself, if only the workers 'take their fate out of the hands of the leaders.' But in this they are profoundly mistaken." (*Works*, Vol. IV., Eng. trans., p. 122.)

Class antagonism can develop into revolutionary class consciousness only under the leadership of a revolutionary political organization. But now, under what conditions do the messages of the revolutionary organization fall upon willing ears? Here we seem to be arguing in a circle. Taking social need and want for granted, the class consciousness of the workers depends upon revolutionary organization, and the effectiveness of the revolutionary message upon the class consciousness of the workers. The circle, however, is only apparent. The conjunction of the two necessary conditions gives us the sufficient condition of radical class consciousness. The program of the political party of the workers wins greater support as the pressure of the environment produces greater misery.

Just as the political party is the agency by which class antagonism comes to life, so there exists a political agency which bends all its energies *to prevent* class antagonisms from rising to class consciousness. This political agency is the state. Through myriads of instrumentalities it seeks to secure the *status quo*. Although it is itself the executor of the interests of the dominant social class, it systematically cultivates the mythology that the state is above all classes and that the well understood interests of all classes are one. Every legal code proclaims this; every school system teaches it. No one can challenge the myth without suffering certain penalties. To the forces of ignorance, inertia and divided allegiance which revolutionary agitation must overcome,

must be added the inverted, official, class-struggle propaganda which teaches that there is no class struggle.

It is a well observed fact that ruling groups are always
more class-conscious than those over whom they rule.
The possession of power and the necessity of making
choices compel them to realize that almost every act in
behalf of themselves is at the same time an act, directly
or indirectly, against other subject classes. Even measures
taken presumably for the good of the whole community,
e.g., protection of the public health, are carried out in
such a way that the larger benefits fall upon those who
need them least.

The state is indirectly involved in every manifestation
of the class struggle. Not only in the obvious sense
that the court, police and soldiers are often brought in
to break strikes with injunctions, clubs and bayonets,
but in the more important sense that every class struggle
which seeks to abolish the social conditions of exploitation out of which class antagonisms arise, is aimed
at the very existence of the state power itself. The *sine
qua non* of political clarity, whether it be in the interest
of reaction or revolution, is the realization that every
class struggle is a political struggle; for the consequences of a class struggle are such as to either weaken
or strengthen the political rule of the class which controls the instruments of production. The fact that every
class struggle is a political struggle suggests why Marx
believed that the class struggle is more fundamental
than any other forms of social struggle whether they
be religious, national or racial. *Only through class*

*struggle can a change in property relationships, i.e.,
social revolution, be achieved.* That is how Marx read
the great revolutions of the past. That is how he evaluated the instrumentalities of social change in the present. He did not deny that other social oppositions—
notably religious, ethical and national—play an important part in historical change. But they never assert
themselves as revolutionary forces unless they are linked
up with the immediate interests of the class struggle.
Cromwell's men marched into battle with hymns on
their lips, but their victories sealed the fate of the feudal
nobility. The rising German bourgeoisie and the rev-
enue-hungry princes backed Luther's fierce attack on
Rome; but church estates and not the doctrine of tran-
substantiation was at issue. Later all parties to this dispute joined in a religious war against the Anabaptists,
peasants and plebeians whose poverty led them to take
the social doctrines of primitive Christianity seriously.

Marx held that religious oppositions in bourgeois society, in contradistinction to the past, no longer paral-
leled class antagonisms. As a consequence of institution-
alization, all influential religions have become wedded
to the existing order of property relations. Doctrinal differences remain, but these are as nothing compared to
the unity of interest in their real estate holdings, educational privileges and practical political power wielded
through their communicants. Any attack upon the sta-
bility of the social order, *i.e.,* upon the existing order of
property relations, is an attack upon their vested interests. Whereas they regard atheism as only a disease of

modern civilization, they denounce communism—free thought in economics—as the enemy of all civilization. In his own day Marx observed that "the English Established Chuch will more readily pardon an attack on 38 of its 39 articles than on 1/39th of its income." Whether or not this be literally and universally true, there can be no doubt that all institutionalized churches have nothing to gain by the abolition of class antagonisms and a great deal to lose. That is why whenever any crucial class issue arises, religious leaders of all denominations make a common front against the common enemy. The daily press offers pointed illustrations.[2]

What is true of the religious differences of the ruling classes is true of their national differences. Tradition, local piety and immediate interests feed the spirit of

[2] Of the many citations available, none is more eloquent than a modest death notice taken from the *New York Times,* Sept. 14, 1925:

"Chicago, Sept. 14 (A.P.)—The death of Max Pam in New York City today closed a noted legal career in which he was associated not only with Judge E. H. Gary, the late E. H. Harriman and the late John W. Gates, but with Vice-President Dawes in the organization of the Central Trust Company of Illinois.

"He had a large collection of paintings and was known as a lover of music, literature and art.

"Mr. Pam was an unrelenting foe of Socialism, and, although a Jew, contributed liberally to several Roman Catholic institutions on the ground that they would oppose the spread of Marxian doctrines. He also was a frequent contributor to the Zionist movement and active in that international organization.

"Burial will be in Chicago."

A frank recognition of the real social issues at stake is contained in the report of the Layman's Foreign Missions Inquiry which summons all denominations to forget their theological differences and to unite in a common struggle against "the real foe" of all "prophets, books, revelations, rites and churches"—the philosophies of Marx, Lenin and Russell. (*New York Times,* Oct. 7, 1932.)

patriotism. But once the class war raises its head at home or in the enemy's country, the fires of nationalism are banked and out of the smouldering flame there springs up the furies of international class interest more relentless than any national zeal can be. Bismarck permitted republican France to live in order to scotch the deadly threat of the Paris Commune; France helped save bourgeois Germany from the proletarian revolution in 1919 and 1923; Miliukov, who had accused the Bolsheviki of being German agents because of their refusal to continue war against Germany, after the October Revolution fled for help and refuge to the arms of the German general staff.

In order to avoid easy simplification, it will bear repeating that class struggles have often been fought, at least in the minds of the participants, as national and religious wars. Marx does not deny this. But he holds that this is the case only when the ruling class within a country has identified itself with one form of religion, so that an attack upon its religion is an attack upon the whole complex of social institutions of which its religious practices are a part. This is the key, as most scholars have admitted, to the attack of the German Reformation and the French Revolution upon Catholicism. Similarly for the national consciousness which becomes a unifying force in most colonial wars. A local class, proclaiming its interests to be identical with that of the whole of the subject nation, may, as in the case of the American Revolution, lead in the attack against the national oppressor. But however it may have been in the past, in the era of monopoly capitalism economic considerations and class divisions overshadow all others. In an era in which the slogan, "where markets and raw materials are, there is the fatherland," expresses an economic necessity, in an era in which all religions are equally true, if only they inculcate respect for the mysterious ways by which God works in the social order, national and religious differences are clearly subordinate to class interests.

What is true for the ruling class is decidedly *not* true for the class over whom it rules. The international working class is torn by the national, racial and religious differences which the culture of capitalism breeds, teaches and systematically intensifies. If these differences and conflicting loyalties did not exist, capitalism would disappear. As it is, until the social revolution takes place, they will never completely disappear. Until then, the class struggle may be regarded legitimately as permanent war between the state and the political party of the working class, in which the state is aided by all the agencies of existing bourgeois culture, and the revolutionary party by all the consequences of existing bourgeois production.

We can now answer the fundamental question, which served as our point of departure, less ambiguously. Class antagonism and opposition is a fact in the sense that its existence does not depend upon class consciousness. Class consciousness is a fact in the sense that sometimes class antagonisms have developed from implicit opposition to explicit struggle. The class struggle is the most important of all other social struggles in the sense that the historical record shows that a change from one social order to another has always been achieved by class struggle and in no other way. The class struggle is a theory in the sense that *to-day* as in the past it is regarded as the most fundamental struggle in contemporary society. As a theory, it is a guide to action. That is what is meant by saying that it is the most fundamental struggle. The proof that the class struggle is the most fundamental of social oppositions in society can be found only in revolutionary action which by socializing the productive base of society therewith transforms all existing national and racial oppositions from anti-social antagonisms to coöperative and mutually fructifying antagonisms. For example, one of the most striking consequences of the still incomplete Russian Revolution is the progressive elimination of national, cultural and racial hostilities among its heterogeneous peoples. This has been accomplished not by suppressing national units or indigenous cultures but by strengthening them— strengthening them by showing that their local political autonomy, natural piety for countryside, and legitimate pride in the best of their language and traditions can be perpetuated most fruitfully by voluntary participation in a socialist economy.

This is not saying that after the socialist revolution has been completed there will no longer be social oppositions. It simply asserts as an hypothesis to be tested in practice that these social oppositions will not be accompanied by economic oppression. Nor is this merely

[*322*]

a matter of definition, as some Marxists believe who argue that since class struggles arise only in class societies, therefore, in the classless society by definition there cannot be any class struggle. It is only in the realm of Platonic essences that anything can be settled by definitions. Here it is a question of the *adequacy* of definition. From the point of view of the materialistic dialectic, definitions, if they are to have any relevance to the things defined, are predictions; and no predictions about anything which happens in time—especially about the social events in which man is an active element—can claim necessity or finality. That is why the apparent paradox is inescapable that the truth of Marx's theory of the class struggle can be established only in the experience of social revolution, *i.e.,* after class society has been overthrown. For a Marxist, there is no other avenue than the concrete experience of social action by which the truth of any theory of human history can be discovered. That is the method by which he tests the doctrines of his opponents. That is the method by which he must test his own. Any other method involves faith, revelation —in short, superstition.

17

THE THEORY OF THE STATE

$\mathbf{I}$N HIS very un-Marxian
*Studien über die Bewegungsgesetze der gesellschaftlichen
Entwicklung,* Karl Liebknecht, the heroic leader of German communism, attempts to revise the materialistic
conception of history from a philosophical basis which
he describes as "more skeptical than Hume's skepticism,
more critical than Kant's criticism, and more solipsistic
than Fichte's solipsism." His attempt to provide a new
philosophical starting point for Marxism is more significant than his failure, for it raises the question of
the degree of organic connection which exists between philosophical theory and political practice. How
much of the general philosophical theory must one accept in order to be a communist? If a Marxist is committed to the philosophy of communism, does it follow
that all who accept this philosophy must be Marxists?
Certainly, from a conventional point of view, Karl Liebknecht, by virtue of his rejection of the Marxian theory
of history and of the labor theory of value, was less of a
Marxist than men like Hilferding and Kautsky; and

yet while he sealed his devotion to the cause of communism with his own blood, these others launched bitter attacks against it. There have been so many other cases in which philosophical heresy has been combined with revolutionary sincerity, that there is a crying need to distinguish between the essential doctrine and the unessential interpretation.

That there is a unity between larger questions of theory and the general direction of practice is indisputable. Every major deviation from the revolutionary practice of the international working class has sought to ground itself upon new philosophical premises or upon some pre-Marxian system—properly cut and trimmed for its purposes. But it is an altogether different matter to assert that every political difference *must* entail a philosophical difference and vice versa. For an attitude of this kind overlooks the empirical fact that human beings are never aware of the full practical implications of their beliefs.[1] Moreover—and this is the crux of the matter—it mistakenly assumes that Marxism is a systematic theory of reality which starts out from self-evident first principles about the nature of being, and rigorously deduces all its other theories and programs—even when the latter are specifically social. A

[1] Despite his fierce polemics against all types of philosophical revisionism, Lenin had a lively appreciation of the fact that variant theoretical beliefs, although potentially a source of different political practice, were not always expressed as such. Even on such a burning question as the conditions of membership in a revolutionary party, he wrote: "A political party cannot examine its members to see if there are any contradictions between their philosophy and the Party program." (*Lenin on Religion,* Eng. trans., p. 22.)

disagreement *anywhere* along the line would have to express itself somewhere else as well. Such a metaphysic, however, is absolutely incompatible with any naturalistic view which regards the world as developing in time, and which views man as an active historical agent. This is a metaphysic which in the past has been associated with mechanistic rationalism or theological idealism. In either case, it involves fatalism.

Marxism is primarily a theory of social revolution. It has wider implications—logical, psychological and metaphysical—which constitute a loose body of doctrine commonly referred to as the philosophy of dialectical materialism. But although Marxism implies a general philosophical position, *e.g.,* the beliefs in the reality of time, in the objectivity of universals, in the active character of knowing, etc., its social theories cannot be *deduced* from its wider philosophy. For they are not logically necessitated by any *one* philosophy. One may accept the Marxist evolutionary metaphysic and not be forthwith committed to its theory of social revolution. At most one can say that Marxism is incompatible with, or rules out, certain philosophical doctrines. Because *A* presupposes *B*, it does not follow that *B* presupposes *A;* although it is legitimate to argue from *non-B* to *non-A*. If space permitted, it could be shown that many of the propositions of dialectical materialism are merely generalized expressions of the findings of the physical and biological sciences, and that of them, one cannot even say that they are *presupposed* by Marxism, but only that they are *compatible* with Marxism. This leaves it an open question whether the opposites of these particular propositions are incompatible with Marxism. One may, for example, with good Marxist conscience substitute relativistic conceptions of space and time for Engels' unclear absolutistic views.

The same considerations apply in the realm of social theory. Although the social doctrines of Marxism possess a much more organic character than the body of its philosophical implications, still, not *all* doctrinal beliefs are equally relevant to the immediate political issues of revolutionary practice. Certainly, one may call into question Engels' literal acceptance of Morgan's scheme of unilateral and universal succession of family relationships and his theory of the nature and extent of private property in primitive communities—theories which modern critical anthropologists have completely discredited—without necessarily being compelled to abandon such important leading principles as the class character of the state.

In strict logic one may go even further. The nature of the state in class society—especially in contemporary bourgeois society—may be submitted to analysis in relative independence of the cluster of problems which surround the historic origin of the state. Whether the state arose in the course of the expansion of the productive forces of society and the division of labor which this entailed, whether it resulted from the military conquest of one people by another, whether, together with the division of labor, it already existed in some primitive tribes before the existence of private property in the means of production—are questions which must be decided by examining separately the evidence for *each* case of transition from primitive to class society. The highly controversial disputes of contemporary anthropologists and sociologists indicate not only that the evidence is not overwhelming for one theory or another, but that the disputants are working with different conceptions of what constitutes a state. It is all the more important, then, that we know *what* it is we are talking about before we embark upon questions as to how and when it arose. *What* the state is can be discovered in the same way that Marx, long before he read Morgan, discovered it, *viz.,* by examining its structure and function in bourgeois society and using the outcome of that analysis as an hypothesis in approaching the state organizations of the past. It can be categorically stated—despite the idealistic Hegelian logic of some Marxists—that the validity of Marx's analysis of the *nature* of the state to-day, and the revolutionary consequences which flow from it, are completely independent of any conclusions anthropologists may reach about the *origin* of the state three thousand years ago. For the purposes of intelligent political action, it is much more relevant to inquire into the function and behavior of social institutions *in the present* than into their presumable *first* origins.

A first step towards clarity may be made by distinguishing between three fundamental concepts which are often confused—society, state and government. For Marx as for Hegel, a *society* is any group of human beings living and working together for the satisfaction of their fundamental economic needs. *Government* is the administrative mechanism by which these economic needs are controlled and furthered. The more primitive the society, the more rudimentary the forms of government. Sometimes the government is nothing more than the order of succession of personal leadership enforced by the spontaneous activity of the group. In modern society, however, with its enormously specialized division of labor, the government is a complex institution with separately delegated powers. The *state* is a special organized public power of coercion which exists to enforce the decisions of any group or class that controls the government. Where the government represents the needs and interests of the entire community, it does not need a special and separate coercive force behind it. In that case it is no longer a specific, political mechanism but an administrative organ, coördinating the economics of production and distribution in both its material and cultural phases. It is extremely important to distinguish between the state and government even though, as in modern societies, the government serves the state, and even though some individuals combine in their very person the social functions of government and the repressive functions of the state. For example, the policeman who directs traffic and gives information, and the teacher who imparts the rudiments of knowledge to his pupils, are workers performing the administrative, governmental services necessary in any complex society. Were the state to be overthrown and another state established, were the state even to disappear, this work would still have to be performed.

The same policeman, however, who clubs striking pickets, and the same teacher who inculcates the ideology of nationalism, are servants of the state. Wherever the state exists, it perverts the administrative function of government to its uses. The distinction nonetheless remains.

The actual or potential exercise of coercion is a necessary constituent element in the existence of the state. But coercion is not its differentiating character. It is the locus and form of coercion which express the characteristic feature of the state. No society is possible, least of all one in which there is a complex division of labor, without the operation of some kind of pressure to strengthen certain modes of behavior and to prevent others. The coercion need not be physical. It may be exercised through public opinion. But so long as there is a recognized difference between conduct which is permitted and conduct which is not permitted, some coercion is being applied. For example, among the Andaman Islanders, where no special state power exists, a man who commits murder is not overtly punished by his tribesmen. He loses standing and is socially ostracized—which is regarded as a severe form of punishment. Among other primitive tribes, although there is nothing corresponding to our police force, physical punishment is meted out to offenders of public morality either by the family of their victims or by the entire community.

In a strict sense, we may speak of a state only where a special public power of coercion exists which, in the form of an armed organization, stands over and above the population. It is only where a *separate organization* exists, ostensibly to keep peace and order by the imposition of penalties, that the distinguishing character of *state* coercion will be found and with it the clue to the rôle and function of the state in society. "The state presupposes the public power of coercion separated from the aggregate body of its members." [2]

Why is it necessary that a special coercive power exist —separate and distinct from the physical and moral force of the collectivity—to enforce peace and order? Obviously because of the presence of *conflicts* and *struggles* in society, and because the organization of society is such that these conflicts, when not actual, are potential, and therefore must be guarded against. What kind of conflicts and struggles makes the existence of the state necessary? Sometimes it is the struggle between nations for territory. But the state power exists and functions *within* the national territory as well as without; its organization is such as to make it as readily available against its own citizens as against others. What internal conflicts, then, make necessary the existence of the whole apparatus of state power? The hypothesis of Marx and Engels is that the state is an expression of the irreconcilable class antagonisms generated by the social relations of economic production. Their subsidiary hypothesis is that wars for territorial expansion are a secondary consequence of the development of the mode of economic production. Where there are no classes, there is no need

[2] Engels, *The Origin of the Family, Private Property and the State,* (1884), Eng. trans., Chicago, 1902, pp. 115-116.

for specially organized instruments of physical coercion. Where there are classes, there is always the danger that the existing property relations, which give wealth and power to one class at the cost of another, may be overthrown. "Political power properly so-called," wrote Marx in the *Communist Manifesto,* "is merely the organized power of one class for oppressing another."

For evidence of the class character of the state, Marx went not to the philosophical concept of the state but to history and experience. Significantly enough, he started out as a believer in the Hegelian theory of the state, but was compelled to abandon it just as soon as he sought to square what Hegel called the *notion* of the state with actual political practices. The abandonment of the Hegelian conception of the state marked a striking turning point in his intellectual biography. It is worth dwelling upon in some detail—all the more so because the specific historical occasion which provoked the shift in Marx's views has striking contemporary analogues.

Like all other Young-Hegelians, Marx started out with a firm belief in Hegel's characterization of the state as "the realization of the ethical idea," as the expression of *Reason* in which the real and reasonable wills of individuals—as distinct from their capricious wills—were taken up in a systematic and harmonious whole, sometimes called the ideal community. Since the state was above man, it was above classes. It expressed the universal and abiding interests, needs and ideals, not of this man or that, nor of this class or that, but of all men and all classes. Without slighting the needs of the living, it claimed to represent the ideal interests of those who had gone before as well as those who were to come after.

Hegel had said that the Prussian state was the perfect fulfillment of the ideal state. The Young-Hegelians knew it was not. They asserted that in his heart Hegel, himself, knew it was not. But they thought they could save Hegel's theory of the state by distinguishing between the truth of the ideal and the necessary imperfection of the real or existent. The actual state uses were in their eyes *abuses* of the ideal; their task was to bring the actual in line with the ideal. They were confident that this could be done by agitation for a democratic, politically free state. The more daring ones called themselves republicans.

When Marx became editor of the *Rheinische Zeitung,* he was obliged to comment upon the day by day activities of the government. He soon realized that his views on the nature of the state were hopelessly inadequate. Even before he resigned from his post to study French socialism and English economics, he came to see that political equality—which the Young-Hegelians aimed at introducing—was a *condition,* not a *guarantee,* of social equality; and that without social equality, all talk about the community of interests and the divinity of the state was empty rhetoric. Where there was no social equality, the state was an *instrument* used by one class in society against another. It was not an expression of the common ideals of the whole of society. For there were no common ideals. There was only a common verbal usage which obscured fundamental class differences.

The occasion upon which this was brought home to Marx was the debate held in the Rhenish Provincial Assembly on the wood theft laws (*Holzdiebstahlgesetz*). The legislators were intent upon putting teeth into the law which made the appropriation of dead wood from the forest a crime. The small landed proprietor was amply protected by the fact that his holding was small. Since he himself lived on his land, he could stop trespassing. The large landed proprietor could not use his wardens to defend his woods unless wood stealing was declared a penal offence and the law enforced. A great deal of ado was made in the Landtag about protecting the large landholders as well as small since, as citizens of the community, both classes were entitled to equal rights of protection. Marx seized upon this principle and hurled it at the heads of the members of the Landtag, barbed with the following question: What protection was the state giving to the poor, the paupered wood stealers themselves, who were also citizens of the political community? The poor were not stealing wood in order to sell it. They merely made sporadic raids on private forests in their vicinity in order to gather fuel for their cottages. The stringency of the winter and the relatively high price of wood had intensified the practice. And as a matter of fact, the poor had always enjoyed the immemorial rights (conveniently forgotten by the historical school of law) of carting off dead wood. But now on the pretext that sometimes injury was done to *living* trees, the poor were to be prohibited from taking *any* wood. The state had stepped forward to defend the property of one class of its citizens. But it did nothing to defend the welfare, indeed, the very life, of a still larger class—those that had no property. If the state was, as it claimed to be, an organization standing above classes, beyond reach of privileged economic interests, its protecting zeal would extend to all sections of the population. Judging it, however, by the specific activity of its courts and legislatures, it appeared very far from being the incarnation of impartial reason which Marx in the first flush of his Hegelianism had regarded it.

The debates on the Wood-stealing Laws marked the definite abandonment on the part of Marx of the Hegelian theory of the state. The state, he now declared, was rooted in a soil other than the self-development of the logical idea. Its voice was the voice of reason, but its hands were the hands of economic privilege. "The organs of the state have now become the ears, eyes, arms, legs with which the interests of the forest owners hears, spies, appraises, defends, seizes and runs." (*Gesamtausgabe,* I, 1, p. 287.) The more closely he studied the behavior of courts and legislatures, the stronger grew his belief that the moving force, ground and motive behind the enactment of any law which affected conflicting interests of different classes, was not an impartial theory of justice but the private privilege of a dominant class whose selfishness and greed were concealed, sometimes even from itself, by juristic rationalizations and mouth-filling phrases about personal rights and liberties. "Our whole exposition," wrote Marx in concluding his discussion, "has shown how the Landtag has degraded [*herabwür-digt*] the executive power, the administrative authorities, the existence of the accused, and the very idea of the state to *material instruments of private interest.*"

When Marx wrote this he was not yet a Marxist. He speaks of the poor and not of the proletariat, and of private interest without linking those interests with the the social relations of production. But in subsequent essays and especially in those chapters of *Capital* which deal with primitive accumulation, capitalist accumulation and the expropriation of the agricultural population, he deepens his analysis by showing that private property in the instruments of production must necessarily carry with it—and always has—political power over those who must live by the use of those instruments. Without the state power there can be no private property, for the legal right to hold private property is nothing but the might of the armed forces of the state to exclude others from the use of that property. The very continuance of production demands the existence of the state, since the immanent logic of the bourgeois system of production intensifies the opposition between classes. It therefore becomes necessary for the state to set itself up as a nominally impartial arbiter working through law and education to dissolve the antagonisms which threaten to wreck society. The state thus insures that the processes of exploitation proceed uninterruptedly.

The fact that the domination of the state is coextensive with that of private property in the instruments of production wrecks not only Hegel's political philosophy but all others, notably that of Lassalle's, which separate bourgeois society from the state, and appeal to the state, as the presumable representative of all classes, to correct the abuses of bourgeois society. Sometimes it is even expected that the existing state will gradually abolish capitalism and introduce socialism. This dangerous illusion disappears once it is realized that the existing state cannot be dissociated from the existing economic society. At any given time, the state is a natural outgrowth of the productive relations, and implicitly pervades the whole of society even when its institutional forms appear to be independent. The economic order is a political order and the political order is an economic order. Against those who asserted that these two were separate and distinct, Marx claimed that the historical record proves that the logical distinction drawn between "property power" and "political power" corresponded to no difference in fact, that in social life, property and political power were but different aspects of the same thing.

"How 'money-making' is turned into 'the conquest of power,' and 'property' into 'political sovereignty,' and how, consequently, instead of the rigid distinctions drawn between these two forces by Mr. Heinzen and petrified into *dogma,* they are interrelated to the point of unity, of all this he may quickly convince himself by observing how the serfs *purchased* their freedom and the communes their municipal rights; how the citizens, on the one hand, enticed money out of the pockets of the feudal lords by trade and industry, and disintegrated their estates through bills of exchange, and on the other hand, aided the absolute monarchy to victory over the undermined great feudal lords and *bought off* their privileges; how they later exploited the financial crises of the absolute monarchy itself, etc.; how the most absolute monarchs became dependent upon the Stock Exchange Barons through the national debt system—a product of modern history and commerce; and how in international relations, industrial monopoly is immediately transformed into political domination. . . ." (*Gesamtausgabe,* I, 6, pp. 306-307.)

Since the forces of political authority serve to support the power of the dominant economic class, and since the mode of economic production determines not only the character of the state but tends to determine the form of the state as well (constitutional monarchy or democratic republic), we can understand Marx's meaning more completely when he writes in the *Communist Manifesto,* "The modern state power is merely a committee which manages the common business of the bourgeoisie."

Does not Marx contradict himself when he speaks, in one place, of the state as a separate public power, and in another, of the state as pervading all the institutions of society and involved in their functioning? No, for the existence of special instruments of oppression is a naked and *formal* expression of the *material* system of oppression, *i.e.,* of the mode of economic production. The history of the state—the succession of its special forms and organization—can best be grasped as an aspect of the history of the economic system. As capitalism develops from the crude competition and duplications of *laissez faire* to the relatively highly organized forms of

monopoly, there takes place a corresponding improvement in the organs of state power. They become more
centralized and efficient. Functionally the state enters
more and more into business and the armed public forces
of the state become, so to speak, the private detective
guard of the business plant. The growing pressure of
class antagonisms compels the employers to see to it that
some special public force is always at hand and that no
other special force exists in the bulk of the population
which can be used against the public one. At the same
time and in the interests of functional efficiency, the
organization of the state machine *seems* to be independent of the organization of business. The concentration of armed forces offers a deceptive plausibility to the
claim that the state stands outside of business and merely
exercises governmental functions of regulation in behalf
of the whole community. When the state takes over
whole industries like the railroads, telegraph and post-
office in the interests of *efficient total production,* it
conceals this under the euphemism of "social service."
As a consequence, the ideology of state neutrality and
supremacy is strongest just when—as under monopoly
capitalism—the state is serving the bourgeoisie most
efficiently.

The era of finance capital and imperialism reveals this
dualism between the actual function of the state and its
professed philosophy most clearly. But by the last third
of the last century Marx had already discerned the
tendency of the state to assume a national form in
bureaucratic organization and in official philosophy pre-

cisely at those moments when its repressive functions came most openly into play. With broad strokes he summarizes the development of the state from the days of the absolute monarchy to the days of the Paris Commune:

"The centralized State power, with its ubiquitous organs of standing army, police, bureaucracy, clergy and judicature—organs wrought after the path of a systematic and hierarchic division of labor—originates from the days of absolute monarchy, serving nascent middle class society as a mighty weapon in its struggle against feudalism. Still, its development remained clogged by all manner of medieval rubbish, seignorial rights, local privileges, municipal and guild monopolies, and provincial constitutions. The gigantic broom of the French Revolution of the 18th century swept away all of these relics of bygone times, thus clearing simultaneously the social soil of its last hindrances to the superstructure of the modern State edifice raised under the First Empire, itself the offspring of the coalition wars of old semifeudal Europe against modern France. During the subsequent régimes the Government placed under parliamentary control—that is, under the direct control of the propertied classes—became not only a hotbed of huge national debts and crushing taxes; with its irresistible allurements of place, pelf, and patronage, it became not only the bone of contention between the rival factions and adventurers of the ruling classes; but its political character changed simultaneously with the economic changes of society. At the same pace at which the progress of modern industry developed, widened, intensified the class antagonism between capital and labor, the State power assumed more and more the character of the national power of capital over labor, of a public force organized for social enslavement, of an engine of class despotism. After every revolution marking a progressive

265

phase in the class struggle, the purely repressive character of the State power stands out in bolder relief." (Karl Marx, *The Paris Commune,* New York Labor News Co., 1920, pp. 70-71.)

The crucial test of the validity of Marx's theory of the state must ultimately be found by analyzing the day by day activities of the legislatures, the courts and executive bodies of the country. The state is what it does and what it does is revealed by experience not by definition. This methodological principle must be kept firmly in mind whenever we approach any body of law as well as the reasons offered for a judicial decision. No law and no agency of the state will openly proclaim that human interests are to be sacrificed for property rights, or more accurately, that where there is a conflict of claims, the interests of the possessing classes take precedence over the interests of the non-possessing classes. Indeed an open admission that this is the case would constitute a violation of the expressed legal principle that all are equal before the law; in theory, such an admission— although truthful—would be illegal. Nonetheless, even with no more knowledge of the law than what it says of itself, one can show that its implicit end is security of property and not justice in its distribution. And as for the law's concern with rights of persons, one need only point to the trivial but highly symbolic fact that in Anglo-American law the punishment for abstracting a small sum of money from a man's pocket is much severer than it is for beating him to within an inch of his life, to illustrate its immeasurably greater concern for the rights of property than of personality.

That *all* law is a direct expression of economic class interests no one can plausibly maintain. Much of it treats of technical commercial matters which are of interest only to private groups who own real property, play the market, etc. Some of it, especially in Anglo-American law, reflects the weight of tradition as in many features of the law of evidence. Some of it expresses the interests of the lawyers as a professional group—often in opposition to the interests of their clients—as in the laws of procedure. Some of it has the character of purely administrative ordinance as in the case of traffic regulation. Nonetheless, the fundamental class character of the law becomes as clear as daylight both in the manner in which it is interpreted and on the occasions in which it is enforced. Just as soon as there is a struggle between capital and labor, the court steps in to protect the interests of the *status quo*. Whether it is the use of injunctions and martial law in labor disputes, the blanket charge of conspiracy against labor organizers, the use of the undefined charge of disorderly conduct to break up a picket line, the arrest of those distributing radical hand-bills on the grounds that they are "littering the streets," the thousand ways in which the phrases "inciting to riot" and "constituting a public nuisance" can be stretched to jail strike leaders—one underlying aim runs through court practice, *i.e.,* the preservation of the existing property relations. In fact, the courts do not hesitate to suspend the constitutional guarantees, which they are

sworn to defend, just as soon as the exercise of the freedom of speech, press and assemblage threaten to be
effective in organizing militant labor.

The economic class divisions of society exercise a profound even if indirect influence upon the whole of
criminal law. Paradoxical as it may appear, criminal law,
although not so immediately concerned with economic
interests and activities, is more overtly repressive and dis-
criminatory than civil law. The purpose of civil law in
the main is to regulate business transactions within the
sphere of exchange and to make possible redress of
business grievances by compelling guilty parties either
to carry out their contracts or to make restitution in the
form of services or money. That civil law can be turned
in case of emergency into an instrument of class repression, is clearly illustrated by the use of damage suits
against labor unions, eviction proceedings against the
unemployed, etc. But the bulk of civil law has, as its
objective, the private detail of the entrepreneur and the
conflicts which arise with other entrepreneurs in the
common quest for profit. The primary purpose of criminal law is punishment—punishment of any individual
whose acts threaten to disrupt the "peace, order and
security" of the social system. These terms are undefined
variables; but whatever meaning they have is determined by the interests which control those who make
the laws as well as those who interpret and enforce
them. Formally, the criminal law is laid down as bind-
ing upon the members of all classes. Actually its enforcement is selective wherever class conflict flares up.

Even where there is no selective bias in the enforcement of criminal law, punishment for the same criminal offence falls with unequal severity upon members of different economic classes. Where there is social inequality, the enforcement of any law—no matter how impartially administered—automatically reflects, in the degree and nature of the punishment, different class divisions. In other words, there can be no strict equality before the law where there is social inequality. Assume, for example, that in an ideal bourgeois society the law is impartially carried out according to its letter—that political favor and financial corruption have no influence upon the integrity of the court. *A,* a worker, and *B,* a banker, are separately arrested on charges of manslaughter. Since they are both formally equal before the law, bail is fixed at the same amount. *A,* who cannot raise the bail or even pay the premium on a bail bond, is confined in jail until his day in court comes; *B,* in virtue of his economic status, is at large twenty-four hours after he is booked. Both are brought to trial. *A* faces a jury, not of his peers, but of men hostile or indifferent to him and his entire class; *B* must meet only the mixed feelings of resentment and admiration which fill the breasts of the less well-to-do among the middle classes at the sight of those who have climbed higher. *A* is dependent for his exoneration upon the skill of an unknown and uninfluential lawyer often appointed by the court; *B* can hire the most eminent counsel in the country and enormously increase the probability of acquittal. At every step in the legal process, no matter how impartially admin-

269

istered, the worker is punished not merely for his crime but for his poverty. No exercise of judicial discretion can alter this fact, for it flows from the class nature of the social system of which the law is the expression not the cause. Indeed, wherever judicial discretion is introduced, the worker fares even worse, since the training and class origins of judges—not to speak of the mechanics of their selection—lead them, as a whole, to mistake their traditional prejudices and class passion for order and security into first principles of justice.

Ultimately, the sanctions behind criminal law are the sanctions behind all law. The sanctions behind all law —the whole array of repressive state forces—is an integral part of the process of production. The habit-patterns of complacency and tradition are not sufficient to keep production running in class society, and the methods of educational indoctrination have their limits. Sooner or later the conflicting needs and interests of different classes become focalized in consciousness and translated into action. No matter how our philosophy may try to escape it, where there are inarbitrable conflicts of interests, force decides which claim will prevail.

We can now return to the question which served as our point of departure. What doctrine is essential to Marxism in the sense that it can be used as a touchstone of allegiance to his thought? If the above analysis is valid, it can be categorically stated that it is Marx's theory of the state which distinguishes the true Marxist from the false. For it is the theory of the state which is ultimately linked up with immediate political practice.

The attempt made by "liberal" Marxists throughout the world—even when they call themselves orthodox—to separate the existing economic order from the existing state, as well as their belief that the existing state can be used as an instrument by which the economic system can be "gradually revolutionized" into state capitalism or state socialism, must be regarded as a fundamental distortion of Marxism. "Liberal Marxism" and "gradual revolution" are contradictions in terms. For Marx, every social revolution must be a political revolution, and every political revolution must be directed against the state. That is why it is more accurate to regard the German Social Democracy as Lassallean rather than Marxian.

Nowhere does Marx state the relation between social and political revolution more clearly than on the final page of his *Poverty of Philosophy,* a work which contains the classic criticism of petty-bourgeois socialism with its theory of public works, fiat money, coöperative workshops, free credit, and a classless theory of the state:

". . . after the fall of the old society, will there be a new class domination, comprised in a new political power? No. The essential condition of the emancipation of the working class is the abolition of all classes, as the condition of the emancipation of the third estate of the bourgeois order, was the abolition of all estates, all orders.

"The working class will substitute, in the course of its development, for the old order of civil society an association which will exclude classes and their antagonism, and there will no longer be political power, properly speaking, since

271

political power is simply the official form of the antagonism in civil society.

"In the meantime, the antagonism between the proletariat and the bourgeoisie is a struggle between class and class, a struggle which, carried to its highest expression, is a complete revolution. Would it, moreover, be matter for astonishment if a society, based upon the *antagonism* of classes, should lead ultimately to a brutal *conflict,* to a hand-to-hand struggle as its final *dénouement?*

"Do not say that the social movement excludes the political movement. There has never been a political movement which was not at the same time social.

"It is only in an order of things in which there will be no longer classes or class antagonism that *social evolutions* will cease to be *political revolutions.* Until then, on the eve of each general reconstruction of society, the last word of social science will ever be:—

> "Le combat ou la mort; la lutte sanguinaire ou le néant.
> C'est ainsi que la question est invinciblement posée."
>
> George Sand.

(*Poverty of Philosophy,* Charles H. Kerr & Co., Chicago, 1920, Eng. trans. by H. Quelch, pp. 190-191.)

The belief in the class character of the state is obviously not a theoretical postulate. It demands that forms of concrete activity be worked out in the struggle against the state power. The chief question to be decided in this connection is what methods and institutions are efficacious in the struggle for the conquest of political power. This introduces for discussion the meaning and function of the "dictatorship of the proletariat" in the philosophy of Karl Marx.

18

THE THEORY OF REVOLUTION

1. "The Revolutionary Situation" and "The Revolution"

IF MARX'S analysis of the state is valid, then it follows that no fundamental change in the control of the instruments of social production is possible without the overthrow of the state. The overthrow of the state means revolution. Since the acceptance of the class theory of the state is the *sine qua non* of Marxism, to be a Marxist means to be a revolutionist. The strategy and tactics of Marxists everywhere must be guided by an evaluation of the consequences of any proposed course of action upon the conquest of political power. When conditions are different, methods of procedure will be different, but the use of one method rather than another is determined by a revolutionary purpose which is constant in all situations. This does not mean that such a purpose can be translated into action at any time. That was the error of the Blanquists who, for almost half a century in France, conceived of revolution

273

as a conspiratorial *coup d'état* on the part of a band of
determined men, whose first task was to seize the state
offices and, independently of the condition of productive
forces and the political maturity of the proletariat, introduce socialism. Such a policy necessarily leads to a
mad adventurism which, for all its heroic qualities, has
disastrous effects upon existing organizations of the
working class.

Many socialists who survived the abortive revolutions
of 1848 were peculiarly subject to the belief that the
sole and exclusive condition of a successful revolution
at any time was the will and power of a political organization. They did not stop to inquire whether the complex of objective conditions, economic, political and
psychological, which had once been favorable for an
uprising, had remained so. In the desperation of their
defeat, they impatiently urged resort to direct action
before the state had an opportunity to take protective
measures in its own behalf and annihilate the revolutionists. Many of these men worked with Marx in
common organizations. But in the interests of the true
revolutionary objective for which these organizations
were founded, Marx was compelled to dissociate himself from the revolutionary Utopians—sometimes to the
point of splitting with them. It was not their sincerity
which he attacked but what was, in its objective consequences, even more important, their lack of intelligence.
"In moments of crisis," he once wrote, "stupidity becomes a crime."

One of the earliest struggles which Marx waged

against this tendency in the international revolutionary movement, took place in London in 1850. On this occasion he split the Communist League by his attack on the Willich-Schapper fraction of direct actionists. In the course of the discussion, he said:

"In place of a critical attitude, you [the minority] substitute a dogmatic one; in place of a materialistic conception, an idealistic one. For you, *pure will* instead of objective conditions is the driving force of revolution.

"While we say to the workers: 'You have to go through 15, 20, 50 years of civil war and national struggles, not only to change conditions but to change yourselves and to acquire the capacity for political mastery,' you say on the contrary: 'We must seize power at once or else we may as well lie down and go to sleep.' While we particularly call to the attention of the German workers, the undeveloped character of the German proletariat, you flatter (in the crudest way) their national feeling and the professional prejudices of the German craftsmen. Certainly, the more popular thing to do. Just as the democrats convert the word 'people' into a holy fetish, so do you the word 'proletariat.' And like the democrats you palm off the revolutionary phrase for revolutionary development. . . ." (*Enthüllungen über den Kommunistenprozess,* Mehring ed., p. 52.)

This note is struck again and again in the history of the European working-class movement. In a different context it appears in the writings of Engels, of Lenin, of Rosa Luxemburg. Sometimes, these passages from their writings will be found quoted in the works of those who call themselves Marxists but for whom revolutionary activity at *any* time is anathema. Such citations may be dismissed as dishonest distortions. For Marx condemns

275

"revolutionists of the phrase" not because he is an advocate of "moral force," but because he is interested in discovering the conditions under which a *successful* revolution is possible.

A political party can prepare itself and large sections of the working class for a revolutionary situation in which its action may be the decisive factor. But it cannot of itself produce the revolutionary situation. That depends, first, upon the breakdown of the forces of production and distribution as measured by the disparity between what the workers receive and what they have produced, by the growing unemployment, by the jamming of the mechanism of credit, by all the familiar phenomena attendant upon an actual or incipient economic crisis. Second, a revolutionary situation is evidenced in the lack of immediate political homogeneity on the part of the ruling classes. This may be the result of an exceptionally prolonged economic crisis or of a lost war or of some natural calamity which demoralizes production. The lack of political homogeneity is reflected in dissensions between different groups over policy. Its objective effects are loss of prestige of the ruling group in the eyes of the mass of the population, a growing sense that "anything might happen," increasing restlessness and unreliability of administrative agencies. To all this must be added, thirdly, spontaneous manifestations of class consciousness and struggle; strikes, riots and mass demonstrations; the disintegration of the habit-patterns of blind response and obedience on the part of the oppressed elements. The revolutionary situation is experienced by *all* classes as one of seething chaos.[1]

It is only in relation to the objective revolutionary situation that the revolutionary act and the rôle of the revolutionary party can be grasped. Psychologically, the seizure of power is felt as an attempt to bring a new order out of the existing confusion. Revolutionary slogans and programs are put forward as ways of saving society. To the mass of the population, without whose support the revolution would fail, the ensuing civil war and destruction appear as the costs of social salvation. Where the revolutionary situation is not conceived of as the condition precedent to the revolution, the latter is regarded as an abstract affair—a *putsch* or *coup d'état*. It is doomed to failure; and if it succeeds, it is only as a superficial, political phenomenon which leaves the essential class relationships unaltered. The proletarian revolution, which is the greatest social upheaval in history, must strike deeper roots. For it marks the transi-

[1] Lenin states this as follows:

"The fundamental law of revolution, confirmed by all revolutions and particularly by the three Russian ones of the twentieth century, is as follows: It is not sufficient for the Revolution that the exploited and oppressed masses understand the impossibility of living in the old way and demand changes; for the Revolution it is necessary that the exploiters should not be able to rule as of old. *Only when the masses do not want the old régime*, and when the rulers *are unable* to govern as of old, then only can the Revolution succeed. This truth may be expressed in other words: Revolution is impossible without an all-national crisis, affecting both the exploited and the exploiters." (*Infantile Sickness of "Leftism" in Communism*, Contemporary Publishing Co., pp. 76-77.)

tion not from one class society to another, but from class society to classless society.

The revolutionary party does not make "the revolutionary situation." Nor does it, by itself, make "the revolution." It organizes and leads it. This is a task heavy with responsibility; a task whose execution is influenced more directly by such "subjective" factors as previous education, theory, personality of leaders than by any one "objective" aspect of the revolutionary situation. A revolutionary situation does not automatically come to fruition. Unless a revolutionary party exists, free from the twin faults of sectarianism and opportunism, and therefore capable of properly exploiting every lead towards the seizure of power, the situation may lose its potentialities for revolutionary change. But it is not only at such moments that the political party is of central importance. Long before the revolutionary situation develops, it must be active on every front on which there is social discontent. It seeks to broaden the base of mass struggles, to organize and educate the working class politically, and to build up its own ranks in preparation for the coming revolutionary situation.

For Marx, questions of revolutionary organization and strategy were of the highest political significance. They were not treated as details incidental to larger problems of theory but as integrally connected with them. This is clearly revealed in that classic statement of tactical first principles, *The Address to the Communist League* (1850). Some illustrations:—In the processes of capitalist production, the wage-workers and agricultural laborers are those who have most to gain by a revolution. Their political party must therefore *lead* the revolution. It must never surrender its independent revolutionary policy and organizational autonomy no matter how closely it works in united action with the political parties of the discontented petty bourgeoisie. Even more important. The international character of capitalist production necessitates an international organization to overthrow it. The social revolution is not complete until it is international. A social revolution in one country creates a breach in the international system of capitalist production which must either become wider or be closed up. As Marx proclaimed in his *Address*, ". . . it is our interest and our task to make the revolution permanent, to keep it going until all the ruling and possessing classes are deprived of power, the governmental machinery occupied by the proletariat, and the organization of the working classes of all lands so far advanced that all rivalry and competition among themselves has ceased." It goes without saying that the uneven character of capitalist development and the varying concomitant political consciousness demand a flexible, concrete application of fundamental principles to specific problems of each nation. But in virtue of the character of the state and of the existence of special bodies of armed men, it is imperative, however, that revolutionary organizations *everywhere be prepared,* when the revolutionary situation arises, for the ultimate overthrow of the state.

2. FORCE AND NON-VIOLENCE

The emphasis on readiness for the ultimate overthrow of the state indicates the kind of revolution Marx is talking about. It raises the most fundamental of all questions concerning revolution, *viz.*, the place and justification of force and violence in social change.

Marx and Engels never discussed the use of force in the abstract. For what could one say of it? Taken by itself, in independence of a concrete historical context and a specific purpose, it is a neutral event devoid of moral quality. It is only in relation to the socio-historical conditions and consequences of its use that it can be intelligently discussed. For example, before one passes moral judgment upon the ancient practice of enslaving prisoners of war, it would be well to ask what the alternative historical methods of treating them were— in this case decimation, and sometimes cannibalism— and why the practice of enslaving prisoners prevailed over others. Where the subdivision of labor has reached a point at which it becomes possible, by the forced labor of prisoners, to provide enough for their wants and a surplus to liberate others for cultural activity, slavery constitutes a distinct moral advance. To condemn slavery as essentially wrong wherever and whenever it is found on the ground that the alternative of freedom always existed as an *abstract* possibility, is to pass moral judgment not upon slavery but upon the natural and social *conditions* out of which ancient life developed and over which one had but limited control.

Abstract moral considerations of this kind have no relevance when it is a question of evaluating between institutions all of which fall short of ideal perfection. Engels properly retorts to Dühring who approached the problem in this abstract fashion: "When Dühring, then, turns up his nose at Greek civilization because it was based on slavery, he might just as reasonably reproach the Greeks for not having steam engines and electric telegraphs." [2]

In contradistinction to economists like Bastiat, who sought to explain social institutions in term of "natural law" concepts of force, Marx denied that the use of force alone—as a naked assertion of power—can ever explain the course of social development. At most it accounts for the destruction of a culture or its retardation. The use of force can achieve higher social and moral ends only when it liberates the productive capacities of the social order from the repressive property relations within which they are bound. That is not merely the condition of its historic justification but of its historic efficacy. "Force is the mid-wife of every old society pregnant with the new. It is itself an economic power." (*Capital,* I, p. 824.)

All this indicates that Marx did not make a fetishism of force. His theory that political force must derive its ethical sanction from some positive social function serves as a guide to its revolutionary use. He had made a close study of the rôle of force in the great English and French revolutions, and knew from first hand experience what

[2] *Anti-Dühring,* 12th ed., p. 191.

it had won and lost in the revolution of 1848. For Marx, the use of force in a revolutionary situation was no more a moral problem than the use of fire in ordinary life; it was only the *intelligent* use of force which constituted a problem. In this position he had to defend himself against two types of anti-revolutionary, theoretical intransigeance. One was the official point of view of the bourgeoisie. Having already made its revolution by force, it now taught that the use of force in political matters was in principle a crime against civilization. And this in the face of the facts that the bourgeois state and law functioned by the use of force; and that the struggle between capital and labor, upon which bourgeois civilization rested, took the form of open civil war whenever workers were driven to defend themselves as a result of intolerable oppression. The second point of view was more sincere, and because it sometimes called itself revolutionary, too,—more dangerous. This was the position of the "moral force" men, Christian Socialists, philosophical anarchists, legalists at any price, and of the perennial Utopians of whom Marx had already written in the *Communist Manifesto* that "they reject all political, and especially all revolutionary action; they wish to attain their ends by peaceful means and endeavor."

Contemporary political thought and practice has witnessed a resurgence of this social philosophy in the doctrines of pacifism and non-resistance. A statement of the Marxist criticism of this view should be timely.

First of all, it should be clear that non-resistance in

politics—if it does not betoken the attitude of complete acceptance—is a species of resistance. Strictly speaking, it means *passive* resistance. It is a *technique* of resistance. On what grounds can it be asserted, then, that the technique of passive resistance is superior to the technique of active resistance? Obviously only in terms of the consequences which follow from their respective use, only in the light of their efficacy in realizing the ends to which they are the technique. In the case in question, the end is the introduction of socialism which will eliminate the remediable horrors and degradation of bourgeois society—war, unemployment, starvation, and the manifold forms of spiritual prostitution that flow from the dominance of the profit motive. To say, then, that passive resistance is more effective than active resistance is to say that by its use socialism may be achieved in the shortest space of time and at the lowest price in human life and suffering. What is the evidence for believing this to be always true? Must not this be redetermined for every situation? If the theoretical possibility is admitted, that this may sometimes *not* be the case, does not the absolutistic foundation of pacifism collapse? And with it the fetishism of the technique of passive resistance?

Whoever denies that passive resistance is a technique to achieve certain ends, is constrained to affirm that it is a religion, since it hypostasizes an attitude which may be valid in some situations into an unconditional postulate of all situations. As a religion it is beyond argument. But its effects are not beyond argument, especially for those who do not share the faith. These effects may be such as to perpetuate and intensify existing evils and disorganize active techniques which aim at their rapid elimination. In such situations the objective implications of the attitude of passive resistance convert it into a religion of acceptance and make its adherents more immediately dangerous to those who urge revolutionary action than the sworn defenders of existing evils. For example, Mr. Gandhi has publicly proclaimed in an address on the future of India:

"I would consider it nothing if we had to pay a million lives for our liberty, but one thing I hope the Congress has set its heart on is the campaign of non-violence. So, whether it is one life or a million we have to pay, I am praying it will be possible for the future historian to say that India fought and won her liberty without shedding human blood." (*New York Times,* Oct. 13, 1931.)

It must be remembered that the imperialistic penetration of India has taken place to the continuous accompaniment of bloodshed; the Amritsar massacre was only a dramatic illustration of the process of "pacification." In the light of this, the implications of Mr. Gandhi's position are very interesting. He does not say, as do some Indian revolutionists, that since the probable cost of attaining national independence by other techniques would come to much more than a million lives, passive resistance is preferable. This is an arguable position. No, Mr. Gandhi declares that he rejects active resistance *even if it could bring national independence at much less than a million lives.* It is Mr. Gandhi, then, who is prepared to justify the shedding of human blood, if only it does not flow as a result of a violent revolution. For what end? The independence of India? Hardly, since he refuses to consider any other methods of attaining it. Out of compassion for those who must suffer? Obviously not, since a humanitarian is one who seeks the least costly road no matter what it is, and who justifies human suffering only when it is either a way of avoiding still greater suffering or the indispensable condition of some greater good. Mr. Gandhi's end or good can be only the *abstract principle of non-violence itself*. But in that case why stop at a million lives? If it is immaterial to the principle whether it is "one life or a million," it cannot be material whether it is one million lives or ten million. In strict consistency Mr. Gandhi must be prepared to say that if India could win her freedom by a campaign of non-violence, he would "consider it nothing" if no Indians were alive to enjoy it. *Pereat mundus fiat principia!*

Let us leave India. A sober analysis of the effects of passive resistance and non-coöperation in social life will reveal that at certain times more privation for the community may follow upon their use than through some forms of militant action. A general walk-out in a key industry may cause more suffering and yet be less effective than a violent demonstration. At other times, a violent revolution may stave off international carnage. If the Second International had been true to its pledged faith in 1914 and had been organized for social revolution, it is unlikely that the costs would have come as high

—to mention only the most conspicuous item—as twenty-five millions of dead and wounded. The punishment for the excessive legalism and pacifism of the Italian socialists in 1920 was Mussolini and Fascism.

The logic of personal relations applies in social affairs, too. An abject humbleness is not always more effective in redressing grievances than a spirited defence. We cannot always get rid of our enemies by loving them. It may make them more furious. And as for the much heralded effects of passive resistance in spiritually disarming the enemy, they cannot be very reliable under conditions where it is not necessary to see men in order to kill them; where bomb, gas and germs do their work in distant anonymity. But under any conditions the technique of passive resistance has its moral limits. For although we may meet force against *ourselves* with charitable forgiveness, we call a man a coward, and not a saint, who forgives the use of brute force against *others* and does not try to stop it—by force if necessary!

It is often declared that application of force demoralizes those who use it and that a new society won by force of arms would be insensitive to truly ethical values. So Dühring. So Tolstoy. So Bertrand Russell. But again it must be emphasized that it is not the use of force but the purpose for which it is used which makes it degrading. Otherwise every engineer, surgeon and soldier in any cause would be a degraded creature. There are many things ethically worse than the use of force: for example, cowardly sufferance or lazy tolerance of degrading social evils and political tyrannies which a resolute use of force might eliminate. Nor is it true that a victory won by arms leads to demoralization. Marx and Engels often point to the moral and intellectual advance which followed the French Revolution. The release of creative collective energy by the Russian Revolution is unparalleled in the history of mankind. In principle, then, the use of force—although always dangerous—cannot be always condemned. It eventuates in brutality no more often than humility leads to hypocrisy and servility.

But that does not yet establish Marx's contention that when the revolutionary situation is ripe the final conquest of power must be won by force of arms. Here we must pick up the thread of our earlier exposition. The existence of the state presupposes the existence of special bodies of armed men obedient to the will of those who control the state. These come into play directly or indirectly even in the ordinary struggles which arise in the course of the class war—a fact which is overlooked by those who profess not to believe in the use of *any* force and yet pay their state taxes which support the soldiery and the police. In a revolutionary crisis, although these forces cannot escape the general ferment and disaffection, the very uncertainties of the situation lead to their wider use on the part of those who are trying to save the old order. The application of force against rising discontent becomes more ruthless and irresponsible. It sometimes appears as if the defenders of the existing state were trying to provoke a violent rather than a peaceful revolution. Even if the parties of social revolution were to be carried to power "legally," their victory would be nugatory unless the armed forces of the state, as well as the defence corps which would be rallied by the leaders of the bourgeoisie, were won over, disarmed or defeated. In such a situation, the "readiness is all." Force must be met by force—by a stronger and more intelligent force. The determining consideration is not one of "legality" but of "revolutionary expediency." In revolutionary situations "legality" is the outworn shibboleth of a system of social repression now in dissolution whose very guarantees of civil rights, such as they were, have long since been abrogated by the bourgeoisie itself. One false step—even hesitation—may be fatal to the revolution. To insure victory strategic places must be seized, points of military vantage occupied, insurrectionary tactics deployed wherever resistance manifests itself.

Marx lived in an age in which the traditions of violent revolution were common to all classes. This was especially true on the Continent. The extension of the suffrage to the entire population did not alter matters, for the crucial question was not the forms by which the strength of the revolutionary ideal was *measured* but the efficacy of the methods by which the ideas were *achieved*. Marx never asserted that the social revolution could take place without the support—active or passive —of a majority of the population. Without the assurance of such support, the revolution must not be undertaken. But although this support is necessary, it is not sufficient unless it is translated into power. Ultimately, whether fifty per cent or ninety per cent of the population support the revolution, state power will be won not by pencil and ballot-paper but by workers with rifles. As late as 1872 in speaking of the continental countries (we shall consider the exceptions below) Marx wrote: "It is to force that in due time the workers will have to appeal if the dominion of labor is at long last to be established."

But it may be asked: Why cannot the revolution be made peacefully? Why may not the ruling class voluntarily surrender its power rather than risk defeat or the destruction of the whole of society in civil war? These questions may be answered by asking others. When has this ever been the case? When has any ruling class permitted itself to be bowed out of power without putting up the most desperate kind of resistance? Again it must be emphasized that the socialist revolution involves not merely the substitution of the power of one class for that of another in the ownership of private property, but of the very existence of private property itself. In past revolutions it was possible for members of one class to save their property by shifting their class allegiance. And still they fought tooth and nail against the rising class who were often more than ready to compromise! How much more fiercely must they fight against the socialist revolution which makes forever impossible the exercise of power over human beings through the possession of property, and which cannot compromise this principle without suffering disaster? It should also be borne in mind that in virtue of their past training,

289

ideology, and class status, the ruling class necessarily regards the defence of its property interests as the defence of civilization against barbarism, the preservation of the refinements of its culture as the preservation of all culture against the vandalism of the rabble. Out of this subjective sincerity there often arises—at least on the part of a sufficient number to constitute a danger— a desire to go down fighting for what they consider honor and the good life.

That the workers will have to resort to force to achieve the socialist revolution, is for Marx, then, as likely as anything can be in history. To disregard the evidence of historical experience, and not to prepare on the basis of it, is to betray the revolution in advance. To be sure, there is always the *abstract possibility* that power may be won peacefully. But history is not determined by abstract possibilities. If peaceful demonstrations on the part of workers for minor concessions of relief and insurance in ordinary times are broken up by savage force and violence, how can it be assumed that the milk of kindness will flow when the demand is made for the abolition of the entire profit system? The socialists captured a legal majority of the Finnish parliament in 1918. Before they could put through their program, they were drowned in rivers of blood by an armed counter-revolution.

3. Some "Exceptions"

We must now consider the exceptions which Marx makes to this general rule. In the very same speech from which we have quoted his remarks about the necessity of a resort to force, he says:

"Some day the workers must conquer political supremacy, in order to establish the new organization of labor; they must overthrow the old political system whereby the old institutions are sustained. If they fail to do this, they will suffer the fate of the early Christians, who neglected to overthrow the old system, and who, for that reason, never had a kingdom in this world. *Of course, I must not be supposed to imply that the means to this end will be everywhere the same.* We know that special regard must be paid to the institutions, customs and traditions of various lands; and we do not deny that there are certain countries, such as the United States and England in which the workers may hope to secure their ends by peaceful means." (Speech at Amsterdam, 1872. Cf. Steckloff, G., *History of the First International,* Eng. trans., p. 240.)

Although the possibility of a peaceful revolution in England and America is stated conditionally, the sense of the passage is clear. In 1886, Engels, in his preface to the first English translation of *Capital,* echoes the same sentiment. He calls upon England to hearken to the voice of a man:

". . . whose whole theory is the result of a life long study of the economic history and condition of England, and whom that study led to the conclusion that, at least in Europe, England is the only country where the inevitable social revolution might be effected entirely by peaceful and legal means." (Kerr trans., p. 32.)

And then immediately after, with an unconsciousness which almost borders on simplicity, he introduces the joker:

"He [Marx] certainly never forgot to add that he hardly expected the English ruling class to submit, without a 'pro-slavery rebellion,' to this peaceful and legal revolution."

As if it were not precisely the danger of a "pro-slavery rebellion"—a counter-revolution—which demanded that the revolution everywhere assure its victory by a resort to force! As if the mandate for its legality were derived from the existing order, which always has a "legal provision" for changing the rules whenever they are working against it, and not from the power of the masses!

Lenin, who, to my knowledge, never challenged a single word in Marx or Engels, instead of calling an error by its right name, attempts to show that Marx and Engels were perfectly justified in holding that a revolution in Anglo-American countries was possible, *at that time,* "without the preliminary condition of the destruction 'of the available ready machinery of the state.'" He hastens to add, however, that at the present time, this is no longer true in virtue of the development of bureaucratic institutions.

He writes:

". . . he [Marx] confines his conclusions [about violent revolution] to the continent. This was natural in 1871, when England was still the pattern of a purely capitalist country, without a military machine and, in large measure, without a bureaucracy.

"Hence Marx excluded England where a revolution, even a people's revolution could be imagined, and was then possible, *without* the preliminary condition of the destruction 'of the available ready machinery of the state.'

"To-day in 1917, in the epoch of the first great imperialist war, this distinction of Marx's becomes unreal, and England and America, the greatest and last representative of Anglo-Saxon 'liberty' in the sense of the absence of militarism and bureaucracy, have to-day completely rolled down into the dirty, bloody morass of military-bureaucratic institutions common to all Europe, subordinating all else to themselves, crushing all else under themselves. To-day both in England and in America, 'the preliminary condition of any real people's revolution' is the break-up, the shattering of the available ready machinery of the State (perfected in those countries between 1914 and 1917, up to the 'European' general imperialist standard)." (*The State and Revolution,* Eng. trans., London and Glasgow, 1919, p. 40.)

Lenin was a political genius but his explanation here is obviously forced and unconvincing. England and America were no different from continental countries, in any respect relevant to the conquest of power by a revolutionary movement, than they were in 1917. If anything, it would have been more difficult to achieve the social revolution peacefully in these countries than elsewhere.

Let us look at England. It was Marx who showed in *Capital* that capitalism had developed in England through the most merciless dictatorship. After the peasants had been forced off their land, they were physically punished if they *would* not work, and driven to the poorhouse when they *could* not work as a result of unemployment. By the eighteenth century Cromwell had become a national hero. Hastings, Clive, and others had carried out England's colonial policy in India, Egypt and elsewhere with the same ruthlessness that Cromwell had used in subduing Ireland. A year after Marx's birth, English workers in peaceful assemblage had been shot down at Peterloo. Marx himself had witnessed the suppression of the peaceful Chartist movement and knew many of its leaders who had languished in jail. At the very time when Marx was making his exception in favor of England, she had the largest navy in the world, standing armies in India, Egypt and Ireland, a highly developed bureaucracy, and as Marx's letters testify, the most astute and class-conscious ruling class in the world. In 1869, at a mass meeting in Hyde Park, Marx introduced a resolution which demanded political amnesty for imprisoned Irish patriots and denounced Britain's "policy of conquest"—a policy which could not be broken without the active coöperation of the English working class. In the same year he wrote to Kugelmann, *"England has never ruled Ireland in any other way and cannot rule it in any other way* . . . except by the most hideous reign of terror and the most revolting corruption"—a sentiment which Engels expressed again and again in his letters to Marx from Ireland a decade earlier. Is this a country in which the social revolution could have taken place peacefully? [3]

Nor is the reference to the United States any more fortunate. A few years before Marx's Amsterdam address, America had gone through her second revolution

[3] "Ireland is the sole pretext of the English government for maintaining a big permanent army which, when it is necessary, will be let loose upon the English workers as has often happened after the army has been turned into a praetorian guard (*Soldateska*) in Ireland." Marx to Kugelmann in 1870.

to break up the semi-feudal slavocracy which barred the expansion of industrial capitalism. At the very moment Marx was speaking, the North was exercising a virtual dictatorship over the South. A few years later profound industrial disturbances, which almost took on an insurrectionary character, shook the country. Was it likely that in a country in which feeble and "constitutional" attempts to abolish chattel slavery had called forth the most violent civil war of the nineteenth century, the abolition of wage-slavery could be effected by moral suasion? Marx was right when he said that "special attention must be paid to the institutions, customs and traditions of various lands," but he did not know nor did Lenin, that already in 1872 the traditions of violence and legislative corruption were stronger in America than in any major European country with the exception of Russia.

It may be argued in defence of Marx, that he merely maintained that in England and America their institutions made it possible, through the "formal processes" of election, to register the will of the people for a social revolution; but that this did not obviate the necessity of using the reconstituted state power to destroy counter-revolutionary elements and consolidate the victory. If this was Marx's meaning, then, first, there was no justification at the very outset for the distinction between Anglo-American and European countries, since the same "formal" procedure was possible in France and Germany; and second, Marx's own historical studies of the transition from one form of state power to another indicate that the weight of probability was against this mode of procedure proving successful.

It remains to be asked, then, what led Marx and Engels into the error of qualifying their general position as they did—an error which could easily be dismissed as unimportant had it not led to intense controversy among Marxist and pseudo-Marxist groups in England and America. After toying with several hypotheses, the author frankly confesses that he does not know.

4. ONE OR THE OTHER

Marx's realistic conception of social revolution has so often been rejected as offensive to the enlightened conscience of well-intentioned men that it is necessary in closing to stress again—at the risk of repetition—its thoroughly human motivation. It is asked: "Do not the costs of social revolution come too high?" This is a question heard more often from those on the sidelines of the class struggle than from those who actually bear the brunt of its struggles. But it is a question which deserves an answer. The Marxist replies that he is willing to judge any project by its cost. But to judge anything *only* by its cost is to condemn everything ever undertaken and carried to completion in this imperfect world. Hardly a major good has come down from the past, from the discovery of fire and speech to the latest developments of scientific technique, for which human beings have not paid a price in blood and tears. Both logic and morality demand, however, that before we reject a proposal because of its cost, we consider the cost of rejecting it for any of the available alternatives. The Marxist contention is that the costs of social revolution are far less than the costs of chronic evils of poverty, unemployment, moral degradation, and war, which are immanent in capitalism; that the ultimate issue and choice is between imperialistic war which promises nothing but the destruction of all culture, yes, of the human race itself, and an international revolution which promises a new era in world history.

19

DICTATORSHIP AND DEMOCRACY

CRITIC of Marx once observed that true believers in democracy were not so much opposed to Marx's ideas as to the emotional associations of the words with which he clothed them. Unfortunately for the accuracy of his remark, the critic forgot to consider the possibility that the words had acquired their associations because of the ideas they expressed. But there is one essential principle of Marx's political philosophy to which, to some extent, the remark applies. This is "the dictatorship of the proletariat."

Dictatorship in popular parlance is used synonymously with terms like despotism, autocracy, and absolutism. And yet historically there have been dictatorships directed *against* absolutism and autocracy, as illustrated in the rules of Cromwell and Robespierre. The popular conception carries with it the connotation of illegality. Yet the constitutions of the ancient Roman Republic and of the modern German Republic make "legal" provisions for a dictatorship; and even the *coup d'état* of Napoleon the Great, as well as that of the Lesser, was confirmed by a popular plebiscite. A dictatorship, it is said, is essentially personal, yet history knows of dictatorships by triumvirates, religious organizations and political parties. None of these popular notions can serve as a clue to what Marx meant by the principle of "dictatorship of the proletariat." It must be considered as an integral part of his philosophy of history and theory of the state.

I. WHAT IS PROLETARIAN DICTATORSHIP?

The key to Marx's conception of proletarian dictatorship is given by Marx himself in his letter to Weydemeyer, March 12, 1852.

"As far as I am concerned the honor does not belong to me for either having discovered the existence of classes in modern society or their struggles with one another. Bourgeois historians had long before me shown the development of this struggle of the classes and bourgeois economists the economic anatomy of classes. What I added was to prove: (1) that the existence of classes is only bound up with certain historical struggles in the development of production; (2) that the class struggle necessarily leads to the dictatorship of the proletariat; (3) that this dictatorship is itself only a transition to the ultimate abolition of all classes and to a society without classes." [1]

Here it is clear that the "dictatorship of the proletariat" is the domination not of an individual, group or party but of one *class* over another. *Its opposite is not "democracy" but the "dictatorship of the bourgeoisie."* The political forms by which dictatorships are imposed

[1] Eng. trans. by Beer, *Labour Monthly,* July, 1922.

are varied, but what all dictatorships have in common is the possession of the state authority which is used in behalf of the dominant economic interest. The ultimate basis of the state authority, as we have seen, is physical power; its specific function, the preservation of the economic order. A dictatorship then, in *Marx's* sense of the term, is not recognized by the name with which its jurisconsults baptize it, but by the objective signs of repression in its social and political life. *Wherever we find a state, there we find a dictatorship.* Whoever believes in a *proletarian state,* believes in a *proletarian dictatorship.* This is Marx's meaning.

Is it adequate to the facts of political life? Does it not overlook important differences between the various forms of "bourgeois dictatorship," *e.g.,* differences between monarchy and republic, limited suffrage and universal suffrage? Marx does not deny the existence of these differences nor their importance for the day by day political strategy of the proletariat. He maintains, however, that the differences are irrelevant to the fundamental facts of social inequality which are common to all political forms of bourgeois dictatorship. In order to see why, we must look at Marx's analysis of "bourgeois dictatorship" a little more closely.

2. The Dictatorship of the Bourgeoisie

In a class society, social equality is impossible; and without social equality, only the political form, but not the substance of democracy can exist. In bourgeois society, the most important matters which affect the lives

of the working masses—the social conditions under
which they live, their opportunities of employment, their
wages—are determined, for the most part, by extra-
political agencies. The bank, the factory, and the market
control the very right of the worker to live, for they
control his means of life. This control is not malicious
and deliberate but is an automatic consequence of existing property relations.[2] "Representative" political institutions cannot control them in turn because within the
frame of the capitalist mode of production (1) political
institutions cannot be "truly" representative, since they
do not provide for democratic control of economic life;
(2) the tendencies towards centralization of industry
and concentration of wealth are not consequences of
political rule but of inherent tendencies in the economic
order and cannot be checked; and (3) the possession of
economic power gives almost complete domination over
the leadership, program and activities of political parties
through the control of campaign funds, the organs of
"public" opinion, and the national budget. The result

[2] Even when the control is conscious the motive is not personal but
arises from the "objective" interest of the business corporation. Mr.
Grace, President of the Bethlehem Steel Corporation, testifying before
the Lockwood Commission, admitted that his corporation was dic-
tating to contractors and builders in New York and Philadelphia, that
"they could buy fabricated steel only on condition that it be erected
under open shop conditions." He declared this to be a national policy.
In answer to a question from Mr. Untermeyer whether he did not
think such dictation on the part of the manufacturers to be arrogant,
Mr. Grace responded: "If they thought it was to protect their interest,
in line with what they considered the right policy for their interest, I
would not consider it arrogant but self-protection." (*New York Times,*
Dec. 15, 1920.)

is widespread indifference among the working population to political processes except on spectacular occasions
once every few years when they are given an opportunity "to decide which member of the ruling class is to
represent them in Parliament." (Marx.) Politics becomes
an annex to business and the principles of public morality are derived from successful commercial practice.

Bourgeois dictatorships may express themselves in
different forms of government. For agitational purposes
these differences are of no little significance to the
working class. Everywhere a struggle must be waged for
universal suffrage—not because this changes the nature
of the dictatorship of capital, but because it eliminates
confusing issues and permits the property question to
come clearly to the fore. "Nowhere does *social* equality
obtrude itself more harshly," wrote Marx as early as
1847, "than in the Eastern States of North America because nowhere is it less glossed over (*ubertünscht*) by
political equality." (*Gesamtausgabe,* I, 6, p. 309.) Twenty-
five years later in his criticism of the Gotha Program, he
repeats: ". . . vulgar democracy . . . sees the millen-
nium in the democratic republic and has no inkling of
the fact that the class struggle is to be definitely fought
out under this final form of State organization of capitalist society." (Eng. trans., S. L. P. Press, p. 49.)

The existence of a formal political democracy is accompanied by sharper expressions of the class struggle between proletariat and bourgeoisie, for now there is only
one issue on the agenda of history—whether man shall
serve property or whether property, for the first time

since the rise of traditional civilization, shall serve man. In the course of the class struggle the bourgeoisie is compelled to abandon its own formal political guarantees whenever the sanctity ot private property and the authority of the state are endangered. The dictatorship no longer remains veiled, but comes into the open. Martial law is proclaimed; freedom of the press and assemblage is suspended; minorities are unprotected, unless they accept bourgeois rule; the hemp rope is substituted for the cord of gold as a measure of repression. In the absence of the objective *social* presuppositions of equality, the formal possession of *political* equality—although it must be used to the utmost—turns out to be inadequate for any fundamental social change.

Bourgeois democracy is not the opposite of bourgeois dictatorship; it is one of its species. It is a dictatorship of a minority of the population over a majority—a minority defined not by the number of votes cast but by the number of those who own the instruments of social production. Bourgeois democracy may be parliamentary, and yet still be a dictatorship; it may be parliamentary, and still be, as Marx said of the French Republic of Louis Napoleon, "a government of unconcealed class terrorism."

True democracy, according to Marx, is possible only in a society where class divisions do not exist, where in virtue of a common administration of the means of production, an objective social morality harmonizes the interests of men and establishes the goals of the social process. True democracy, therefore, cannot be bourgeois democracy (dictatorship) nor proletarian democracy (dictatorship). But how is it to be achieved? Only by substituting for the dictatorship of the bourgeoisie, which declares itself to be the perfect enduring expression of democracy, the dictatorship of the proletariat, which regards itself as transitional and paves the way towards communism.

3. The Tasks of the Proletarian Dictatorship

In his critical analysis of the Gotha Program, Marx wrote:

"Between the capitalist and communist systems of society lies the period of the revolutionary transformation of one into the other. This corresponds to a political transition period, whose State can be nothing else but the *revolutionary dictatorship of the proletariat*." (*Op. cit.,* p. 48.)

Communism does not spring full born from the shell of capitalist society, for the latter can only create the presuppositions of communism. The proletariat must do the rest. When a revolutionary situation arises, it seizes power with the aid of other oppressed groups of the population. After it seizes power, it must organize to hold it against the practically certain attempts which will be launched, from within and without, against it. It uses its power to carry out the measures of socialization and cultural education which lead to communism. The organization of power is known as the proletarian dictatorship.

The proletarian dictatorship, like all dictatorships, is based on force. But it is not lawless or irresponsible. Its acts are strictly determined by the dictates of revolutionary necessity. It justifies what it does by principles which, in the course of time, it proceeds to codify—as all other states do. In the eyes of those who suffer by their application, these principles are regarded as spawned of hell, infamous and unnatural—a judgment often uttered before by those who have lost power.[3] But if anything, revolutionary principles make a greater and more sustained demand upon the integrity, courage, strength and intelligence of those who profess them than the principles they have replaced.

The first task the proletarian dictatorship must accomplish is to crush all actual or incipient counter-revolutionary movements. Otherwise, it cannot survive and goes down in a blood-bath which, as historical experience indicates, surpasses anything the proletariat is capable of. Marx cherished the lessons of the June days of 1848, the October days of the same year in Vienna and, bloodiest of all, the May days after the fall of the Commune in 1871. Revolutionary terrorism is the answer of the proletariat to the political terrorism of counter-revolution. Its ruthlessness depends upon the strength of the resistance it meets. *Its acts are not excesses but defensive measures.* Its historic justification is the still greater tragedies to which it puts an end. It was as the result of his studies of the successful French Revolution of 1793, which could never have been won with-

[3] "At present you seem in everything to have strayed out of the high road of nature. The property of France does not govern it." (Edmund Burke, "Letters on the French Revolution," *Works,* Bohn ed., Vol. 2, p. 325.)

out the Terror, and of his experience of the unsuccessful revolutions of 1848 and their bloody epilogue, that Marx wrote:

"The fruitless butcheries since the June and October days, the protracted sacrifice-festivals of victims since February and March, the cannibalism of the counter-revolution itself, will convince the people that there is only one means by which the torturous death agonies of the old society and the bloody birth-pangs of the new society, may be shortened, simplified and concentrated—only one means—revolutionary terrorism." (*Aus dem literarischen Nachlass von Marx und Engels,* Bd. 3, p. 199.)

The suppression of the counter-revolution is the first of the tasks which must be accomplished by the proletarian dictatorship, but it is by no means the most important. The problems of economics and educational reorganization are far more fundamental. Although the material bases of the new social order will already have been laid under capitalism, only mechanical Marxism—which is the obverse of fantastic Utopianism—can understand this to mean that when the revolution occurs, the maximum socialization of the processes of production will have been achieved, that adequate mechanisms of distribution will necessarily be at hand, and that all small independent producers, peasants and craftsmen will have disappeared. Were this ever to be the case, there would be no need of revolution; capitalism would collapse of its own internal weight. But that collapse would be a far cry from the inauguration of socialism. For before capitalism could have developed to such a point, it would have long since crushed out of existence an *active* independent working-class movement. Its collapse would mean absolute social chaos.

Having assumed power with the help of the discontented petty bourgeoisie and peasantry, the proletarian dictatorship carries the tendencies of capitalist production to completion in such a way as to secure the foundations of the socialist society. In the process of reconstruction it must watch very carefully to see that the political tendencies of its allies—whose intermediate position in production has generated an ideology which is anti-capitalist rather than pro-socialist—does not flower into a program demanding small independent production, complete administrative decentralization, and other non-socialist measures. Concessions to these groups must, of course, be made but only with an eye to their ultimate withdrawal, or more accurately, with relation to a program of social activity which, by nullifying the anti-social effects of these concessions, render them in time superfluous. Here the exigencies of the specific situation, together with first principles, dictate what is permissible and what is not.

The force of habit is stronger and more insidious than the force of arms. After the first flush of revolutionary enthusiasm has subsided, the traditional habits of the old order, which have been made part of the unconscious by the educational agencies of capitalism, reassert themselves. In the long run the processes of social reconstruction will effect a psychological transformation; meanwhile the obstructive consequences of anti-social motivation may result in serious obstacles to carrying through the program. A strenuous effort must therefore be made to overcome the cultural and psychological lag of the masses. New incentives to conduct must be fostered; new moral values made focal. Consciousness of the *creative* possibilities of a socialist order must be furthered and the educational system remade in the light of new social objectives.

The relative difficulty of these tasks will vary with different countries, but if Marx's guess is right, they cannot be accomplished anywhere in less than a generation. The proletarian dictatorship, in order to survive, must carry on a struggle on all fronts. Lenin, who not only studied the theory of proletarian dictatorship but tested it in practice, wrote:

"The dictatorship of the proletariat is a resolute, persistent struggle, sanguinary and bloodless, violent and peaceful, military and economic, pedagogic and administrative, against the forces and traditions of the old society. The force of habit of the millions and tens of millions is a formidable force." (*The Infantile Sickness of "Leftism" in Communism,* Eng. trans., p. 31.)

4. The Organs of Proletarian Dictatorship

The dictatorship of the proletariat is not a despotism. It expresses itself through representative institutions whose fundamental pattern was first revealed in dim outline in the political organization of the Paris Commune. The constitution of the Paris Commune showed that Marx said:

"It was essentially a working-class government, the product of the struggle of the producing against the appropriating class, the political form at last discovered under which to work out the economic emancipation of labor." (*The Civil War in France,* S. L. P. ed., p. 78.)

The representative institutions projected by the Commune—which served as the forerunners of the Russian Soviets of 1905 and 1917—distinguished themselves from the representative institutions of bourgeois democracy in several important ways. First, since the means of production, land and capital, were to be socialized, the government was to be a government of *producers.* All administrative functions were, therefore, to be performed at workmen's wages. Second, all delegates to representative bodies could be recalled at any time by those who had elected them. Third, the commune was to be, in the words of Marx, "a working, not a parliamentary body, executive and legislative at the same time." This would make officials more sensitive to the needs of those whom they represented, and more capable of checking and coördinating their administrative functions with the processes of production. Fourth, the source of power was to be "the nation in arms," and not a special army.

The logic of this scheme was completed in the Soviet system of 1917 in which the unit of representation was shifted from a territorial to an occupational basis—an idea already expressed by Daniel De Leon in America in 1904.

Despite all this, the Commune or the Soviet is still a

state, *i.e.,* a dictatorship. It exercises its repressive powers against those elements of the population which resist the transformation of society into a coöperative socialist commonwealth. It is therefore not yet a true democracy. Nonetheless, it more closely approaches true democracy than any previous political democracy in that it is a dictatorship of producers over non-producers, and, therefore, of a majority over a minority. Within the ranks of the producers the principles of true democracy prevail. Further, its activities are directed to making its own repressive functions superfluous. This is the justification of their use.

But in a society where there are no classes, will there not be conflicts between the majority of the population and the minority? How will these be solved? By force? But, by definition, the state—the organ of repression— no longer exists. Peacefully? Then why cannot the conflicts between the majority and minority be solved without acts of repression even before the state has disappeared? These questions overlook again the distinctive character of class oppositions. The proletarian state does not set itself up to be a true democracy. It frankly asserts that no true democracy is possible where a majority *represses* the minority. In a true democracy—due to the homogeneity of interests produced by the absence of economic class divisions—the minority, after discussion and decision, *voluntarily* subordinates itself to the majority. In a class democracy—bourgeois or proletarian—the presuppositions of social homogeneity are lacking and society is divided into two inarbitrably hostile camps.

Since the subject class cannot be relied upon voluntarily to subordinate itself, the state power is necessary. If ever a time comes when in a class democracy the group which controls the state uses it in the interests of the class which its economic institutions oppress, or if ever in a true democracy a situation arises in which a minority resorts to force to overthrow the decision of a majority—the Marxian theory will have to be revised.

One further question. What guarantee is there that after the class enemy has been eliminated from the social scene, the proletarian dictatorship will disappear, or that it will not give way to a new type of dictatorship—the dictatorship of the leaders over those whom they lead? May not one form of oppression then be substituted for another? Robert Michels has developed this point into a system of sociology.[4] The nature of every organization —especially political organizations—is such that they cannot function without leaders. In the course of time, oppositions arise between the leaders and those who are led which are analogous to the oppositions between classes. The power of the leaders, derived from control of the party machine, enables them to constitute themselves into a virtual oligarchy which is self-perpetuating. Where democratic forms prevail, the leaders, due to their control of the strategic positions in the political bureaucracy, can get themselves "legally" voted into power again. If they are overthrown by organized mass protest or revolt, then the leaders of the revolt—those who have

[4] *Zur Soziologie des Parteiwesens in der modernen Demokratie,* Leipzig, 1925.

311

rallied the masses—take their places. A new bureaucracy arises and the process continues forever. Michels calls this the "iron law of oligarchy" and holds that it is valid for *all* societies. He, therefore, concludes that "socialists may be successful but socialism [true democracy] never." History is the succession of one set of politicians for another.

That personal abuse of power will always be possible is undeniable. But what Michels overlooks is the social and economic presuppositions of the oligarchical tendencies of leadership in the past. Political leadership in past societies meant economic power. Education and tradition fostered the tendencies to predatory self-assertion in some classes and at the same time sought to deaden the interest in politics on the part of the masses. In a socialist society in which political leadership is an administrative function, and, therefore, carries with it no economic power, in which the processes of education strive to direct the psychic tendencies to self-assertion into "moral and social equivalents" of oligarchical ambition, in which the monopoly of education for one class has been abolished, and the division of labor between manual and mental worker is progressively eliminated—the danger that Michels' "law of oligarchy" will express itself in traditional form, becomes quite remote. In addition, the organization of the communes or soviets demands that all producers in the course of their work be drawn into the "social planning activities" of society. Of necessity they must become politically conscious. And where political consciousness is widespread and the means of production held in common, bureaucracy cannot flourish. For limited periods, especially in the period immediately after the revolution, evils may appear, but it is impossible to predict in advance what specific form they will take. This bare and abstract possibility, however, is much too weak a foundation for the heavy sociological structure which Michels builds upon it.

5. COMMUNISM AND DEMOCRACY

Hostile critics of Marxism have often designated it as the last system of Utopian socialism. Marxism, they have said, envisages the social order of the future as one in which there are no material lacks and no political constraint, in which human beings are moved only by altruistic motives. This is a millenary dream. From an opposite quarter, their fellow critics have protested that Marxism is the last theoretical expression of capitalism, that it assumes the same values and motives of human behavior and gives no indications of the criteria of a desirable society. The same evils, they remind us, may be produced by different causes. Unless mankind is guided by a more adequate schedule of ethical values than those illustrated in the class war to-day, the meanness, cruelty and vulgarity of contemporary culture will reappear in a different guise in the culture of to-morrow.

Both criticisms—cancelling one another though they do —fall wide of the mark because they share two theoretical presuppositions which are utterly foreign to Marxism. Both assume that ethical values are relevant and meaningful in independence of a concrete social and historical context. The first school of critics, on the basis of the patent hollowness and inapplicability of all past schemes of "universal" and "truly human" morality in class society, argue that no objective system of social morality will ever be possible.[5] The second school desire to work out now, and to propagate in full detail, a system of morality which can only be realized and understood after social conditions have been changed. Both schools further assume that communism springs into existence immediately after the revolution, and overlook the *gradual* interactive effects between human ideals and social existence which result from the activities of socialization. They do not view social experience as an educational and transformative process in which, by the control of social institutions, human motives and ideals are themselves changed.

According to the Marxist philosophy the content—the very meaning of moral ideals—is a function of a concrete situation in the process of historical development. Ideals must be redetermined from time to time in relation to what the forces of production make possible and what human beings *will* as desirable. Marx, therefore, never invoked a natural rights theory of ethics.

[5] This is a generalized and illicit form of Marx's specific line of criticism of all "classless" morality in class society. Of the humanitarian Heinzen, Marx wrote: ". . . Mr. Heinzen professes to be unconcerned either with the bourgeoisie or with the proletariat in Germany. His party is the 'party of humanity,' that is, the noble and warm-hearted enthusiasts who champion 'middle-class' interests disguised in the form of 'human' ideals, without ever realizing the connection between the idealistic phrase and its realistic kernel." (*Gesamtausgabe,* I, 6, p. 321.)

The only formal ethical invariant he recognized, was man's desire for "the better." In class societies there are to be found only class moralities, for just as the "good" of one class, is the "bad" of another, "the better" of the first is "the worse" of the second. This is most obviously true of such political shibboleths as liberty, equality, and democracy. Just as soon as we give a concrete content to these terms we find that what is liberty for one class is wage-slavery for another; what is democracy for one class is the formal cloak of dictatorship for another.

After the socialist revolution, social morality will only gradually lose its antinomic character, for classes will not have been immediately abolished. But class divisions will not be relevant to the overwhelming majority of the population since it will consist of producers. The chief consideration *now* which determines the principles of justice, in accordance with which social wealth will be distributed, is the level socialized *production* will have reached. Even under communism, then, abstract principles of justice by themselves will not be adequate to settle the specific problems of distribution.

It is in his discussion of the principles which are to guide the distribution of the social product under communism that Marx appears at his realistic best. He avoids the abstract morality of the Utopians and at the same time transcends the morality of the *status quo*. This question is bound up with the problem of democracy. Since there can be no social equality without "just distribution," and since political democracy, according to Marx's earlier critique, is an empty form without social equality, his analysis of "just distribution" is part of his analysis of democracy. This discussion will be found in his *Critique of the Gotha Program*.

The "right to the full product of one's labor" had always been an agitational demand of the Utopian socialists. Due to the influence of Lassalle's thought, a variant of this demand had slipped into the platform of the German Social Democratic Party. It called for a system of society in which "the proceeds of society [*Arbeitsertrag*] belong to all the members of society, unabridged and in equal right." The presupposition of their demand is that the social revolution has just been accomplished.

Marx protests that it is obviously impossible at such time both to reward "all members of society," *including those who do not work,* and, at the same time, to give those who do work the full and unabridged products of their labor. If it is meant that only those who work are to receive the full product of their labor, while those who do not work are to be permitted to starve, then all talk about "equal rights" on the part of these two groups must be dropped. Besides, it is nonsense to demand that those who work should receive the full product of their labor, for (*a*) the product is *social* and cooperative, not private and individual, (*b*) deductions from the social product must be made for wear and tear of social capital, expansion of production, etc., (*c*) deductions must be made for administrative expenses, education, public hygiene, and (*d*) deductions must be made for those who are *unable* to work. Making allowance for all these deductions and reservations, the principle of distribution in the *first* stage of communist society— a society which, as Marx says, has not *"developed* on its own basis, but, on the contrary, is just *issuing* out of capitalist society"—amounts to this: *Each individual is to be rewarded in proportion to what he produces.* What he produces is measured by his labor time.

"Accordingly, the individual producer gets back—after the deductions—exactly as much as he gives to it. . . . He receives from the community a check showing that he has done so much labor, and with this check he draws from the common store as much of the means of consumption as costs an equal amount of labor. The same quantity of labor that he has given to society in one form, he receives back in another form." (*Op. cit.,* p. 29.)

But this is not yet genuine social democracy or justice, Marx adds. It is, however, the best attainable in a "society that still retains, in every respect, economic, moral, and intellectual, the birthmarks of the old society from whose womb it is passing." It is not genuine justice because it makes possible inequality of wage payments. *A,* who enjoys natural strength, may in the same span of time produce, with less exertion, twice as much as *B.* If he receives in payment twice as much as *B, B* is being punished for his natural weakness, for which he is no more responsible than *A* is for his strength. Or *A* and *B* may produce the same amount and get the same reward, and yet, because *B* is the head of a family and *A* is not, inequality will result.

Both *A* and *B* are equal before the law of the new

society because, together with their fellow producers, they own and control the means of production. In this there is a definite advance over capitalism. But it is not yet communism. In respect to *distribution* one person may acquire more wealth than another and certain groups may be able to enjoy a higher standard of living. This will not constitute a danger to the social order because the ownership of the instruments of production will be common. But the incentives and motives of the old order will have survived down to this period. The possibility of social disorder will be quite real. A certain vestigial state apparatus will therefore be necessary to keep the peace. Coercion will still have to be employed. The principle that each one has an equal right to what he produces (and not to what he needs) is just, then, only under those social conditions in which productive forces have not been developed to a point where, by purely voluntary labor, everyone's fundamental needs can be gratified. But "just" though it be under the circumstances, the principle of equal right is still a hangover from capitalism.

"*Equal right* is here, therefore, still according to the principle, *capitalist right.* . . . The equal right is still tainted with a capitalist limitation.

"However, one person is physically or intellectually superior to the other, and furnishes, therefore, more labor in the same time, or can work a longer time; and in order to serve as a measure, labor must be determined according to duration or intensity, otherwise it would cease to serve as a standard. This *equal* right is unequal right for unequal labor. It does not recognize class distinctions, because everyone is only a workingman like everybody else; but it tacitly recognizes unequal individual endowment, and hence, efficiency, as natural privileges. *It is, therefore, in its substance, a right of inequality, like all right.* According to its nature, right can consist only in the application of a common standard; but the unequal individuals (and they would not be different individuals if they were not unequal ones) can be measured according to a common standard only in so far as they are brought under the same point of view, or, are regarded from a *particular* side only. For example, in the given instance they are regarded *only as workingmen;* we see nothing more in them, we disregard everything else. Moreover, one workingman is married, the other is not married; one has more children than the other, etc. Hence with equal contribution of labor and, therefore, equal shares in the social consumption-fund, the one receives actually more than the other, the one is richer than the other, etc. In order to avoid all these shortcomings right would have to be not equal, but unequal.

"But these shortcomings are unavoidable in the first phase of Communist society, as it has just issued from capitalist society after long travail. Right can never be superior to the economic development and the stage of civilization conditioned thereby." (*Critique of the Gotha Program,* S. L. P. ed., pp. 30-31.)

Marx, at this point, stops short of specific description and contents himself with indicating the communist ideal of social distribution. This is: *"Production according to one's capacities, and distribution according to one's needs."* He does not say when and how it will be realized, or even assert that it is some day certain to be achieved. After all, it is an ideal. But the conditions for its realization are stated and some intimations are offered of intermediate stages in the progress towards complete communism.

"Need" is an ambiguous term; "reward according to need" even more so. One man's need may be another man's luxury. Certainly, except in paradise, not all individuals can be rewarded in accordance with their "fancied" needs. During the first stage of communist society, all who are willing to work will receive sufficient for their fundamental needs—food, clothing, shelter, education, etc. But due to the inequality of wage payments, some will be able to gratify needs which are not fundamental. Later, when equality of wage payments has been established, it may be possible to redefine "fundamental needs"—another elastic concept—in such a way that it will include the need for what were formerly regarded as luxuries—material or cultural. As production increases, the equal minimum wage is increased. But equality of payment in a world in which human beings are unequal, Marx showed, involved inequality. The true ideal of social equality must respect these human differences and seek to give each individual the opportunity to develop himself in accordance with his own moral ideal. The presupposition is that technology will be sufficiently advanced, and the educational processes of the new society sufficiently enlightened and effective, to make it possible that the material prerequisites necessary for a free career for all—will be produced by *voluntary* labor. Where this is not so, the principle of need will have to be modified by the principle of desert, *i.e.,* specific reward for individual effort.

Marx is not very much concerned with the higher phase of *communism*. His life-work and thought were primarily directed to overthrow the highest phase of *capitalism*. But he permits us to catch a glimpse of the social ideal which gave added meaning and justification, not alone to his own heroic struggles, but to the struggle of the international working-class movement of which he was a part. It is an ideal whose complete realization is not as important as its directive power:

"In the higher phase of communist society, after the enslaving subordination of the individual under the division of labor has disappeared, and therewith also the opposition between manual and intellectual labor; after labor has become not only a means of life, but also the highest want in life; when, with the development of all the faculties of the individual, the productive forces have correspondingly increased, and all the springs of social wealth flow more abundantly—only then may the limited horizon of capitalist right be left behind entirely, and society inscribe on its banners: 'From everyone according to his faculties, to everyone according to his needs!'" (*Critique of the Gotha Program*, p. 31.)

APPENDIX

FOUR LETTERS ON HISTORICAL MATERIALISM

by Frederick Engels

Translated by Sidney Hook

1. Engels' Letter to Conrad Schmidt

London, Oct. 27, '90

Dear Schmidt:

I seize the first free moment to write you. I think you would be well advised to accept the position at Zurich.[1] You can always learn considerably about economic matters there especially if you bear in mind that Zurich is still only a third-rate money and business market, and that, consequently, the effects which make themselves felt there are weakened, and indeed deliberately falsified by double and triple-fold manipulations. But one acquires a practical knowledge of the business and is compelled to follow first-hand market reports from London, New York, Paris, Berlin, Vienna—and that's the world market in its reflected form as money and security market. Of the economic, political and other reflections the same thing is true as of the images in the human eye. They all pass through a convex lens and therefore appear upside down, standing on their head. Only the nervous system is lacking to set

[1] Conrad Schmidt had written Engels that he intended to take over the commercial section of a Zurich newspaper.

them right on their feet again. The money-market expert sees the movements of industry and the world market only in the inverted reflections of the money and security market, and takes the effect for the cause. I saw that take place already in the forties in Manchester. The London market reports were absolutely useless as a guide to the development of industry and its periodic maxima and minima because m'lords wanted to explain everything as arising from the crises in the money market which were, after all, only symptoms. Behind the matter at that time was the desire to explain away the fact that industrial crises arose out of temporary overproduction; in addition there was a bias which invited distortion. This last is now for us irrelevant; besides it is a fact that the money market can also have its own crises in which direct industrial disturbances play only a subordinate rôle or none whatever. In this connection there is much to be investigated especially in the last twenty years.

Wherever there is division of labor on a social scale, there will also be found the growing independence of workers in relation to each other. Production is in the last instance the decisive factor. However, as soon as the commercial exchange of commodities separates itself from real production it follows a movement which, although as a whole still dominated by production, obeys in its particular details and within the sphere of its general dependence, its own laws. These flow from the nature of the new factors involved. This movement has its own phases and reacts in turn upon the course of production. The discovery of America resulted from the hunger for money, which had already driven the Portuguese to Africa (Cf. Soetbeer's *Edelmetall-Produktion*), because the tremendous expansion of European industry in the fourteenth and fifteenth centuries together with the corresponding commercial activity demanded more currency than Germany—the great silver

country from 1450 to 1550—could provide. The conquest
of India by the Portuguese, Dutch, and English from 1500
to 1800 was undertaken for the sake of *imports from India.*
At that time no one thought of exports. And yet what
colossal counter-effects these discoveries and conquests
which were determined purely by interests of trade, had
upon exports from those countries and upon the development of large scale industry.

The same is true for the money market. Just as soon as
dealing in money [*Geldhandel*] is separated from commodity exchange it develops its own special laws and
phases. These follow from its own particular nature, yet
they all take place within the given limits and conditions
of production and commodity exchange. Where dealing in
money is extended to include securities that are not merely
government consols but industrials and railroad stocks, and
thereby wins direct control over a phase of the production
which as a whole controls it, the reaction of the money
market upon production becomes all the stronger and more
complicated. The investment bankers are the owners of
railroads, mines, steel mills, etc. These means of production
take on a double aspect. Business has to be run now with
an eye to the immediate interests of production, and now
with an eye to the needs of the stock-holders in so far as
they are money lenders. The crassest illustration of this is
furnished by the activities of the North American railroads
which at the present time depend completely upon the
market operations of Jay Gould, Vanderbilt and others—
operations that are totally foreign to the needs and interests
of the railroads as common carriers. And even here in
England we have witnessed years of struggle between
different railway companies in competitive territories in
which an enormous amount of money went up in smoke
not in the interest of production and communication but
solely because of a rivalry whose main function was to

make possible the market operation of the wealthy stock-holders.

In these few words about my conception of the relation between production and commodity exchange, and of both to the money market, I have already answered in essence your questions concerning *historical materialism* in general. The matter can most easily be grasped from the standpoint of the *division of labor*. Society gives rise to certain public functions which it cannot dispense with. The people who are delegated to perform them constitute a new branch of the division of labor *within society*. They acquire therewith special interest in opposition to those who have elected them; make themselves relatively independent of them, and the *state* is already here. The same thing takes place, as we observed, in commercial exchange and later in money exchange. The new independent power must, of course, submit to the movement of production as a whole. But it also *reacts,* by virtue of the strength of its immanent, *i.e.,* its once borrowed but gradually developed relative independence, upon the conditions and course of production. There is a *reciprocity* between two *unequal* forces; on the one side, the economic movement; on the other, the new political power which strives for the greatest possible independence and which having once arisen is endowed with its *own movement*. The economic movement, upon the whole, asserts itself but it is affected by the reaction of the relatively independent political movement which it itself had set up. This political movement is on the one hand the state power, on the other, the opposition which comes to life at the same time with it. Just as the money market reflects as a whole, with the qualifications indicated, the movement of the industrial market, but naturally in an *inverted* fashion, so there is reflected in the struggle between government and opposition, the struggle between already existing and opposing classes but again in an inverted form, no longer direct but indirect, not as open class struggle but as a struggle between *political principles*. So inverted is this reflection that it required thousands of years to discover what was behind it.

The reaction of the state power upon economic development can take a three-fold form. It can run in the same direction, and then the tempo of development becomes accelerated; it can buck up against that development in which case to-day among every large people the state power is sure to go to smash before long; or it can block economic development along some directions and lay down its path along others. This last case is ultimately reducible to one of either of the foregoing two. It is clear that in the second and third cases the political power can do great damage to the course of economic development and result in a great waste of energy and materials.

We must add to the above the cases of conquest and brutal destruction of economic resources in which under certain circumstances it was possible in the past for a local or national economic development to be completely destroyed. To-day situations of this kind produce opposite effects at least among the large nations. Often it is the conquered who in the long run wins more economically, politically and morally than the conqueror.

The same is true for law. Just as soon as the new division of labor makes necessary the creation of *professional jurists,* another new independent domain is opened which for all its dependence upon production and trade in general, still possesses a special capacity to react upon these fields. In a modern state, law must not only correspond to the general economic situation and be its expression; it must also be a *coherently unified expression* and free from glaring internal inconsistencies. In order to achieve this, the fidelity with which the law directly reflects economic conditions becomes less and less. This is all the truer, in those rare cases, when

327

the legal code expresses the harsh, unrelieved and naked fact of class rule. For that contradicts the very *principle of justice* and law. The pure and consistent jural concept of the revolutionary bourgeoisie of 1792-96 already appears falsified in many respects in the Code Napoleon. And in so far as it is carried out, it is subject to daily modification because of the growing power of the proletariat. That doesn't prevent the Napoleonic code from serving as a legal model for new codifications of law in all parts of the world. The course of legal development is to be explained in large part first by this attempt to erect an harmonious system of law by eliminating the contradictions between jural propositions which are themselves the direct translation of economic relations; and then by the influence and compulsion exerted by the further economic development which keeps on upsetting the system and plunging it into new contradictions. (I speak here for the time being only of civil law.)

The reflection of economic relations as principles of law is necessarily an inverted one. The process takes place without the participants becoming conscious of it. The jurist imagines that he is operating with *a priori* propositions while the latter are only reflections of the economic process. And so everything remains standing on its head. This inverted reflex so long as it is not recognized for what it is constitutes what we call *ideological conceptions*. That it is able to set up a counteraction on the economic basis and within certain limits to modify it, seems to me to be self-evident. The foundations of the law of inheritance, corresponding stages in the development of the family being presupposed, are economic. Nonetheless it would be very hard to prove that, *e.g.,* the absolute freedom of testamentary disposition in England, and the strongly restricted right in France, in all particulars have only economic causes. Yet both methods react in a very significant way upon the economic system in that they influence the distribution of wealth.

And now as concerns those ideological realms which tower still higher in the clouds—*religion, philosophy,* etc.— they all possess from pre-historical days an already discovered and traditionally accepted fund of—what we would to-day call bunk [*Blödsinn*]. All of these various mistaken ideas of nature, of the creation of man, of spirits and magical forces have as their basis, in the main, negative economic grounds. False ideas of nature are supplementary to the primitive economic development of the pre-historical period; but in places they are often conditioned and even caused by economic development. However, even if economic need has been the chief driving force in the advance of natural knowledge, and has become even more so, it would be altogether pedantic to seek economic causes for all this primitive original superstition. The history of science is the history of the gradual elimination of this superstition, *i.e.,* its replacement by new, but always less absurd, superstitions. The people who supply it belong again to a special sphere in the division of labor and imagine that they are working in an independent domain. And in so far as they constitute an independent group within the social division of labor, their production, inclusive of their errors, exerts a *counter-acting influence* upon the entire social development, even upon the economic. Nonetheless they still remain under the *dominant influence of economic development.* For example, in philosophy this is easiest to demonstrate for the bourgeois period. Hobbes was the first modern materialist (in the sense of the eighteenth century) but an absolutist at a time when in the whole of Europe absolute monarchy was enjoying the height of its power and in England had taken up the struggle against the people. Locke was, in religion as in politics, a son of the class-compromise of 1688. The English Deists, and their more consistent followers, the French materialists, were the genuine philosophers of the bourgeoisie—the French, even of the bourgeois revolution. In German philosophy from Kant to Hegel the German philistine makes his way—now positively, now negatively. But as a definite domain within the division of labor the philosophy of every age has as its presuppositions a certain intellectual material which it inherits from its predecessors and which is its own point of departure. That is why philosophy can play first violin in economically backward countries; *e.g.,* France in the eighteenth century as opposed to England upon whose philosophy her own was based; and later Germany as opposed to both. But in France as in Germany, philosophy and the general outburst of literary activity of that time, were a result of an economic upswing. The final supremacy of economic development even in these realms is established but it takes place within the conditions which are set down by the particular realm; in philosophy, *e.g.,* through the effect of economic influences (which again exert influence through disguised political, etc., forms) upon the existing philosophical material which our philosophical predecessors have handed down. Of itself economics produces no effects here directly; but it determines the *kind of change* and development the already existing intellectual material receives, and even that, for the most part, indirectly, since it is the political, jural and moral reflexes which exercise the greatest direct influence upon philosophy.

I have said what is necessary about religion in the last section of my *Feuerbach.*

If Barth [2] imagines that we deny all and every counteraction of the political, etc., reflexes of the economic movement upon that movement itself, *he is simply contending against windmills.* Let him take a glance at Marx's *Eight-*

[2] Schmidt had called Engels' attention to the book of Prof. Paul Barth—*Die Geschichtsphilosophie Hegels und seiner Nachfolger.*

eenth Brumaire, which almost restricts itself to the treatment of the *special* rôle that political struggles and events play, naturally within the sphere of their *general* dependence upon economic conditions; or in *Capital, e.g.,* the section on the working day, where legislation, which certainly is a political art, operates so decisively; or the section on the history of the bourgeoisie (Chap. 24). Why are we struggling for the political dictatorship of the proletariat, if political power has no economic effects. Force (*i.e.,* the state authority) is also an economic power!

But I have no time at present to criticize the book. The third volume must first come out, and besides I believe that Bernstein can do the job quite well.

What all these fellows lack is dialectic. They see cause here, effect there. They do not at all see that this method of viewing things results in bare abstractions; that in the real world such metaphysical polar opposites exist only in crucial situations; that the whole great process develops itself in the form of reciprocal action, to be sure of very unequal forces, in which the economic movement is far and away the strongest, most primary and decisive. They do not see that here nothing is absolute and everything relative. For them Hegel has never existed.

Yours, etc.

2. ENGELS' LETTER TO J. BLOCH

London, Sept. 21, 1890

Dear Sir:—

Your letter of the 3rd inst. was forwarded to me at Folkestone; but as I did not have the book in question there, I could not answer you. Returning home on the 12th I discovered such a pile of important work waiting for me, that only to-day have I found the time to write you a few lines. This in explanation of the delay which I hope you will kindly pardon.

To Point I.[1] First of all you will please note on p. 19 of the *Origin* that the process of development of the Punaluan family is presented as having taken place so gradually that even in this century marriages of brother and sister (*of one mother*) have taken place in the royal family of Hawaii. And throughout antiquity we find examples of marriages between brother and sister, *e.g.* among the Ptolemies. Secondly, we must here distinguish between brother and sister deriving from the side of the mother, or deriving only from the side of the father; *adelphos, adelphä* comes from *delphos,* womb, and originally signified, therefore, only brother and sister on the *side of the mother*. The feeling had survived a long time from the time of the *Mutterrecht* that the children of the same mother who have different fathers are more closely related than the children of the same father who have different mothers. The Punaluan form of the family excludes only marriages between the first group (*i.e.,* children of one mother but of different fathers) but by no means between the second who according to the existing notion are not even related (since *Mutterrecht* rules). As far as I know the cases of marriage between brother and sister in ancient Greece are restricted either to those individuals who have different mothers or to those about whom this is not known, and for whom, therefore, the possibility is not excluded; nor is it in absolute contradiction to the Punaluan usage. You have overlooked the fact that between the time of the Punaluan family and the time of Greek monogamy there lies the jump from the matriarchate to the patriarchate, which alters matters considerably.

According to Wachsmuth's *Hellen. Althertümern,* in the heroic age of Greece, "there is no sign of any concern

[1] Bloch had asked how it came about that even after the disappearance of the consanguine family, marriages between brother and sister were not forbidden among the Greeks.

about the too close blood relationship of husband and wife except for the relation of parent and child." (III, p. 156.) "Marriage with the *leiblichen* sister was not disapproved of in Crete" (*ibid.,* p. 170). The last also according to Strabo (Bk. X), (for the moment however I cannot find the passage because of the absence of chapter divisions). By *leiblichen* sister I understand, unless there is proof to the contrary, sisters on the father's side.

To Point II.[2] I qualify your first major proposition as follows: According to the materialistic conception of history, the production and reproduction of real life constitutes in the *last instance* the determining factor of history. Neither Marx nor I ever maintained more. Now when someone comes along and distorts this to mean that the economic factor is the *sole* determining factor he is converting the former proposition into a meaningless, abstract and absurd phrase. The economic situation is the basis but the various factors of the superstructure—the political forms of the class struggles and their results—constitutions, etc., established by victorious classes after hard-won battles—legal forms, and even the reflexes of all these real struggles in the brain of the participants, political, jural, philosophical theories, religious conceptions which have been developed into systematic dogmas, all these exercise an influence upon the course of historical struggles, and in many cases determine for the most part their form. There is a reciprocity between all these factors in which, finally, through the endless array of contingencies (*i.e.,* of things and events whose inner connection with one another is so remote, or so incapable of proof, that we may neglect it,

[2] Bloch had asked how the fundamental principle of the materialistic conception of history was understood by Marx and Engels themselves; whether the production and reproduction of life constituted the *sole* determining factor or was only the foundation upon which all other relations developed a further activity of their *own.*

regarding it as non-existent) the economic movement asserts itself as necessary. Were this not the case, the application of the theory to any given historical period would be easier than the solution of a simple equation of the first degree.

We ourselves make our own history, but, first of all, under very definite presuppositions and conditions. Among these are the economic, which are finally decisive. But there are also the political, etc. Yes, even the ghostly traditions which haunt the minds of men play a rôle albeit not a decisive one. The Prussian state arose and developed through historical, in the last instance, economic causes. One could hardly, however, assert without pedantry that among the many petty principalities of North Germany, just Brandenberg was determined by economic necessity and not by other factors also (before all, its involvement in virtue of its Prussian possessions, with Poland and therewith international political relations—which were also decisive factors in the creation of the domestic power of Austro-Hungary) to become the great power in which was to be embodied the economic, linguistic and, since the Reformation, also the religious differences of North and South. It would be very hard to attempt to explain by economic causes without making ourselves ridiculous the existence of every petty German state of the past or present, or the origin of modern German syntax, which reinforced the differences that existed already in virtue of the geographical separating wall formed by the mountains from Sudeten to Taunus.

Secondly, history is so made that the end result always arises out of the conflict of many individual wills in which every will is itself the product of a host of special conditions of life. Consequently there exist innumerable intersecting forces, an infinite group of parallelograms of forces which give rise to one resultant product—the historical event. This again may itself be viewed as the product of a force acting as a Whole without consciousness or volition. For what every individual wills separately is frustrated by what every one else wills and the general upshot is something which no one willed. And so the course of history has run along like a natural process; it also is subject essentially to the same laws of motion. But from the fact that the wills of individuals—who desire what the constitution of their body as well as external circumstances, in the last instance economic (either personal or social) determine them to desire—do not get what they wish but are sunk into an average or common result, from all that one has no right to conclude that they equal zero. On the contrary, every will contributes to the result and is in so far forth included within it.

I should further like to beg of you to study the theory from its original sources and not at second hand. It is really much easier. Marx hardly wrote a thing in which this theory does not play a part. The *Eighteenth Brumaire of Louis Napoleon* is an especially remarkable example of its application. There are many relevant passages also in *Capital*. In addition, permit me to call your attention to my own writings, *Herrn E. Dühring's Umwälzung der Wissenschaft* and *L. Feuerbach und der Ausgang der klassischen deutsche Philosophie* where I give the most comprehensive exposition of historical materialism which to my knowledge exists anywhere.

Marx and I are partly responsible for the fact that at times our disciples have laid more weight upon the economic factor than belongs to it. We were compelled to emphasize its central character in opposition to our opponents who denied it, and there wasn't always time, place and occasion to do justice to the other factors in the reciprocal interactions of the historical process. But just as soon as it was a matter of the presentation of an historical chapter, that is to say, of practical application, things became quite different; there, no error was possible. Unfortunately it is only too frequent that a person believes he has completely understood a new theory and is capable of applying it when he has taken over its fundamental ideas—and even then in an incorrect form. And from this reproach I cannot spare many of the recent "Marxists." They have certainly turned out a rare kind of tommyrot.

To Point I again. Yesterday (I am writing now on the 22nd of Sept.) I found the following decisive passage, in Schoemann's *Griechische Altertümer* (Berlin, 1855, I, p. 52), which completely confirms the view taken above: "It is well known that marriages between half-brothers or sisters of *different mothers* was not regarded as incest in late Greece."

I hope that the appalling parenthetical expressions which for brevity's sake have slipped from my pen won't frighten you off.

Yours, etc.

3. ENGELS' LETTER TO HANS STARKENBURG

London, January 25, 1894

Dear Sir:—

Here are the answers to your questions: [1]

1. By economic relations, which we regard as the determining basis of the history of society, we understand the way in which human beings in a definite society produce their necessities of life and exchange the product among themselves (in so far as division of labor exists). Consequently the *whole technique* of production and trans-

---

[1] (I) To what extent are economic relations *causally* effective, *i.e.,* are they sufficient causes or necessary conditions or occasions, etc., of social development? (II) What rôles do the factors of *race* and historical *personality* play in Marx-Engels' conception of history?

portation is therein included. According to our conception, this technique determines the character and method of exchange, further, the distribution of the products and therewith, after the dissolution of gentile society, the relationships of ruler to ruled, and thence, the state, politics, law, etc. Under economic relations are included further, the geographical foundations upon which they develop and the actually inherited remains of earlier economic stages of development which have persisted, often through tradition only or *vis inertiae,* and also, naturally, the external surrounding milieu of society.

If the technique, as you properly say, is to a large extent dependent upon the state of science, how much more is science dependent upon the *state* and *needs* of technique. If society has a technical need, it serves as a greater spur to the progress of science than do ten universities. The whole of hydrostatics (Torricelli, etc.) was produced by the needs of controlling the mountain streams in Italy in the sixteenth and seventeenth centuries. We only acquired some intelligible knowledge about electricity when its technical applications were discovered. Unfortunately, in Germany, people have been accustomed to write the history of the sciences as if the sciences had fallen from the sky.

2. We regard the economic conditions as determining, in the last instance, historical development. But there are two points here which must not be overlooked.

(a) The political, legal, philosophical, religious, literary, artistic, etc., development rest upon the economic. But they all react upon one another and upon the economic base. It is not the case that the economic situation is the *sole active cause* and everything else only a passive effect. But there is a reciprocal interaction within a fundamental economic necessity which *in the last instance* always asserts itself. The state, *e.g.,* exerts its influence through tariffs, free-trade, good or bad taxation. Even that deadly supine-ness and impotence of the German philistine which arose out of the miserable economic situation of Germany from 1648 to 1830 and which expressed itself first in pietism, then in sentimentalism and crawling servility before prince and noble, were not without their economic effects. They constituted one of the greatest hindrances to a progressive movement and were only cleared out of the way by the revolutionary and Napoleonic wars which made the chronic misery acute. It is not true, as some people here and there conveniently imagine, that economic conditions work themselves out automatically. Men make their own history, but in a given, conditioning milieu, upon the basis of actual relations already extant, among which, the economic relations, no matter how much they are influenced by relations of a political and ideological order, are ultimately decisive, constituting a red thread which runs through all the other relations and enabling us to understand them.

(b) Men make their own history but until now not with collective will according to a collective plan. Not even in a definitely limited given society. Their strivings are at cross purposes with each other, and in all such societies there therefore reigns a *necessity* which asserts itself under the form of contingency. The *necessity* which here expresses itself through all those contingencies is ultimately, again, economic. Here we must treat of the so-called great man. That a certain particular man and no other emerges at a definite time in a given country is naturally pure chance. But even if we eliminate him, there is always a need for a substitute, and the substitute is found *tant bien que mal;* in the long run he is sure to be found. That Napoleon— this particular Corsican—should have been the military dictator made necessary by the exhausting wars of the French Republic—that was a matter of chance. But that in default of a Napoleon, another would have filled his place, that is established by the fact that whenever a man was necessary he has always been found: Caesar, Augustus, Cromwell, etc. Marx, to be sure, discovered the materialistic conception of history—but the examples of Thierry, Mignet, Guizot, the whole school of English Historians up to 1850 show they were working towards it; and its re-discovery by Morgan serves as proof that the time was ripe for it, and that it *had* to be discovered.

So with all other accidents and apparent accidents in history. The wider the field we investigate, the further removed from the economic, the closer to the domain of pure, abstract ideology, the more we find that it reveals accidents in its development, the more does the course of its curve run in zig-zag fashion. But fit a trend to the curve and you will find that the longer the period taken, the more inclusive the field treated, the more closely will this trend run parallel to the trend of economic development.

The greatest obstacle to the correct understanding of the theory in Germany is the inexcusable neglect of the literature of economic history. It is hard not only to get rid of historical conceptions which have been drummed into one's head at school but even more so to gather the material together necessary to do it. Who has even read, *e.g.,* old G. v. Gülich whose dry accumulation of material nonetheless contains so much stuff which explains innumerable political facts?

In addition I believe that the beautiful example which Marx himself gives in his *Eighteenth Brumaire* ought to give you considerable information on your questions just because it is a practical illustration. I also believe that in the *Anti-Dühring,* ch. I, 9-11; II, 2-4; III, 1, as well as in the introduction and final section of *Feuerbach,* I have already treated most of the points.

I beg of you not to weigh gingerly each separate word of the above by itself but to take the connections into account. I am sorry that I have not the time to work things out and write you with the same exact detail that I would have to do for publication.

Yours, etc.

4. FROM A LETTER OF ENGELS TO F. MEHRING

July 14, 1893

You have expressed the main facts admirably and for every open-minded person convincingly.[1] If I were to take exception to anything it would be to the fact that you ascribe more credit to me than I deserve, even if I include everything I could have possibly discovered in the course of time by myself; but which Marx with his quicker *coup d'oeil* and wider view, discovered much sooner. When one has had the good fortune to work together for forty years with a man like Marx, one does not during his lifetime receive the appreciation one believes he deserves. But just as soon as the greater of the two dies, the lesser is easily overrated. That seems to be true for me now. History, however, will take care of all that and by that time one is happily here no longer and cares nothing at all about it.

Only one point is lacking which Marx and I did not sufficiently stress and in relation to which we are equally to blame. We both placed and *had to place* the chief weight upon the *derivation* of political, legal and other ideological notions, as well as the actions which they led up to, from fundamental economic facts. In consequence we neglected the formal side, *i.e.,* the way in which these ideas arose, for the sake of the content. That gave our opponents a

---

[1] The reference is to an essay of Mehring's reprinted as an appendix to the first edition of his *Lessinglegende.* Mehring reprinted this section of Engels' letter in his *Geschichte der deutschen Sozial-democratie,* 2nd ed. (1903), Vol. I, pp. 385ff.

welcome occasion for misunderstanding. Paul Barth is a striking example.

Ideology is a process which of course is carried on with the consciousness of so-called thinkers but with a false consciousness. The real driving force which moves it remains unconscious otherwise it would not be an ideological process. It imaginatively creates for itself false or apparent driving forces. Because it is a thought process, it derives both its content and form from pure thought, either its own or that of its predecessors. It works with pure conceptual material which it unwittingly takes over as the product of thought and therefore does not investigate its relations to a process further removed from and independent of thought. Indeed it seems to be self-evident that since all activity is mediated by thought, it is ultimately *grounded* in thought. The historical ideologist (and historical means here political, jural, philosophical, theological, in short, all domains which belong to society and not merely to nature)—the historical ideologist is confronted in every scientific field by material which has been built up independently out of the thought of earlier generations, and which through the minds of these successive generations has undergone an independent development peculiar to itself. External facts from this or other fields may have contributed to determine this development, but these facts, according to the tacit presuppositions made, are themselves mere fruits of a thought process. And so we still remain in the realm of pure thought which has succeeded so well in digesting the hardest facts.

It is this appearance of an independent history of state constitutions, systems of law, of ideologies in every special field, which, above all, has blinded so many people. When Luther and Calvin "transcend" the official catholic religion; when Hegel "transcends'" Fichte and Kant; and Rousseau, indirectly with his social contract, the constitutionalist, Montesquieu,—it is a process which remains within theology, philosophy, and political science. It merely reveals a stage in the history of these intellectual domains and never emerges from the field of pure thought at all. Ever since the illusion of the eternity and ultimacy of the system of capitalist production arose, the refutation of the Mercantilists through the physiocrats and A. Smith has been regarded not as the intellectual reflection of different economic facts, but only as a victory of thought, as a correct insight, won at last, into actual conditions existing always and everywhere. If only Richard the Lion-hearted, and Philip Augustus had introduced free trade, instead of involving themselves in crusades, five hundred years of misery and stupidity would have been spared us.

This side of affairs, which I can here only indicate, we have all neglected, more than is necessary. It's the old story. In the beginning the form is always neglected for the content. As already said, I myself have made that error and it has always been thrown up to me. I am far from reproaching you with it. As an older sinner in this respect I have hardly the right. But I wish to call your attention to this point for the future.

This is bound up with the stupid conception of the ideologists. Because we denied that the different ideological spheres, which play a part in history, have an independent historical development, we were supposed therewith to have denied that they have any *historical efficacy*. At the basis of this is the ordinary undialectical notion of cause and effect as fixed, mutually opposed, polar relations, and a complete disregard of reciprocity. These gentlemen forget, almost intentionally, that an historical factor, once it has been brought into the world by another—ultimately economic fact—is able to re-act upon its surroundings and even affect its own causes. . . .

FROM IDEOLOGY TO PHILOSOPHY

SIDNEY HOOK'S WRITINGS ON MARXISM

BY LEWIS S. FEUER

TODAY, when we discuss
the work of a philoso-
pher, its generational coordinates have to be assigned. We
speak of the "early Marx" and the "early Russell," and
then their middle-age and old-age ideas. In part, this is
because the actual historical situation and crises which the
successive generations have had to meet have changed so
basically within short periods. Of all living American
thinkers, Sidney Hook has been the one most responsive to
his times, and one might add, the one also the most
responsible. The problems raised by Marxism have been
central to his thinking and action; and what he has written,
bearing the impress of successive periods, falls into a succession of stages.

The young Sidney Hook was a Marxist activist; from

Originally published in *Sidney Hook and the Contemporary World: Essays
on the Pragmatic Intelligence*, edited by Paul Kurtz (New York: John Day
Company, 1968), pages 35–53. Copyright © 1968 John Day Company.

that era came his *Towards the Understanding of Karl Marx* in 1933 and the delayed *From Hegel to Marx* in 1936. Those were years moved by the revolutionary longings which arose from the Great Depression; it was in 1932 that Hook had a principal part in organizing a group of leading American intellectuals to endorse the Communist candidate for the Presidency of the United States:

> We of this generation stand midway between two eras. . . . When we look ahead, we see something new and strange, undreamed of in the American philosophy. What we see ahead is the threat of cultural dissolution. . . . We who write this, listed among the so-called "intellectuals" of our generation, . . . we strike hands with our comrades. . . . We have acted. As responsible intellectual workers we have aligned ourselves with the frankly revolutionary Communist Party. . . .[1]

The next years, however, brought the corruption of Stalinism; the socialist hope became ambiguous. The trials in Moscow of the old Bolshevik leaders raised ethical problems of a kind which no activist previously had had to face. The latter thirties were Hook's most polemical period; a few years earlier he had been the only Marxist professor in an American university; in the latter thirties, it often seemed that he was the only professor who had the courage to speak out against the evil of Stalinism. To the polemical stage belong also his critical writings against the orthodox variant of "dialectic." Meanwhile, Adolf Hitler was stamping his mark of evil on Europe and the world. One individual could

---

1. League of Professional Groups for Foster and Ford, *Culture and the Crisis* (New York, 1932), pp. 3, 32.

shape an era to his horrible image. Something was fundamentally wrong in the impersonal and optimistic standpoint of dialectical materialism. Hook the polemicist gave way in the early forties to the mature scholar of *The Hero in History*, a work in which with an amazing strength of character this man in his own early forties undertook to reexamine his basic assumptions. He emerged with a philosophy which was surprisingly similar in its argument to that which he had heard in the classroom of his teacher, Morris R. Cohen, on the philosophy of civilization, except that in Hook the argument was weighted with an immense personal involvement and experience of history.[2] This was Hook, the post-Marxist. But even the post-Marxist became vestigial in Hook during the years after the Second World War. He explained in an article published in 1947:

> For the last twenty years I have presented an interpretation of Marx which has run counter to customary views and conceptions of his fundamental doctrines. . . . It would appear that if I were justified in my interpretation of Marx's meaning, I would be perhaps the only true Marxist left in the world. This is too much for my sense of humor, and so I have decided to abandon the term as a descriptive epithet of my position. . . . Certainly, if the Stalinists and their international salon of fellow-traveling litterateurs and totalitarian liberal politicos, whose ignorance of the subject is as broad as their dogmatism is deep—are Marxists, then I am cheerfully resigned to being non-Marxist.[3]

2. *Cf.* Morris R. Cohen, "Notes on Prof. Hook's Understanding of Marx," *Student Outlook* 3, nos. 2–3 (November–December 1934): 31–34.

3. Sidney Hook, "The Future of Socialism," *Partisan Review* 14 (January–February 1947): 25.

One can imagine the emotion which went through this transitional experience and the acknowledgment that a social thought experiment was being written off. The battles of a lifetime and their banners are, however, not easily forsworn. Hook still joined as a powerful controversialist to keep the legacy of Marx from being purloined by totalitarians. For the twenty years after the Second World War he became the symbol of political integrity, feared because he had remained immune to mass fashions and caste pressures; he had been proved too often right and remained indefatigably ready to argue with and expose the latest demagogic fraud. His numerous articles and book reviews were unswerving in their loyalty to reason. That is why the New Left disliked him almost as much as had the Old.

If Sidney Hook failed to see his socialist philosophy become the guiding principles of a political party, he achieved in the course of his effort the most unique contribution which has been made in America to Marxist thought. To this we must now turn.

It is hard to convey to readers today the significance of *Towards the Understanding of Karl Marx*, and the still earlier formative articles when they first appeared. For here indeed was the first original American Marxist, one who could join in ideological debate with the European Marxists, with Eduard Bernstein, Kautsky, and Trotsky, one who comprehended the nuances which divided Rosa Luxemburg and Lenin, and could take issue with the abstruse commentaries of Lukács. There had been erudite men in the American socialist movement before the First World War who had written ably on socialist economics and history—Louis B. Boudin and Morris Hillquit—but they belonged to an immigrant generation which lacked the training for original work.

One American, William English Walling, had actually proposed to conjoin the pragmatism of William James with
Marx's socialism, but he too was unable to give substance to
his insight. Here, however, was Sidney Hook, writing with
an unparalleled vigor and authority; his articles, read by college and university students, were like the reports of the
great theologians' disputes which spread through the European universities in the Middle Ages. Copies of the *Symposium* and *Modern Monthly* articles were passed among impe-
cunious undergraduate hands. Soon, however, a warning
spread through the left-wing grapevine: Hook is a revisionist. The signal was especially sounded by two articles of
Earl Browder's in *The Communist* entitled ominously "The
Revisionism of Sidney Hook."[4] This young philosopher was
original and independent-minded, and the orthodox hierarchy suspected such qualities. I recall how at Harvard a
fellow graduate student approached me and suggested in the
language of the academic underground that perhaps I might
be interested in joining a "neo-Hegelian" discussion circle.
His enthusiasm waned when I asked if they would discuss
Sidney Hook's new book.

Hook in the first phase of his thought was the spokes-
man of what might be called "epistemological activism."
His argument was an adaptation of John Dewey's instrumentalism; unlike European Marxism, it was suffused
with a sense of the open universe of possibilities whose
realization depended on human decision and action. It was
an interpretation of Marxism which placed a tremendous
meaning on Marx's now celebrated eleventh thesis on

---

4. Earl Browder, "The Revisionism of Sidney Hook," *Communist*
12 (1933): 133–46, 285–300. See also V. J. Jerome, "Unmasking an
American Revisionist of Marxism," *Communist* 12 (1933): 50–82.

Feuerbach: "Philosophers have only interpreted the world differently; the point is, however, to change it." This was in Hook's eyes more than a political-ethical summons to action; he maintained that revolutionary action brought with it as well the highest sociological knowledge. This then was a "revolutionary epistemology" which Hook advocated; he went so far as to regard every perception as a natural revolutionist, as an incipient "revolutionary act." The only point at which he criticized Lenin was when Lenin adopted what Hook took to be Engels' nonactivist epistemology, that "sensations are copies, photographs, images and mirror-reflections of things"; such a notion, said Hook, departed from the requirements of Marxism as "the theory and practice of social revolution." Hook warned of the social dangers of such a theory of knowledge. "Whoever believes that sensations are literal copies of the external world, and that of themselves they give knowledge, cannot escape fatalism and mechanism." The "dualistic Lockean epistemology," Hook felt, had exactly such pernicious consequences. Sensation, he said, was not a passive occurrence; perception was an "interacting process within which sensations are just as much the resultant of the active mind (the total organism) as the things acted upon." Moreover, Hook believed that an activist theory of knowledge resolved all of Hume's anxiety about causal connections. With Engels, Hook held that the practical use of causal connections in industry refuted Hume's doubts: "It is only in so far as we can produce things, or bring situations to pass that we can conquer the well-known Humean difficulties about causation."[5] Thus the

---

5. Sidney Hook, *Towards the Understanding of Karl Marx* (New York: John Day, 1933), pp. 63, 95, 114, 173.

youthful activism of the early thirties was projected by
Sidney Hook into an epistemological ideology, which was
indeed a hymn to action in 1933. Its theses from a post-
Marxian, nonideological, scientific standpoint scarcely
seem cogent. Hume, for instance, would hardly find his
anxiety dissolved by Hook's practicalism. He would make
the obvious reply that human industrial actions and
achievements were just special instances of "constant conjunctions" which in no way alleviated his skepticism concerning the uniformity of nature. Nor can one see that the
"dualistic Lockean epistemology" carries with it any pernicious social consequences. Jefferson and his followers
were disciples of Locke, and their democratic faith was in
no wise diminished by their high regard for Locke's
account of perception, primary and secondary qualities.
One can be either a social revolutionist or conservative,
and accept the notion that sensations are copies of things.

In short, there was a strong voluntarism in Hook's early
philosophy which impelled him to superimpose an ideological demand on the theory of knowledge. Only that
kind of perception and knowledge were to be called
"knowledge" which contributed to the revolutionary
reconstruction of the world. On such grounds, Hook was
led, furthermore, to a decision in favor of the labor theory
of value which otherwise he regarded as beset with logical
and empirical difficulties: "The labor theory of value is
worth saving if the struggle against capitalism is worth the
fight."[6] One finds oneself stirred by this activist ideology,
this mysticism of the revolutionist-participant-observer,
but one's misgivings are more quelled with emotion than

---

6. Ibid., p. 223.

with logic. What gave a certain credence to Hook's epistemological activism was that the great social scientists were often associated with programs for social reform—Smith, Ricardo, Mill, Keynes. The great historians from Thucydides to Trotsky had also experienced with the utmost directness the inner throb of events. Hook's epistemology was a healthy revolt against the "masochistic theory of knowledge" which found truth in the merger of knower with the known, in the fusion of the subject with object. Not passive contemplation but active interaction was the avenue to knowledge, according to Hook.

Nonetheless, the emphasis on action was essentially an ideological intrusion into the definition of knowledge, and one which quickly politicized the meaning of knowledge.

To begin with, much observation depends for its scientific character on reducing the "active" contribution as much as possible. An anthropological fieldworker trying to be as unobtrusive as he can while he observes tribal rituals, an instrument maker fashioning his instruments so that they will alter as little as possible the phenomenon which is being measured, are familiar cases of observation which is optimal when the "active" contribution is minimal. Since Hook was so much influenced in his interpretation of Marx by Dewey's analogy of knowledge to an "instrument," it is especially well to remember how the designer of an ammeter, for instance, uses wires with unusually low resistance so as to change as little as possible the current which is being measured; the voltmeter, on the other hand, is fashioned with wires of high resistance in order to change as little as possible the potential difference in the segment of the circuit which is being measured. To be sure, the desire to change social reality will often inspire researches which reveal otherwise undisclosed possibilities of social change; aspects of the social environment which were regarded as constants will be seen to be instances of social variables which are accessible to human intervention. But one cannot make this latter situation into a universal requirement for scientific knowledge. If knowledge, as Bacon had it, confers the power to change, it just as often, as Ecclesiastes recognized, delineates the eternal sameness of things.

Further, the social role of perception seems to depend on cultural circumstances. Thus perception in Western societies is often motivated by activist, reconstructive intentions; in Asian societies, the norm of perception is much more passive, submissive, a "masochist mode of perception" (as I have called it).[7] This very variation in the character of perception from society to society undermines the notion that every perception is a prelude to social action (unless "action" is defined tautologically as whatever response takes place). Hook, in other words, was imposing a revolutionary a priori on the sociology of perception. And the extent to which our sensations are copies of external objects is likewise a problem for specific studies in psychophysics rather than a question to be settled by a general philosophical argument.

An image of Marx as the great scientist-activist seems to have inspired much of Sidney Hook's writing as a Marxist. Yet it is probably true that the Marxist tradition has largely created a false image of Marx the "activist." Unlike Lenin, Marx had little taste for the hurly-burly of politics. He never tried to build a party. For almost fifteen

7. Lewis S. Feuer, *The Scientific Intellectual* (New York: Basic Books, 1963), p. 254.

years in London he abstained from any involvement with the political groupings of the German exiles. Compare him with Lenin in exile, arguing with every petty faction, attending every conference, desperately trying to control the course of the Russian movement. By contrast Marx dismissed all the "war of the frogs and mice" with an aloof historicism, rejoiced that he was without a party, took pleasure in his "public isolation," and betook himself to the British Museum.[8] When the chance came to return to Germany to work as Lassalle did to help build a workers' party, he chose to remain in Britain. He was brought into the International Workingmen's Association almost by accident. As a British resident, he provided a convenient delegate for Germany in the General Council. His influence grew because he was one of the few educated men in the International and could write manifestos, knew his way around the foreigners' intrigues, and opposed the Continental extremists. Though he was a member of the General Council, Marx attended only one of the congresses of the International, the very last one at the Hague; he was too busy with *Capital* to go to the Lausanne meeting although important debates with the Proudhonists on the strike weapon and collectivism were in the offing. Probably Marx's principal reason for transferring the General Council to New York in 1872 was that when it came down to it, he preferred his books and the British Museum to political battles with the Bakuninists and Blanquists. He publicly celebrated the Paris Commune but privately felt

8. Franz Mehring, *Karl Marx*, trans. Edward Fitzgerald (New York: Covici, 1935), pp. 235–39. Boris Nicolaievsky and Otto Maenchen-Helfen, *Karl Marx: Man and Fighter*, trans. G. David and E. Mosbacher (Philadelphia: Lippincott, 1936), p. 219.

they had acted ridiculously in pressing matters to the point of civil war.[9] He was often the social scientist who regarded "activism" as misplaced zeal. His "dialectic method" by 1867 could not be described as a theory for making social revolution; it was rather the model for theories as to how impersonal forces make for the transition from one social system to another.

Hook in his early phase gave a distinctive and original interpretation to Marx's dialectic method. He tells in a self-portrait written more than thirty years ago: "When Marx's early manuscripts were published, I took the occasion to make a systematic re-study of all his works. . . . I became convinced that his dialectic method by which he strove to combine realism and activism to do justice to the facts of objectivity and relativity . . . involved a nascent experimental naturalism. This was essentially the same position which John Dewey had independently arrived at. . . ."[10] What Hook then did was to interpret Marx as a Left Pragmatist; the dialectic method held, according to Hook, that every theory is a guide to some determinate action: "Its meaning is an implicit prediction that certain consequences will follow upon certain actions and its truth or falsity is established by the set of actions which realizes or fails to realize the predicted consequences. This is the basic proposition of Marx's methodology." More particularly in our time, the dialectic method was "the theory and practice of social revolution."[11]

9. Bertram D. Wolfe, *Marxism: One Hundred Years in the Life of a Doctrine* (New York: Dial Press, 1965), pp. 105 ff.

10. Sidney Hook, "Experimental Naturalism," in *American Philosophy Today and Tomorrow*, ed. Horace M. Kallen and Sidney Hook (New York: Lee and Furman, 1935), pp. 223–24.

11. Sidney Hook, ed., *The Meaning of Marx; A Symposium* (New York: Farrar & Rinehart, 1934), pp. 30–31.

From the purely historical standpoint, Hook's interpretation of Marx's dialectic is at variance with Marx's own summation of his method. The principal passage in Marx which shaped the views of several generations as to the meaning of "dialectic" occurs in the second preface to *Capital*. Marx does not present his dialectic as a theory of action: it is simply a statement of a form, a model (as we would call it today) of sociological law. The dialectic method as applied to societies, he says, aims to ascertain "the law of their variation, of their development, i.e., of their transition from one form into another, from one series of connections into a different one." It aimed "to show, by rigid scientific investigation, the necessity of successive determinate orders of social conditions, . . . into which the first must inevitably pass over; and all this the same, whether men believe or do not believe it, whether they are conscious or unconscious of it." The social movement, Marx indicated, was to be taken as "governed by laws not only independent of human will, consciousness, and intelligence, but rather, on the contrary, determining that will, consciousness, and intelligence." This is clearly a long way from Dewey's method of intelligence and the notion of dialectic as action to test the consequences of a theory for whose validation the action itself is a necessary condition. Marx is little concerned with the methodology of how to make a revolution; the latter would presumably consist of a set of propositions of applied social science— how to write propaganda, slogans; how to heighten discontent; how to recognize revolutionary situations. Rather his dialectic method is the study of how societies evolve through unresolvable disequilibria through successive stages. Hook's dialectic makes it dependent on acts of

will; certain actions must be taken to see if certain consequences are realized. Marx's whole point in *Capital* is that
whether you take action or not, this process of social history must realize itself.

Perhaps Hook's method of interpretation in the early
thirties was not unlike that of the alienational neo-Marxists
in the sixties. He went back from the mature Marx of *Capital* to an early Marx of age twenty-seven; they went back
to the still earlier one of alienation, age twenty-six, rather
than stopping with the midway Marx of the Feuerbachian
theses. The "alienational" Marx was akin to an ethical exis-
tentialist; the slightly older one whom Hook followed was
more decisional and materialistic. Hook actually was
reaching for a Jamesian version of Marx; the will to act, the
social decision, was the arbiter among the categories; the
necessities of action superimposed themselves on polar
categories. In other words, the social situation required a
one-sided commitment which violated the principle of
polarity of his philosopher-father, Morris R. Cohen.[12]

In 1936, Sidney Hook's *From Hegel to Marx* was published; it is the unsurpassed work of Marxian scholarship
in the United States, a masterpiece of interpretation in
intellectual history. Harold J. Laski, the foremost British
Marxist of that era, justly observed that Hook had established himself "as one of the three or four outstanding
Marxist authorities of the time"; he hoped that our age
would see the discovery of a philosophy which would do
for us what Marx did for the Young Hegelians. Unless
such a philosophy emerged, Laski felt fascism would triumph: "For the cause of that triumph lies always in the

12. Hook, "Experimental Naturalism," p. 221.

failure of those who feel the need to transform the world
to produce a philosophy."[13] Such an avowal in the power
of ideas was hardly to be expected from a Marxist, but
Hook's book awoke this enthusiasm.

This was a drama of ideas which Hook wrote of Marx—
the young Promethean wrestling with his contemporaries
and forging in combat the revolutionary philosophy for his
time. The circle of the Doctors' Club, the restless ferment
of the Young Hegelians, the arrogance of their generational revolt, all came alive in Hook's book. Now, in retrospect, the book's imperfection comes from the very
completeness of Hook's identification with Marx. Always
the adversaries are vanquished—Bruno Bauer, Arnold
Ruge, Max Stirner, Moses Hess, Ludwig Feuerbach. Marx
engages them in dialectical joust, and his argument thrust
is always judged as a clear victory for dialectical materialism. Today we would be less certain. In every case, we
would think of what each of these men might have
answered Marx. And perhaps each of them had a truth
which when cast aside made for a cumulative poverty in
Marxism. Bruno Bauer's doubts concerning the political
capacity of the masses were not dispelled by Marx's
emphasis on social determinants of character; would the
abolition of capitalism really set the stage for man to
become truly human? Arnold Ruge was more than a *naïf*,
tired liberal when he advocated making the state a "classless" one. Was it wise to exacerbate political differences
by always insisting that they stemmed from unresolvable
class conflicts? Were controversies ineluctably beyond the
bounds of the values of a common peoplehood? Did not

13. Harold J. Laski, "From Hegel to Marx: By Sidney Hook,"
Nation 143 (13 August 1936): 188–89.

the insistence that "every philosophy of politics is a class philosophy expressing class politics" finally make for political amorality? Was the concern for individual liberties to be so easily put aside? When Moses Hess and the "true socialists" asserted that the driving impulse behind socialist reform must be an ethical conception of man, did Marx add to the stature of socialism by ridiculing the ethical ingredient? Did the endless emphasis on man's malleability under different social circumstances overlook the fact that some societies repress man more than others, that there is an underlying common human nature? Were Marx and Hook too confident in assuming that class struggle was a "school" which would educate the working class to a higher integrity even if ethics was removed from the curriculum? Was Feuerbach perhaps right in holding against Marx that man was indeed a religious creature? To correlate historical religions with social circumstances does not show that the religious impulse itself originates from the latter; for the religious feeling may be invariant in all societies, even as its expression varies with social conditions. Even Max Stirner's individualism had a truth which Marx ignored. For Stirner's "pure ego" was not an abstraction but consisted precisely of the underlying substratum of human needs, which Stirner proposed to use as the criterion by which to test every social ideal and idol. Marx's dismissal of Stirner as "petty bourgeois" may have helped pave the way for the fetishism of party to arise; party loyalty became party idolatry, and Koestler's Rubashov had painfully to rediscover the "I." Granted that the Young Hegelians had their extravagances; that Stirner, for instance, reads at times like the ideological precursor of the "beats" and "hippies." Nevertheless we cannot today share the confidence of the young Sidney Hook, that it was all a forward movement from Hegel to Marx.

Hook's *From Hegel to Marx* was far superior in its scholarship to the contemporary neo-Marxian tracts which exalt "alienation." Long before this trend of mythological Marxism, Hook without fanfare noted the concept's role in Feuerbach's philosophy and its transitional appearance in Marx. Though the word "alienation" didn't appear in the index, the index in this case belied the text.[14] The religious fact in Feuerbach, wrote Hook, was "the alienation of man from himself," a concept extended by the Young Hegelians to politics, ethics, and economics. When Feuerbach traced the roots of religious dogma to sexual repression, Hook noted his direction was much like Freud's ("a fashionable contemporary psychology"); Marx instead moved toward the study of economic relationships. In recent years, Hook has rebuked those who, trying to fashion a Marx after their own image, make a new sacred text of the unpublished juvenilia about "alienation" which Marx himself subsequently repudiated.[15] Yet Hook himself, prior to the revival of alienational neo-Marxism, recognized an underlying humanist component in Marx's "concern with human alienation and his view that it can be overcome by creative fulfillments. . . ."[16]

---

14. Daniel Bell wrote quite erroneously: "In Sidney Hook's pioneer account of Marx's intellectual development, *From Hegel to Marx* published in 1936, the word 'alienation' does not occur once in the text." One must set this down as an example of generational misperception in Marxian scholarship. *Cf.* Daniel Bell, "The Rediscovery of Alienation," *Journal of Philosophy* 56 (1959): 934.

15. Sidney Hook, "Karl Marx's Second Coming," *New York Times Book Review*, 22 May 1966, p. 2.

16. Sidney Hook, "What's Left of Karl Marx?" *Saturday Review* 42 (6 June 1959): 58.

Toward the end of his first phase as a Marxist, Hook began his notable polemics against the dogmas of Soviet Marxism. In *From Hegel to Marx* he assailed the Soviet doctrine that the dialectic was applicable to nature; this doctrine, he argued, was incompatible with naturalism. The counterpart of such a debate in Anglo-American philosophy would be one, for instance, as to whether Spencer's law of evolution applies to the planetary system as well as to social systems, and what relevance this would have for the validity of economic liberalism. One agrees with Hook's rejection of orthodoxy in philosophy while wondering whether his methodological critique of "dialectic" is too extensive. For if dialectic is taken as the formal patterns of systems in disequilibrium and their equilibration, there is no a priori reason why the evolution of stellar systems, for instance, could not be regarded as exemplifying such forms. Hook, however, wrote: "Only an idealist can adhere to the distinctive connotation of dialectic . . . and still believe that nature, independent of man, is an illustration of it."[17] But this was tantamount to prescribing that human consciousness is a necessary part of "dialectical" processes, which thus by definition are restricted to the human domain. In his desire to combat the absurdities of Communist ideologists, Hook restricted the "dialectical" forms to social processes in a way which reminded one of the traditional separation between the *Geisteswissenschaften* and the *Naturwissenschaften*. Curiously, in this respect Hook was led to depart from the principle of continuity so dear to Dewey, according to which

17. Sidney Hook, *From Hegel to Marx* (New York: John Day, 1936), p. 75. Also, the essay, "Dialectic and Nature," reprinted in Hook's *Reason, Social Myths and Democracy* (New York: John Day, 1940), p. 183.

the operation of dialectical patterns in the social foreground would have constituted evidence for their presence in the natural background.

The notion of *praxis* was at this time Sidney Hook's central concept. *From Hegel to Marx* culminated in a series of glosses on Marx's Theses on Feuerbach which exalted *praxis*, or as we would say today, activism. At times, under positivist influence, Hook would assimilate *praxis* to the activity of scientific verification, but then he would return to its more basic significance, revolutionary practice. In part, *praxis* included what sociologists later called "self-fulfilling prophecies," but it was more than that. For Hook called for *actions*, not mere predictions based on a theory; theory had to be a guide to action, not mere prediction. Herein, says Hook, we have a type of judgment whose truth could never be established by the idealistic or traditional materialistic theories.[18]

This was the distinctive American variant of Marxism—the notion that action-involvement to realize a theory's truth is a necessary condition for its confirmation. Yet it is hard to see that any traditional idealist or materialist would feel himself balked by it. Traditional philosophers were certainly aware of the power of fanatical beliefs to achieve social action; Voltaire had written *Mahomet*. Hook's judgments of *praxis* could be translated with the help of a few provisos into traditional hypothetical ones, as, for instance: Provided that enough people believe in the advent of socialism and provided that they act with firmness and vigor, then given certain objective

---

18. Hook, *From Hegel to Marx*, pp. 284–85.

economic and political circumstances, a socialist society
will eventuate.[19]

Oddly enough, if "scientific socialism" were put to
people in terms of such "provisos" and "possibilities" it
would lose that whole irrational fervor which the mytho-
poeic "inevitable" calls forth. The modality of revolutionary "logic" is necessity, not possibility; and a scientifi-
cally conceived socialism might be a condition for the
undoing of a revolutionary emotion. Probably a component
of Promethean myth safeguarded from analysis is part of
praxis. Hook, despite some appreciative pages on myth,
like Marx shied away from any epistemological mysticism.
Is there a necessary disunity between revolutionary political theory and revolutionary political practice? Does it
have its counterpart of the Platonic "noble lie"?

From Hegel to Marx failed to have an influence on
American thought. In part, this was because it was virtually proscribed by the American Communist Party which
exerted an immense influence, not only on its members,
but on wide circles of fellow travelers. If one wishes to see
what American Marxism would have been like if the party
machine had not been able to dictate the thinking and

19. This was essentially Max Eastman's criticism of Hook's version of "dialectic." Max Eastman, *The Last Stand of Dialectic Materialism: A Study of Hook's Marxism* (New York: Polemic Publishers,
1934), p. 45. For the controversy in retrospect, *cf.* Sidney Hook, "Marx,
Dewey and Lincoln," *New Leader* 40 (21 October 1957): 16 ff.; Max
Eastman, *Love and Revolution: My Journey through an Epoch* (New
York: Random House, 1964), pp. 499–500. Dewey himself refused to
play favorites among his old students and declined to take sides. *Cf.* Max
Eastman, *Great Companions* (New York: Farrar, Straus & Cudahy,
1959), p. 200. Also *cf.* Max Eastman, "Lincoln Was No Pragmatist," *New
Leader* 40 (23 September 1957): 19–20.

reading of so many intellectuals, one can find it in Sidney Hook's first two books on Marx. As it was, Hook's work had no social base, no audience, no sense of an imparted direction, except for a handful of Marxian independents. Also Hook's books were far more Marxist than his own evolving beliefs and practice. *From Hegel to Marx* was published even as the Moscow trials were sharpening the significance of ethical choices and dilemmas, the problem of means and ends. Ethics had hitherto occupied a subordinate place for Hook as simply the formulation of class demands.[20] Now, however, in his polemics there was a return of the repressed, a sense of human values more overriding than class or party mandates. Hook's masterpiece of Marxist scholarship was published on the eve of events which were to take him far from Marxism. In another century, in the eighties or nineties, when the historical tempo was slower, Sidney Hook might conceivably have found sufficient answers available in Marxian premises. But the thirties and forties brought a succession of political crucial experiments which shattered one theory after another. The party faithful and fellow travelers sealed off their thinking and seeing so as to evade a confrontation with social realities. Hook, the only clear-headed Marxist philosopher in the United States, was always testing theory against social actualities. Physical theory has gone through rapid successions of such crises, but the equivalent of such experiences for a social scientist entails a severe personal toll. While Marxism became for many intellectuals an emotional anodyne, Hook became all the

---

20. Hook, *From Hegel to Marx*, pp. 51–53.

more one who was philosophizing for a generation which had lost its way.

Hook's definitive rejection of Marxism came with *The Hero in History* published in 1943. It was his most sustained intellectual achievement and represented a laborious rethinking of his most basic postulates. Here he broke through the chief shibboleths which had enthralled his time. He dared, for instance, to argue that the net consequences of the Bolshevik Revolution had been baneful. Few of the Marxist critics of Stalin's regime had ventured to go so far. Leon Trotsky, the greatest of them, could never bring himself to question the Soviet creation itself. But Hook traced the consequences and the alternatives with a new persistence and doggedness. It was a bold construction in historical hypotheticals which probably severed his last attachment to Leninist activism. If the October Revolution had not occurred, he noted, the world economic crises might not have been so devastating; the Russian market, withdrawn by the Soviets from the world economy, might have absorbed great quantities of goods and services. A monolithic Communist International would not have imposed its throttling mass on democratic socialist movements. The fear of Bolshevism would not have fed the reaction of Fascism: "Without the Russian Revolution, there would have been a Hitler movement anyway, but it would not have triumphed."[21]

The argument of *The Hero in History* was no longer formulated in terms of instrumentalist epistemology. Rather it was straightforwardly scientific and sociological. When he

---

21. Sidney Hook, *The Hero in History* (New York: John Day, 1943), pp. 87, 200.

wrote the *Understanding*, he had the conventional Marxist outlook toward such personages as Hitler and Gandhi. They were of no crucial historical significance, he said: "It is no exaggeration to maintain that if they had not been what they were, then historically speaking, others would have been what they were."[22] This was the orthodox Marxist standpoint of Engels and Plekhanov. But the experience of Hitler, with sheer individual demonry set loose in history, and the experience of Stalinism had undermined one's faith in a law of history in which the emergence of a higher ethic was synchronous with the development of productive forces. Hook now distinguished between cases in which the impersonal "determining tendencies" were sufficient and those where alternative paths of development existed and where consequently "heroic action can count decisively." He left little standing of Engels' easy view that "in default of a Napoleon, another would have filled his place. . . ." The Bolshevik Revolution itself, Hook argued, would not have occurred without Lenin's personal influence: "But from first to last it was Lenin. Without him there would have been no October Revolution." In this sense, Lenin was an "event-making" personality rather than just an "eventful" man. Moreover, history could fail one remarkably when it came to providing heroes. "If there had been a great figure in Germany capable of unifying the left and appeasing the center, Hitler might never have become Chancellor."[23]

Insofar as its basic tenet was involved, Sidney Hook had returned to the insight of William James' classical protest against sociological determinism in *Great Men and Their*

---

22. Hook, *Towards the Understanding of Karl Marx*, p. 166.
23. Hook, *The Hero in History*, pp. 109, 203, 116.

Environment, as he had heard it often from the interme-
diary teacher, Morris Cohen.[24]

The old arguments, however, as Hook presented them,
were spoken with a new significance. Every age redis-
covers, if it is blessed, ancient philosophical truths in
terms of its own experience; otherwise it may be immured
in new versions of falsehood.

Where one cavils with *The Hero in History* is the ambiguity of its central concept. How would one identify a hero
in operational terms? Before October, 1917, the chief
European Marxists thought of Lenin as a quarrelsome,
fanatical, unrealistic man, who was dividing and morally
compromising the Russian Social Democracy. An
abnormal, improbable situation created the historical
occasion for a man who otherwise might have been
remembered in Trotsky's early characterization of him as
an egomaniac who wanted the power to "guillotine" those
who disagreed with him.[25] The World War and the breakdown of the Russian government transformed Lenin in
people's eyes from an unhistorical "loner" into the protag-
onist of a new historical era. The man's traits were the
same throughout. The "hero" can be known only after the
fact, and people then endow him with almost supernatural
attributes (charisma) which they never would have seen in
him before.[26] The concept clearly retains poetic overtones

24. Morris R. Cohen, *The Meaning of Human History* (La Salle,
Ill.: Open Court, 1947), pp. 214 ff.

25. Bertram D. Wolfe, *Three Who Made a Revolution* (reprint,
Boston: Beacon Press, 1962), p. 253.

26. Max Weber, the sociologist of charisma, saw no charisma in
Lenin's leadership before or after 1917. *Cf.* Richard Pipes, "Max Weber
and Russia," *World Politics* 8 (1955): 392, 397. For Lenin's polemic with
Weber, *cf.* V. I. Lenin, *Lecture on the 1905 Revolution* (Moscow,

which project peoples' longings under certain conditions for a redeemer. Then, of course, there is the strange problem of the heroes who failed to shape history, from the Carthaginian Hannibal to the fallen Indian chiefs Tecumseh and Pontiac. Their heroism was all the greater in their defeat.

Moreover, arguments from historical hypotheticals ("contrary-to-fact conditionals," more precisely), from what might have happened *if*, while they may chasten certitude with ignorance, still leave us unable to affirm an alternative position. The Soviet apologists emphasize (what we might call) the "sociological sequence line" of actual occurrences; Hook selects another possible sequence line. But there were of course many others. A military dictatorship, for instance, was regarded by many in 1918 as the only alternative to Bolshevik rule; to what extremities of ferocity would the militarists have gone, and with what consequences? Would the trend to reactionary dictatorship have spread more quickly in Europe? Would a Russian capitalism have added to the intensity of the depression? We are left with an admixture of historical skepticism, with the recognition of the limits of our sociological knowledge. There are questions which may have no answer.

Since the end of the Second World War, Hook has engaged in numerous discussions concerning academic freedom and the status of a conspiratorial party. Although often harshly attacked for his stand against political conspiracies, it is noteworthy that Hook's view represented a

undated), p. 114. For a third notion of the "hero" as neither event-making nor eventful, but events-representative, as *cf.* Isaiah Berlin, *Chaim Weizmann* (New York: Farrar, Straus & Cudahy, 1958), p. 26.

return to classical Marxism. For Marx even in 1848 objected to the Communist League's retaining any of the appurtenances of the political secret society, and he demanded the ouster of the Bakuninists from the International Workingmen's Association in 1872 on the similar ground that a secret apparatus had no place in a democratic movement. Hook had thus made a full return from Lenin to the mature Marx.

From Sidney Hook's Marxist writings there emerged certain contributions to American sociological theory. For one, Hook was one of the first theorists of what came to be called "structural functionalism," the emphasis, that is, on the interrelations of institutions in a social system: "The mutual determination of function and structure becomes intelligible only from the point of view of the whole system." Hook, however, was free of the "static" bias of the later functionalists. He combined the emphasis on the social system with the dialectic (or polar) interaction of disequilibrating forces. His article on determinism for the *Encyclopedia of the Social Sciences* was formative for this mode of thought. To make the purely functional concept of causation consistent with the Marxist view of the primacy of economic factor, Hook proposed to define "cause" as that variable in a functional relation which is accessible to human action: "The element which must be changed we regard as the cause."[27] Whether Marxism was translatable

---

27. Hook, *From Hegel to Marx*, pp. 64–65. Sidney Hook, "Determinism," *Encyclopedia of the Social Sciences*, vol. 5 (New York: Macmillan, 1931), pp. 110–14. No one has heretofore noted that Parsons' analysis of the social "act" repeats exactly Hook's analysis of the dialectical structure of action. *Cf.* Talcott Parsons, *The Structure of Social Action* (reprint, Glencoe, Ill.: Free Press, 1949), p. 44.

into such functional equations, however, remained open to
question. For a Marxist would hold that the primacy of the
economic factor for inducing social change indicated a
causal, existential primacy as well. Indeed, where social
systems were relatively unalterable, it was because their
economic basis presumably could not be affected by
human decisions.

Finally, a distinctive conception of the role of philosophy in the history of civilization emerged from Hook's
Marxist writings. A critical, experimental approach, said
Hook, is associated with those groups pressing for social
reform. The dominant groups, the vested interests, he
argued, look for support in the obscurities of idealistic philosophy. The reformers, on the other hand, eager to stress
"the empirical facts of discrimination and under-privi-
lege," could afford to be experimental in their outlook.
Thus, Hook wrote, a "significant connection is to be found
between social movements and philosophical doctrines."[28]
Hook, the philosopher, however, was at odds with Hook
the Marxist. Elsewhere he had written that not class allegiance but temperament was the basic causative factor in
philosophical standpoint: "I believe that the connection
between temperament and philosophy is more fundamental and more readily ascertainable than that between
class allegiance and philosophical belief."[29] Would idealistic, "tenderhearted" temperaments then tend to enroll
among the reactionaries? The facts of American intellectual history scarcely confirmed Hook's Marxist interpreta-

28. Sidney Hook, "Metaphysics and Social Attitudes," *Social Frontier* 4 (February 1938): 153–58.

29. Hook, "Experimental Naturalism," p. 222.

tion. The transcendentalists, apriorists and Platonists, were the eloquent social critics of slavery before the Civil War; the defenders of slavery were often found to be materialists and positivists. In Latin America, empirical positivism became the ideology of dictatorial rule. In the Soviet Union today, the words spoken against the dictatorial regime tend to come from idealistic existentialists; they see materialism as tied to a bureaucratic rule. There is an ambiguity in the social rule of philosophies which one must trace to certain cyclical and generational movements.

Sidney Hook has led the discussion in all these problems. He has made the first hypotheses, experimented with ideas, and always remained open to new fact. He has been the symbol of courage in almost forty years of discussion and debate. He has ventured too far ahead in argument on political issues to have a supporting school behind him, but as time goes on, it becomes clearer that the one significant political philosopher that our country has produced this century has been Sidney Hook. He was far in advance of the European Marxists. Only the novelists Koestler and Silone equaled him in the depth of analysis; thinkers like Camus after the Second World War painfully went over ground which Hook had long since traversed. Of all America's philosophers, Sidney Hook was the one who kept its conscience alive.

Ideologists have always tried to change the world; they become philosophers when they transcend ideology and ask questions concerning the inner aims, means, and consequences of ideologically motivated change for human lives. Not to change the world, but to change it only wisely.

MARX IN LIMBO:
AN IMAGINARY CONVERSATION

BY SIDNEY HOOK

I T was not difficult to find the shade of Karl Marx in limbo. His spectral beard was trimmed, his monocle was gone and he seemed much more benign than his pictures show him—indeed, almost grandfatherly. Flanked by Engels and Kautsky, he was arguing a technical point with Keynes, Veblen and Schumpeter. Lenin was not in the circle. Later my guide told me he was waiting with brooding impatience for Stalin, who, although due, was still missing; there were rumors that limbo would not receive him.

Marx detached himself from his fellow shades when he learned that a visitor from earth had arrived. Instead of introducing myself as an author of several studies of his thought (I had heard that biographers and critics sometimes

Originally published in the *New Leader* 38 (2 May 1955): 14–17. Reprinted with permission of the *New Leader*, 2 May 1955. Copyright © The American Labor Conference on International Affairs, Inc.

got an unspiritual reception when they met their subjects face to face), I announced at once that I had news for him.

"News?" he said. "I hope it's agreeable for a change. For the last twenty years or so, it has been uniformly unpleasant. Almost every new arrival prominently connected with public affairs has picked an argument with me, as if I were responsible for what's happening on Earth."

"My news is more personal," I replied. "The Marx-Engels-Lenin Institute at Moscow is issuing a new corrected edition of your works at the command of the Central Executive Committee of the Russian Communist party."

"Corrected edition, indeed!" he remarked bitterly. "They have been correcting me by word and deed ever since 1917. Every last outrage they commit is laid at my door—even by people who should know better."

"Well," I pointed out, "isn't it natural? You called yourself a Communist at one time and they call themselves Communists."

"That, my dear Professor," Marx interrupted, "is known as the fallacy of the undistributed middle term, according to the logic you teach, whose laws, I gather from our cosmic news ticker, the Kremlin has just rediscovered. As well say that, because both sides in the Thirty Years War called themselves Christian, they really were in agreement with each other. Soviet Communism and mine are quite different."

"In what respect?" I inquired.

Marx's retort surprised and alarmed me a little because it indicated either that his reading habits were still omnivorous or that the cosmic ticker paid attention to him. "You ought to know, since you've read the material. We called ourselves Communists in order to differentiate ourselves from sentimental socialists who had their eyes so fixed on a Utopia that they couldn't see what the necessary steps were in the process of realizing it. As you recall, when my friends and I were members of the Communist League we wrote that *'we were not among those Communists who were out to destroy liberty and who wished to turn the whole world into one huge barracks or into a gigantic warehouse. There certainly were some Communists who with easy conscience refused to countenance personal liberty.'*[1] But for me personal liberty was the very oxygen of any decent society. My criticism of capitalism was based on my desire to diffuse freedom among those who were suffering from lack of it."

"But if that's true," I objected, "why have the leaders of Communist Russia canonized you and built a cult around you? Surely, to use a favorite phrase of theirs, it is no accident that—"

"It's a long story," Marx interjected, "and there *are* accidents in history even if this isn't one. The Russians were always difficult and different. More than once I had to say *'I am no Marxist.'* Bakunin, who also once called himself a Marxist, I disowned on Earth. The Communists are people of *his* kidney, and even Bakunin rages against them up here. I don't recognize the present-day Communist brood as my legitimate offspring no matter what they call themselves."

"I've heard other fathers *say* that," I replied, "but saying it is not enough to disprove parentage. Legitimate or not, they claim to be inspired by your ideas and to have built a socialist society. You may not like *how* they got there, but they *are* there, are they not?"

---

1. All italicized material is quoted from the writings of Marx.

"By no means," Marx replied with a vehemence that seemed to make his beard-tip glow. "A Socialist society as I always conceived it is one in which '*the free development of each is the condition of the free development of all.*' That excludes the dictatorship of a party, and especially the rule of despots. A socialist society is based on equality, even if it cannot be absolute, and, in the beginning, on equality of wage payments for equal working time. The Communists have substituted a new and worse system of exploitation of the workers—through piecework, speed-up devices, and differences in earned income and living conditions greater than existed in the early days of capitalism. Why, they claim to be Marxists and socialists and yet they frankly admit that labor power is still a commodity subject to the law of value. The surplus value sweated out of them goes to their masters. . . ."

Fearing that Marx was going to ride his ancient economic hobby horse, I interrupted. "Surely not all of it. Some of it goes into new plants, and they do have trade unions."

By this time Marx's whole beard was incandescent. "Trade unions!" he burst out. "Their trade unions are worse than company unions. They are auxiliaries of the secret police whose function is to intimidate the workers into producing more. I have always taught that the working class '*regards its courage, self-confidence, independence and sense of personal dignity as more necessary than its daily bread.*' How is this possible under a regime of a ruthlessly censored press, regimented schools from kindergarten to universities, forced labor, juridical frame-ups, mass deportations and executions? No, the Soviet Union is not a socialist society."

"Nor is it a capitalist society," I added while he paused to draw a fresh breath, "since all the major instruments of production, distribution and exchange are collectivized. What kind of a social system is it, then? Your theory of social development seems unable to account for it."

"This is a terminological matter," Marx declared with a touch of asperity. "The main point is that Soviet society, wherever it exists, outrages all the democratic traditions for which the socialist movement fought as well as those of the great revolutionary movements of liberation whose heirs we always considered ourselves to be."

"Very well," I said hurriedly, "I grant your social philosophy is not theirs. But there is nothing in the notion of a completely collectivized economy which insures that *your* social philosophy will prevail rather than theirs. What I am asking you to explain, however, is the origin and development of the Soviet social system on the basis of your own theory of history. Didn't you say over and over that '*no social order ever perishes before all the productive forces for which there is room in it have developed*'? There was certainly plenty of room for the development of productive forces in Russia in 1917, even more than in the United States of 1917, which was decades ahead of Russia and which has enormously increased its productive capacities since then."

"Quite right," retorted Marx with a triumphant air. "I predicted that socialism would come first to England and the United States because those countries are ripe for it. And certainly not in a backward, undeveloped, semi-barbarous country like Russia. You see how presumptuous the Communists are in calling themselves Marxists."

I wondered why he sounded so triumphant. "I see," I

exclaimed, "that the Communists are not Marxists as they claim to be and that, if you came to life again in Moscow, the Grand Inquisitors of the Kremlin would probably throw you into the cellars of the Lubianka as an agent of American imperialism. But it seems even clearer to me that the Communists have refuted the central doctrine of Marxism in the name of Marxism. According to that doctrine, the mode of economic production determines political events, not conversely. But the Communists seized political power, nationalized the economy, industrialized the country, collectivized agriculture. Their culture may not be democratic, but their economy is collectivist. It is quite apparent that it was not, as you proclaimed, *'historical laws working with iron necessity toward inevitable results'* which were the driving force of events in Russia but the driving will of the Communists. Doesn't this show that men control economic forces, for good or evil, wisely or unwisely, and are not controlled by them to the extent that you taught? In other words, haven't the Communists refuted the central proposition of the theory of historical materialism?"

"Not so fast, Professor," Marx quietly replied. "If you take my words literally, you may be right. But let's look for the meaning behind the mere words. When I wrote about what was historically necessary or impossible, I assumed that there was a certain level of civilization which we could take for granted, certain basic human needs and values which would guide human action, or at least limit what human beings would do to other human beings. I was a humanist before I became a socialist, and therefore I believed it was impossible to build a socialist economy in a backward country like Russia except at a morally prohibitive cost. But if we are completely indifferent to questions of human cost and suffering, only physical and biological necessities limit our action and we are all reduced to the level of clever beasts of prey."

"Nothing can grow in a desert," he continued after a pause, "but we can make even a desert bloom like a flower garden if we are prepared to fertilize it with human corpses and water it with rivers of blood. A country which doesn't grow into socialism on the basis of an already prepared economic foundation, a tradition of skill, management, democracy and culture, will defeat the very ends in behalf of which the socialist movement came into existence."

"It is a pity," I observed, "that you didn't spend more time in elaborating on these ends. By concentrating mainly on the economic conditions of achieving them, you gave the impression that collectivism was the be-all and end-all of socialism; that, once it was achieved, all the other virtues would be added to society. The fault is not completely attributable to those of your disciples who converted a necessary condition into a sufficient one. The sentimental socialists may have ignored the means, but *you* lost sight of the ends. It seems to me that your fault is graver."

"No," said Marx, "my Hegelian teachers had convinced me that means and ends are so intertwined that they couldn't be separated. It may be I took too much for granted. But, remember, I wasn't writing textbooks or manuals or recipe books for revolutions everywhere at any time."

"Then tradition becomes an important constraining force in what men can make of man," I pointed out, "and under some conditions as decisive in influencing the direction of social change as the mode of economic production."

"I have never denied it. On the contrary. *'Men make*

their own history, but not just as they please. They do not choose the circumstances for themselves, but have to work on circumstances as they find them. The legacy of the dead generations weighs like a nightmare upon the brains of the living. At the very time when they seem to be creating something perfectly new, the past often creeps back.' The Russian past could not be wiped out by any Commissar's decree; it still lives in the present. As of old, for the Russian ruler progress consists in extending the domain of their despotism. What I said at the time of the suppression of Poland by Tsarist Russia is even truer today: *'The policy of Russia is changeless. Its methods, its tactics, its maneuvers may change, but the polar star of its policy—world domination—is still a fixed star.'* "

Not wishing to discuss foreign policy in limbo, I shifted to another question.

"Well, now," I asked, "what about China. Surely here is something you didn't foresee. Do you think China can build socialism, even with the help of the Soviet Union?"

"My analysis of the Soviet Union," Marx spoke scornfully, "is even more valid for China. I predict that the attempt to introduce socialism in China will fail even more badly than it has in the Soviet Union."

"Agreed," I replied, "but what you didn't predict is that the attempt would be made! Since the consequence of the attempt, whether it fails or succeeds, is bound to give rise to momentous historical changes—indeed! it already has—something important about history is left unexplained."

"My main interest, as you should know," Marx patiently explained, "has always been in the Western world, and the truth or falsity of my theories rests primarily upon developments there. I predicted *the growth and centralization of large-scale industry, increasing mechanization, the con-centration of capital and monopoly, the entanglement of all peoples in the net of the world market, and periodic crises of production.* By and large, all these things have come to pass."

"Quite true," I rejoined, "but there are a number of other things you predicted which didn't come to pass. You pre-dicted the pauperization of the working classes, the disap-pearance of the middle class, the atrophy of nationalism and patriotism. Large groups of workers in Western Europe, and especially in the United States, enjoy a stan-dard of living higher than the privileged classes of some previous societies. Nationalism is as strong as ever. The middle class has not disappeared. And the plain fact is that the workers in non-collectivist economies have incompa-rably more freedom, political power, and a greater share of what they produce than the workers in presumably collec-tivist economies."

"I cheerfully admit it," Marx smilingly responded, "but I believe I can take some credit for it since I taught the necessity of political action and called attention to the influence of factory legislation."

"But, in addition to the predicted things which didn't happen," I objected, "there are other things which hap-pened that you did not predict—the birth of new indus-tries, the expansion of productive forces, the rise of fas-cism, the emergence of the welfare state."

"I underestimated the vitality of capitalism," said Marx, "and the extent to which the democratic process could be used to strengthen social control and responsibility. But this is a matter of detail and degree. I always argued that *in countries like Great Britain, Holland and the United*

States the transition from capitalism to socialism could be effected peacefully. Similarly with the development of the technological revolution. I believe I was the first to recognize the impact upon society of *'conscious technical application of science to industry and agriculture.'* "

"But you claimed that technology was always a subordinate instrument to war and industry," I protested. "Yet neither you nor anyone else guessed that some day the choices we would have to make concerning its dread uses might affect the very existence of civilization as such."

"The effects of certain discoveries," he agreed, "as well as their significance, cannot always be measured by their origins. Whatever the causes of technological change in the past, unless men today think and plan better than they have in the past, they may not even survive. Limbo will become rapidly overpopulated."

I turned to ask a last question. "Do you believe the basic issue of our time is still between capitalism and socialism?"

Marx spoke deliberately. "Capitalism and socialism as they were traditionally conceived are today irrelevant abstractions in understanding social reality. Wherever free institutions exist, they have been used to make capital more socially responsible and labor more powerful and prosperous. Aside from the defense of freedom itself, the great problems arise in the West not from a quest for new forms of property but for new modes of democratic human experience which will enrich human life and multiply the possibilities of creative fulfillment. The choice is not between *either* capitalism *or* socialism but of *more* or *less* insofar as they bear upon the possibility of maximizing in each specific situation the opportunities of freedom.

Socialism must today be conceived as a principle of welfare and fraternity integral to the democratization of culture on every level—economic, educational and social. It is democracy as a way of life. It relies on creative intelligence to conceive, modify or transform any or all institutions with one goal in view: the development of a community of free persons—each one different from the other and yet enjoying or respecting one another's differences.

By this time, the space ship which was to take me back to Earth had arrived, and Marx escorted me to the ectoplasmic gangplank. I told him that it was not likely that credence would be given to my report of our conversation. His last words to me were the sentence from Dante with which he completed the preface to his chief work: *"Segui il tuo corso, e lascia dir le genti—follow your own course and let people talk."*

COMMUNISM IN HELL

AN INTERVIEW WITH SIDNEY HOOK
FROM BEYOND THE GRAVE

BY PAUL BERMAN

$\mathcal{S}$IDNEY Hook, the brilliant
American philosopher, died
last July [1989]. The following interview took place several
months *after* his death, on a bright asteroid where Mr.
Hook's spirit resides. In one of his books, Mr. Hook conducted just such a posthumous interview with Karl Marx,
who turned out to agree on all matters with Sidney Hook.

PAUL BERMAN: *Do you mind if I ask some questions
about the world of ideas?*

SIDNEY HOOK: You! Aren't you the one who made fun
of me in the *Village Voice*?*

Originally published in the *Village Voice* (December 1989). Reprinted by
permission of the author.

*Editor's note: This refers to an earlier article by Paul Berman in the
Village Voice (13 March 1984). For Hook's thoughts on the piece, see pp.
341–42, 344 in his *Letters of Sidney Hook*, ed. Edward S. Shapiro
(Armonk, N.Y.: M. E. Sharpe, 1995).

Berman: *You did vote for Richard Nixon, sir.* You were fearsome in your later years. Still, I called you America's greatest writer on Marxism.*

So allow me, please, to ask if you have noticed, from your place in the stars, the Eastern and Central European revolution?

Hook: Missing it would be impossible. The vast international revolution that Marx predicted and that Marxists have confidently awaited ever since, the revolution that I myself expected throughout my younger years—this revolution has finally occurred. Except it is against the Communists, not against the West.

Berman: *Ironic, no?*

Hook: Striking, not ironic. A good student of the *real* Marx cannot be surprised.

Berman: *Gorbachev recently called for Marxism to be revived in the Soviet Union. You must think, then, that Marxism has a value and its revival has a chance.*

Hook: Under Gorbachev? Don't be illogical. Marxism for the Communists long ago became a mystical, irrational doctrine of totalitarian domination. There is nothing for them to revive. Their only relation to Marx is through corruption of terminology.

Murderers can't revive their victims. Communists can no more revive Marxism than can American professors.

---

*Editor's note: Hook votes for Hubert Humphrey in 1968, Nixon in 1972, Jimmy Carter in 1976, and Ronald Reagan in 1980.

Berman: *Still, what if Gorbachev, persisting in this idea, turns for advice, via* Sputnik, *to America's greatest writer on Marxism? He's turning to America for advice in every other field.*

Hook: I would tell him that reviving elements from Marxism is not, finally, a question of intention. It is partly a matter of moral right, which no Soviet leader can have. And it is a matter of reality: how much of Marx lives, objectively?

Berman: *And how much is that?*

Hook: The theory of historical materialism was refuted long ago. I challenge anyone to argue otherwise. If Marx's theory of surplus value were true, the working class would have starved to death generations ago. Marx never understood nationalism.

Berman: *Latvian separatism, to cite a random example, proves that Marx was, as Daniel Patrick Moynihan says, basically wrong.*

Hook: Basically wrong? Not at all. Consider Marx's prophecies. He was right about mechanization, the concentration of industry and capital, the entanglement of all people in the net of the world market, and the periodic crises of production—which is a respectable number of predictions. And his political and moral values—

Berman: *Values! Aren't Marx's values the fundamental cause of everything that is calamitous in Communism?*

Hook: It depends whether you think Marx was a democrat or an antidemocrat.

Berman: *Unfortunately, an ambiguous point.*

Hook: Not at all. Marx advocated the democratic liberation of the working class. He was a fighter for freedom— not for totalitarianism.

Berman: *So Marx would, in your view, have been an anti-Communist?*

Hook: Exactly to the degree that Communism suppresses the democratic rights of the working class, which is totally.

Berman: *But, Mr. Hook, do you seriously mean to persist with old-fashioned Marxist phrases like "the working class"? Today's European revolutions are democratic and national—not proletarian.*

Hook: You are not very observant. The Great Revolution of 1989 began in a Polish shipyard and was led by an electrician. Also by, it's true, a Czechoslovakian playwright, who has so far succeeded because of a general strike by labor. The result is the largest, grandest working-class revolution in history.

Berman: *Even so, look at what these workers are demanding—capitalism! No Marxist formula there.*

Hook: What formula do you mean? Marx imagined a struggle between socialism versus capitalism. But anyone with a Marx-like respect for scientific inquiry has long recognized that, in the real world, the authentic alternatives pit *more* socialism against *more* capitalism.

Berman: *People speak about the free market, though.*

Hook: The free market is gibberish. Labor unions and democratic regulations abolished the free market ages ago.

Berman: *Still, even if capitalism and socialism are relative terms, it was, you must admit, right wingers who most forcefully opposed the Communist dictatorships.*

Hook: That's propaganda, not scientific observation. In the United States, free-marketeers and right-wingers have been anywhere but in the lead.

Berman: *In the age of Reagan and Bush? Can you be serious? But then, you, Mr. Hook, seemed to like Reagan.*

Hook: You, if I recall your writings correctly, have not always admired the AFL-CIO, without which, incidentally, you would long ago, young man, have lost your dental plan. I remind you nonetheless that, among all the powerful elements of American society, the AFL-CIO alone stood behind Polish Solidarity during the years when Solidarity's future looked grim.

Everyone loves a winner. But American labor had the moral values to love a loser, too. This is an instance of the international working-class solidarity that Marx believed in.

Berman: *There you go again with that ancient Marxist rhetoric! Surely its day is done.*

Hook: Quite right: I myself, more than 40 years ago, advised Marxists to abandon the rhetoric of dialectical thought, which only serves to obscure Marx's authentically scientific intentions. Marx came to agree with me about that, by the way.

But should we abandon good and decent phrases like *social democracy* and the faith in labor just because of an association with Marx? I can understand why, in some countries, the temptation to do so may exist. Adopting the free-market rhetoric will only make for problems in the future, though. It will mean that Communism's evil influence will persist even after the last Communist government has been driven from the face of the earth. But that is a problem for the future.

Berman: *Driven from the face of the earth? Where will the Communists go?*

Mr. Hook did not answer. He sat at an empty table already set up for a public debate, with one microphone for himself and another marked "Communists of the World." And he chuckled.

When the Communists are gone from the earth, they will be condemned to debate with Sidney Hook, America's greatest writer on Marxism. They will be in hell.

APPENDIX

WORKS BY AND ABOUT SIDNEY HOOK

I have compiled these lists from Barbara Levine's checklist supplemented by additional material in my possession. By "books" I mean stand-alone publications. A very small number are pamphlets. It is highly likely that this list of his books is complete. Regarding biography or other reviews of the life or work of Sidney Hook, or some aspects of it, there may well be as yet unpublished theses and the like of which I am unaware. There is almost certainly a good deal more in journal literature, especially in the commentary shortly after his death. There is also an enormous vehemently denunciatory literature on Sidney Hook. This starts with the work of members of the American Communist Party in the early 1930s. First, they denounced the "revisionism" of Marx they perceived in the volume reprinted here. Earl Browder, the General Secretary of the U.S. Communist Party, in his 1935 book, *Communism in the United States*

(New York: International Publishers), devotes an entire
chapter to "the Revisionism of Sidney Hook" (pp.
316–33), the only person so honored by a chapter of
denunciation all his own. The 15 February 1935 newspaper of Washington Square College of New York University reported Sidney Hook had just been denounced
by a speaker on campus as "a slimy revolutionary and a
reptile," moreover, a reptile "of the lowest sort." (As the
attack came from a Communist, almost certainly the
speaker had called him a "slimy *counter*-revolutionary.")
Later the attacks from the Party focused upon Sidney
Hook's anti-Stalinism. These written and verbal assaults
continued as long as the American Party lasted. This was
even supplemented with a specific targeted diatribe
direct from the Kremlin—I regret I cannot provide a specific reference—a signal honor for a political philosopher who was not a politician. Then there is a literature
starting in the 1940s and 1950s from friends and fellow
travelers of the Communist Party which is continued to
the present time by those who still sympathize with its
perceived mission, although they still do seem to have
recognized its ultimate goals. They deliberately misread
his work, unlike confused liberals who do not seem to
have read his work carefully, and whose critiques also
continue. (Hilton Kramer analyzes an example from one
of the latter, Arthur Schlesinger, in *New Criterion* 19, no.
7 [March 2001]: 57–61.) Quite independent of the Communists, numerous Trotskyites and Independent Marxists
began chiming in heavily with anti-Hook attacks in 1939
and 1940 because Hook supported war against the Nazis.
Attacks from Trotskyite and other independent Marxist-
Leninists intensified in the 1950s, and ironically and

hypocritically began to denounce him for his anti-Stalinism.[1]

Sidney Hook was fortunate. None of these denunciations of him throughout his life, from hostile totalitarians and their sympathizers to misguided liberals, resulted in any worse fate than, in the 1960s and later, diminished acclaim or simply willful dismissal by a large portion of the academy and the influential press, because he was viewed as "politically incorrect" and overly concerned with Stalinism. Those in other countries have paid a much harsher price for his views. But now, at least secure in the knowledge that he has not, we can view an anthology of denunciations of Sidney Hook as an entertaining testament to expressions of human folly.

Ernest B. Hook
Berkeley, California
26 June 2002

---

[1] My favorite denunciation of Sidney Hook comes from James Cannon. In 1935 he led a faction of several hundred Trotskyites within the revolutionary (not-all-Trotskyite) Workers Party of the United States (WP-US). In early 1936 they were allowed into the nonrevolutionary Socialist Party led by Norman Thomas, to its great subsequent discomfiture. Sidney Hook, a member of the WP-US but much closer than Cannon and others in the party to Thomas in spirit, was the schatkin. Around December 1935 he arranged and mediated at his apartment the crucial meeting between Cannon and Thomas that led to the agreement. According to Cannon, the arrangement of this meeting by Hook ("then dabbling in socialism") was the "*last progressive act in the* life *and career of Sidney Hook*"! (My emphasis. James P. Cannon, *The History of American Trotskyism: 1928–1938* [New York: Pathfinder, 1995], pp. 211, 270.) I was born in March 1936. So my life has been damned to a nonprogressive upbringing. But I console myself with the thought that at least my *conception* could still be politically immaculate.

The best source concerning Sidney Hook's life and work is his autobiography, *Out of Step* (1987). An almost complete "checklist" of his writings has been published by Barbara Levine (1989). Two Festschrift edited by Paul Kurtz (1968 and 1983) include a number of essays on his life and aspects of his career, as does a Hoover Institution "memorial" (1989). Two biographies have appeared. One focuses on the younger Sidney Hook and finds little useful contribution in his post-"revolutionary" work (i.e., after 1939), political or nonpolitical. The other takes a more balanced view and goes up to 1956. Full bibliographical information on all of these sources appears below. As the one-hundredth anniversary of Sidney Hook's birth (twentieth of December 1902) occurs later in the year of publication of this expanded edition, likely additional centenary commentary on his life and work will appear in the near future.

Books or Pamphlets by or Edited by Sidney Hook

The Metaphysics of Pragmatism. Chicago: Open Court, 1927.

Towards the Understanding of Karl Marx: A Revolutionary Interpretation. New York: John Day, 1933.

The Meaning of Marx. Edited by Sidney Hook. Symposium by Bertrand Russell, John Dewey, Morris R. Cohen, Sherwood Eddy, and Sidney Hook. New York: Farrar and Rinehart, 1934.

American Philosophy Today and Tomorrow. Edited by Sidney Hook and Horace M. Kallen. New York: Lee Furman, 1935.

From Hegel to Marx: Studies in the Intellectual Development of Karl Marx. New York: John Day, 1936. (Reprinted with a new introduction by Hook. Ann Arbor: University of Michigan Press, 1962. A reprint by Columbia University Press [1994] contains a foreword by Christopher Phelps.)

John Dewey: An Intellectual Portrait. New York: John Day, 1939.

Reason, Social Myths, and Democracy. New York: John Day, 1940. (Reprinted with a new introduction by Hook. New York: Harper and Row, 1965.)

The Hero in History: A Study in Limitation and Possibility. New York: John Day, 1943. (An afterword and further reflections on the theme of this volume in view of subsequent developments was issued as a pamphlet, in 1978 by Hoover Institution Press.)

Education for Modern Man. New York: Dial Press, 1946. (An enlarged and revised second edition with a slightly different title was issued in 1963. See below.)

Freedom and Experience: Essays Presented to Horace M. Kallen. Edited by Sidney Hook and Milton R. Konvitz. Ithaca, N.Y.: Cornell University Press, 1947.

John Dewey: Philosopher of Science and Freedom. Edited by Sidney Hook. New York: Dial Press, 1950.

Democracy and Desegregation. New York: Tamiment Institute, 1952.

Heresy, Yes—Conspiracy, No. New York: John Day, 1953. (Reprinted with a new introduction by Hook. Westport, Conn.: Greenwood Press, 1973.)

Dialectical Materialism and Scientific Method. Manchester, England: J. B. Foy and Co., 1955.

Marx and the Marxists: The Ambiguous Legacy. Princeton, N.J.: D. Van Nostrand Co., 1955.

American Philosophers at Work. Edited by Sidney Hook. New York: Criterion Books, 1956.

Common Sense and the Fifth Amendment. New York: Criterion Books, 1957.

Determinism and Freedom in the Age of Modern Science. Edited by Sidney Hook. First Symposium, New York University Institute of Philosophy. New York: New York University Press, 1958.

John Dewey: His Philosophy of Education and Its Critics. New York: Tamiment Institute, 1959.

Political Power and Personal Freedom: Critical Studies in Democracy, Communism, and Civil Rights. New York: Criterion Books, 1959

Psychoanalysis, Scientific Method, and Philosophy. Edited by Sidney Hook. Second Symposium, New York University Institute of Philosophy. New York: New York University Press, 1959.

Dimensions of Mind. Edited by Sidney Hook. Third Symposium, New York University Institute of Philosophy. New York: New York University Press, 1960.

The Quest for Being and Other Studies in Naturalism and Humanism. New York: St. Martin's Press, 1961.

Religious Experience and Truth. Edited by Sidney Hook. Fourth Symposium, New York University Institute of Philosophy. New York: New York University Press, 1961.

The Paradoxes of Freedom. Berkeley: University of California Press, 1962. (Reprinted with a new introduction by Hook. Amherst, N.Y.: Prometheus Books, 1987.)

Education for Modern Man: A New Perspective. Enlarged edition. New York: Alfred A. Knopf, 1963. (A modest revision and expansion of *Education for Modern Man* [1946, see above] but with new material including a new introduction by Hook.)

The Fail-Safe Fallacy. New York: Stein and Day, 1963.

Philosophy and History. Edited by Sidney Hook. Fifth Symposium, New York University Institute of Philosophy. New York: New York University Press, 1963.

Law and Philosophy. Edited by Sidney Hook. Sixth Symposium, New York University Institute of Philosophy. New York: New York University Press, 1964.

Art and Philosophy. Edited by Sidney Hook. Seventh Symposium, New York University Institute of Philosophy. New York: New York University Press, 1966.

Religion in a Free Society. Lincoln: University of Nebraska Press, 1967; Don Mills, Ontario: Burns and MacEachern, 1967.

Human Values and Economic Policy. Edited by Sidney Hook. Eighth Symposium New York University Institute of Philosophy. New York: New York University Press, 1967.

Language and Philosophy. Edited by Sidney Hook. Ninth Symposium, New York University Institute of Philosophy. New York: New York University Press, 1969.

The Essential Thomas Paine. Edited by Sidney Hook. New York: New American Library, [1969].

Academic Freedom and Academic Anarchy. New York: Cowles Book Co., 1970.

In Defense of Academic Freedom. Edited by Sidney Hook. New York: Pegasus, 1971.

Education and the Taming of Power. La Salle, Ill.: Open Court, 1973.

Pragmatism and the Tragic Sense of Life. New York: Basic Books, 1974.

The Idea of a Modern University. Edited by Sidney Hook, Paul Kurtz, and Miro Todorovich. Amherst, N.Y.: Prometheus Books, 1974.

Revolution, Reform, and Social-Justice-Studies in the Theory and Practice of Marxism. New York: New York University Press, 1975.

The Philosophy of the Curriculum: The Need for General Education. Edited by Sidney Hook, Paul Kurtz, and Miro Todorovich. Amherst, N.Y.: Prometheus Books, 1975.

Ethics, National Ideology, Marxism and Existentialism: Discussions with Sidney Hook. Edited by Harsja W. Bachtiar. Jakarta, Indonesia: Djambatan, 1976. In Indonesian and English.

The Ethics of Teaching and Scientific Research. Edited by Sidney Hook, Paul Kurtz, and Miro Todorovich. Amherst, N.Y.: Prometheus Books, 1977.

The Hero in History: Myth, Power, or Moral Ideal? Hoover Institution on War, Revolution and Peace, Stanford University, 1978.

The University and the State: What Role for Government in Higher Education? Edited by Sidney Hook, Paul Kurtz, and Miro Todorovich. Amherst, N.Y.: Prometheus Books, 1978.

Philosophy and Public Policy. Carbondale and Edwardsville: Southern Illinois University Press, 1980.

Marxism and Beyond. Totowa, N.J.: Rowman and Littlefield, 1983.

Out of Step: An Unquiet Life in the 20th Century. New York: Harper and Row, 1987. (Autobiography)

Soviet Hypocrisy and Western Gullibility, by Sidney Hook, Vladimir Bukovsky, and Paul Hollander. Washington, D.C.: Ethics and Public Policy Center, 1987.

Convictions. Amherst, N.Y.: Prometheus Books, 1990. (With an introduction by Paul Kurtz)

Letters of Sidney Hook: Democracy, Communism and the Cold War. Edited by Edward S. Shapiro. Armonk, N.Y.: M. E. Sharpe, 1995.

Publications with Commentary about
the Life or Work of Sidney Hook

Festschrift (each includes some directly pertinent essays):

Sidney Hook and the Contemporary World: Essays on the Pragmatic Intelligence. Edited by Paul Kurtz. New York: John Day, 1968.

Sidney Hook: Philosopher of Democracy and Humanism. Edited by Paul Kurtz. Amherst, N.Y.: Prometheus Books, 1983.

Published Memorials:

Sidney Hook: A Service of Remembrance. 18 July 1989. Stanford, California: Hoover Institution, Stanford University. As I wrote one of the six essays in this volume, and helped to choose the other contributors, understandably I may be biased in my enthusiasm about the value of this 28-page pamphlet.

Obituary (among many):

"Sidney Hook, Political Philosopher Is Dead at 86," by Richard Bernstein. *New York Times*, 14 July 1989, A10 (National edition).

Biographies:

Hook's autobiography, *Out of Step* (1987, see above), is the best and most complete source to date. Two other works have appeared, but neither is comprehensive.

"Young Sidney Hook: Marxism and Pragmatism, Revolution and Democracy," by Christopher Brooks Phelps. Ann Arbor, Mich.: UMI, 1995 (Ph.D. diss., Department of History, University of Rochester). Expanded and published as *Young Sidney Hook: Marxist and Pragmatist*. Ithaca, N.Y.: Cornell University Press, 1997. In my view, a "Leninist" or at least an "anti-anti-Leninist" presentation of Hook's life and career, which is unbalanced and misleading on events after about 1940, when Hook concluded fighting the Nazis had much greater priority than fighting capitalism at home.

"The Perils of Pragmatism; Sidney Hook's Journey Through Philosophy and Politics, 1902–1956," by Richard Downing Horn. Ann Arbor, Mich.: UMI, 1997 (Ph.D. diss., Department of History, Princeton University).

List of Writings:

Sidney Hook: A Checklist of Writings. Compiled by Barbara Levine. Carbondale and Edwardsville, Ill.: Southern Illinois University Press, 1989. Extends and expands earlier bibliographies compiled by John Dennis Crowley (in the 1968 Festschrift) and by Jo Ann Boydston and Kathleen Poulos (in the 1983 Festschrift).

Books of Sidney Hook Currently in Print
by Prometheus Books

Convictions

The Ethics of Teaching and Scientific Research (edited with Paul Kurtz and Miro Todorovich)

John Dewey: An Intellectual Portrait

The Metaphysics of Pragmatism

Paradoxes of Freedom

The Philosophy of the Curriculum (edited with Paul Kurtz and Miro Todorovich)

The Quest for Being

Reason, Social Myths, and Democracy

Towards the Understanding of Karl Marx

INDEX

Editor's note: Page numbers listed in the index denote both the original and expanded editions. Page numbers not in brackets refer to the original edition and appear at the bottom of the reprinted text. Page numbers in brackets refer to the expanded edition and appear in brackets at the top of each page. For example, "absolute idealism, 169 [243]" indicates that this subject occurs on page 169 of the original edition that also has the bracketed page number [243] in the expanded edition.

[518]

[301]–248 [322]
dialectic of, 90 [164]–93
[167]
social reform
gradual, 20 [94]
and theory of Marxism, 24
[98]
social relations: correlated
with psychological atti-
tudes, 125 [199]
social relations of production,
89 [163], 142 [216], 256
[330]
identified with technical
forces of production, 141
[215]–147 [221]
social revolution, 51 [125],
110 [184]–114 [188],
248 [322], [427]
Marxism is a philosophy
of, 9 [83]
not complete until it is
international, 279 [353]
and political revolution,
271 [345]
theory, 25 [99]
thoroughly human motiva-
tion, 296 [370]–297
[371]
social service: euphemism for
monopoly, 264 [338]
social theories: different
classes choose differ-
ently, 105 [179]
social: wrongly reduced to

complicated effect of the
non-social, 128 [202]
society
confused with state and
government, 253
[327]–255 [329]
definition, 253 [327]–254
[328]
economic structure of, 133
[207]
Socrates, 86 [160]
Soetbeer (*Edelmetall-Produktion*), 324 [398]
Solon, S. L., [29 n–30 n]
Sombart, Werner (*zwei Seelen*
theory of Marx), 65
[139]
sophistry: and dialectic, 77
[151]
Sophists, 77 [151]
Sorel, Georges, [64], 1 [75],
11 [85], 53 [127]
*De l'Utilité du Pragma-
tisme*, 52 n [126 n]
on duty, 47 [121]–48 [122]
*Matériaux d'une Thérie du
Prolétariat*, 45 n [119 n]
opposed Jaurès and
Kautsky, 46 [120]
Reflections on Violence,
47 n [121 n], 48 [122],
49 [123]
relation to Marx misunderstood, 46 [120]
revision of Marx, 45